NEW TESTAMENT
WITNESSES of CHRIST

PETER, JOHN, JAMES, & PAUL

Cover painting *Go Ye Therefore* by Harry Anderson, © Intellectual Reserve, Inc.

Cover design copyrighted 2002 by Covenant Communications, Inc.

Published by Covenant Communications, Inc.
American Fork, Utah

Printed in the United States of America
First Printing: November 2002

09 08 07 06 05 04 03 02   10 9 8 7 6 5 4 3 2 1

ISBN 1-59156-118-3

NEW TESTAMENT
WITNESSES of CHRIST

PETER, JOHN, JAMES, & PAUL

↪ John F. Hall ↩

Covenant Communications, Inc.

Covenant

Patri Optimo

John Franklin Hall, Jr.

FOREWORD

Through the composition of this work I have increased my admiration and even come to think of as friends the four remarkable individuals whose lives and service form the subject of the volume. Distinct in their persons, methods, and varying labors, the early Christian leaders, Peter, John, James, and Paul, shared a common devotion to their beloved Master, the Lord Jesus Christ. It was this dedication to fulfilling apostolic callings from Him that motivated their tremendous lifetime missions in the face of never abating opposition. They tirelessly proclaimed the glad tidings that Jesus was the Christ, the Only Begotten Son, and Savior. In teaching and serving His flock, they returned to Christ's followers the same love they received from Him. By examining the inspiring lives of these special witnesses, the volume seeks to encourage the similar application of love, faith, and devotion to the Savior.

The volume has two additional ends: first, to provide an accurate depiction of their background and the world in which they lived by recounting the lifework of the four "pillars" of early Christianity; secondly, to enlighten modern sectarian misunderstanding of apostolic authority and function, as well as to counter hypercritical scholarly technique that calls into question the authority of Peter, John, James, and Paul, and variously challenges their authorship of certain works of scripture by tradition long attributed to them. Developing a book designed both to provide basic knowledge for a general audience and also to address, if only in small part, pertinent issues and problems of current scholarship, is wrought with difficulty. Nevertheless, I have not hesitated to make the reader aware of certain scholarly issues, but have discussed them in what I hope is accessible terminology that avoids academic jargon. Most importantly, I have endeavored to demonstrate that the surviving writings of the early Christians themselves disagree not only with later Christians of the third and fourth centuries, but also with the views of modern sectarian scholarship, and instead, accord with the revealed doctrines of the Restoration.

I appreciate the efforts of all who were part of the production of this volume. Special thanks must be given to Tyler Moulton, Acquisitions at Covenant Communications, Inc., who suggested that I write a book on the subject of my lectures about "The Four Pillars of Early Christianity" delivered for several years at BYU Education Week; to Shauna Nelson, Managing Editor at Covenant Communications, Inc., whose friendly and efficient professionalism has made the preparation of this book a most pleasant experience; and to Kris Swinson, whose talented editing of the volume produced a tighter and better text, yet one that maintained eccentricities of form and style favored by the author. Also to be thanked are Liza Anne Hall for her proofreading of the manuscript, and Jefferson Hall for several suggestions for interpreting the original Greek of New Testament texts. Particular thanks are due my longtime assistant, Victoria Franklin Johnson, whose devotion to this project ensured its fruition.

—JOHN F. HALL

TABLE OF CONTENTS

SECTION ONE

The World of the Four Pillars

CHAPTER ONE

The Four Pillars

The spread of the gospel and the establishment throughout the Roman Empire of the Church of Jesus Christ in the dispensation of the meridian of time was chiefly the work of four men, united in their devotion to the Savior and steadfast in their shared apostolic calling. Paul recognized their role by naming as "pillars" Peter, John, and James, the brother of the Lord (Gal. 2:9). To the three pillars identified by Paul, a fourth must be added—Paul himself. Together they stood as four great supports of the edifice for which Jesus Christ Himself was the chief cornerstone (Eph. 2:20).

The Glad Tidings

With no less glorious an event than the Ascension of the Lord, Luke chose to begin his chronicle of the spread of the early Christian message of glad tidings (Acts 1:2–9). These glad tidings[1] proclaimed the divine Sonship, atoning mission, and resurrection of Jesus of Nazareth, the prophesied Messiah, the Christ. They comprised the foundation of the gospel message to be carried throughout the world, a charge entrusted to His disciples by the Savior Himself. Indeed, Luke records Jesus' words of final address: "ye shall be witnesses unto me both in Jerusalem, and in all Judea, and in Samaria, and unto the uttermost part of the earth" (Acts 1:8).[2]

The narrative of Acts continues by describing the ascent of Christ while the disciples watched Him lifted up, until "a cloud received him out of their sight" (Acts 1:9). What wonder these men who loved the Savior must have felt as they witnessed His ascent! Surely feelings of inexpressible joy filled their hearts as they realized this was very much a triumphant culmination of His mission. But their awe was not permitted to continue long, for two men in white apparel appeared and declared, "Ye men of Galilee, why stand ye gazing up into heaven? this same Jesus, which is taken up from you into heaven, shall so come in like manner as ye have seen him go into heaven" (Acts 1:11). The time had come to begin their own work of spreading the glad tidings.

That labor of love—and devotion to the person and mission of Jesus Christ—continues even today as the charge for true disciples. The Father's plan of salvation is again declared in this era of restoration, just as it was in the days of the meridian of time. The glad tidings remain the same, defined anew for the Prophet Joseph Smith in that great vision of the Son of Man.

> And this is the gospel, the glad tidings, which the voice out of the heavens bore record unto us—That he came into the world, even Jesus, to be crucified for the world, and to bear the sins of the world, and to sanctify the world, and to cleanse it from all unrighteousness; That through him all might be saved whom the Father had put into his power and made by him (D&C 76:40–42).

Until the Savior comes again in the manner in which He ascended into Heaven, there abides His charge to declare these glad tidings.

The men of Galilee who witnessed the Ascension were true to the command their Master gave them. The Lord's Apostles faithfully taught and testified of the Christ, sealing their witness with their life's blood.[3] The mission of proclaiming the glad tidings and teaching the gospel was shared by many who labored under the leadership of the Twelve Apostles. From the record of Acts, in particular, and from the letters of the New Testament, in general, much can be adduced about this process. Examination of the scriptures, as well as other early Christian writings, leads to the conclusion that of all those who dedicated themselves to the spread of the gospel and the establishment of the Church of Jesus Christ, four men are revealed as preeminently stalwart in the faithfulness of their labor.

The Three Pillars

The scriptures give evidence of only one occasion when these four men were together. Paul came from Antioch to bring to the attention of the other three, Peter, John, and James, the brother of the Lord, a problem that threatened the nascent Christian movement, especially outside of Judea in places like Antioch. Converted Jews and Gentiles came from differing traditions, and some were trying to impose their old beliefs on those around them. The four Apostles met in Jerusalem, probably in the year A.D. 49,[4] to resolve this crisis. They clarified that those who followed the Christ were not merely another separatist Jewish sect, but a different religion from the Judaism of the day, a renewal of the faith once followed by Abraham and the patriarchs, extending back even to Adam and the foundations of the world.[5]

Antioch had been founded over three hundred years earlier as the capital of the Seleucid Empire, one of the three great Hellenistic successor kingdoms to the empire of Alexander the Great, that had stretched from Greece eastward to India and southward to include Egypt, encompassing within its borders the entire Middle East. In the first century A.D., Antioch was the second most populous city in the Mediterranean world, exceeded only by Alexandria, the capital of Greek Ptolemaic Egypt. Although Antioch's population was heavily Greek, a large concentration of Jews had come to settle there. From both groups Paul, Barnabas, and other Christian missionaries converted such great numbers that Antioch began to rival Jerusalem as the largest Christian center.[6]

Acts 15:1 reports that certain men came from Judea and taught the Gentile converts at Antioch that "except ye be circumcised after the manner of Moses, ye cannot be saved." These men may have been of that group of Jewish Christians described as "certain of the sect of Pharisees which believed, saying, That it was needful to circumcise them, and to command them to keep the law of Moses" (Acts 15:5). Whatever their identity, they were considered credible by enough of the Antioch Church members to create a serious problem of fellowship between Jewish and Gentile Christians and to distress the Gentile converts. Paul refers to them as "false brethren" who had tried to compel the circumcision of Titus (Gal. 2:3–4). Their actions were undertaken without the authorization of Church leaders at Jerusalem (Acts 15:24).[7]

The Apostle Paul, moved by revelation, journeyed to Jerusalem to lay the matter before the presiding brethren.[8] This occasioned the meeting of leaders that came to be known as the Jerusalem Council. Before the public meeting, however, Paul met privately with "them which were of reputation" (Gal. 2:2). Of those present he identifies the three whom he names "pillars," and who are described as extending to Paul and Barnabas "the right hands of fellowship; that we should go unto the heathen, and they unto the circumcision" (Gal. 2:9).[9] The three pillars were the same Peter, John, and James.

Peter's primacy among the Twelve is well established. With the brothers James and John, called the *Boanerges* or "sons of thunder," Peter was part of a privileged inner circle of three. Alone of the Apostles, these three participated in certain events, witnessed the Transfiguration, and accompanied the Savior to Gethsemane. Peter, James, and John also received the priesthood keys which they themselves restored to Joseph Smith when they ordained him to the apostleship (D&C 27:12).[10] John, Peter's constant companion in performing miracles and testifying of the Messiahship of Jesus (Acts 2–4), had continued to labor side by side with Peter these many years; but James was the first of the Twelve to be killed. No later than the year A.D. 44 he was put to the sword by Herod Agrippa to curry the favor of his Jewish subjects (Acts 12:1–2). This James, the son of Zebedee, was often called James the Greater to distinguish him from the other James among the Twelve, James the son of Alphaeus. However, the James who figures prominently in the Jerusalem conference and other later events was the James whom, along with Peter, Paul had met many years earlier upon his return to Jerusalem after his conversion (Gal. 1:18–19). This James is regularly identified in the New Testament and other early Christian writings as "the brother of the Lord."[11]

The Jerusalem Council

The A.D. 49 meeting of Apostles and other Church leaders, sometimes called the Jerusalem Council, offers insight into not only the problems that confronted the Church in its early years, but also the manner by which they were resolved. In this instance, as in so many other events which followed (sometimes collectively, more often individually), the Four Pillars provided the inspired leadership that the Lord's flock needed.

Two scriptural accounts report the causes and proceedings of the conference. Paul himself alluded to the meeting and the policy formulated at it, as he endeavored to counteract among the Galatians destructive activities of "Judaizers" that violated the newly established Church policy. The second chapter of Galatians preserves Paul's summary of the pertinent issues. In the Acts chronicle, several notations may refer to this gathering of similar meetings, but chapter 15 most likely treats the same conference as Galatians 2. In effect, here "Luke opens the council room so we can see revelation in action."[12]

The occasion for the conference was as already mentioned. A group of Pharisees who had nevertheless affiliated with the followers of Jesus in Jerusalem journeyed to Antioch, apparently representing themselves as authorized by the leadership, in order to impose observance of the Mosaic law on Gentile converts. For several hundred years it had not been uncommon for Gentiles to convert to Judaism, incurring the obligation not only of circumcision but of all other aspects of the law of Moses.[13] Clearly, a segment of the Church considered themselves to still be practicing Jews who had discovered the Messiah in Jesus, and presumed that all converts must also conduct themselves as practicing Jews.

The Jewish religion of the first century A.D. was not that of Old Testament revelation but a religion that had been restructured during a period of apostasy following the return from Babylonian captivity. It was during this era of almost 500 years between the conclusion of the Old Testament and the beginning of the New Testament account that the foundations of rabbinical Judaism were laid, with the origin of factional and theological politics between Pharisees and Sadducees and a variety of separatist movements, including various Essene and Zealot groups.[14] Nevertheless, for most Jews adherence to the law of Moses was the mechanism by which salvation could be secured. Moses had been augmented by the rabbis, and

God's holy law was being buried under a load of human traditions, which Paul calls "the traditions of my father" (Gal 1:14), the entire "*halakah*" or body of Jewish oral law which supplemented the written law. . . . By means of obedience to the entire Mosaic law as interpreted by all these traditions, many of them trivial and at times directly contrary to the very intention of the commandment as originally given, the Jews, including Paul before his conversion, tried to work their way into the "kingdom of heaven."[15]

No doubt the object of the "Judaizers" within Christianity was not limited to concern that new converts be compelled to follow Mosaic law to ensure their salvation, but also to guard against any contamination of themselves through contact with Gentiles, whom they considered unclean.

Members of Christian congregations are said to have partaken together in a ritual meal as a symbol of their new covenant. While this may, in fact, have been the sacramental ordinance, it has also been referred to as a Christian version of "table fellowship," a practice followed in the ancient world among a number of religions, including Judaism, by which co-religionists dined together to foster unity.[16] Under Mosaic law, a Jew who ate with the impure, whether Gentile or non-observant Jew, was himself tainted. Indeed, Pharisees condemned Christ for eating with persons they considered unworthy (Matt. 9:10–13; Mark 2:15–17; Luke 5:29–32); Peter was involved in a controversy of eating, and then *not* eating with Gentile members (Gal. 2:11–14); the vision that instructed Peter to extend the gospel to Gentiles was itself cast in the symbology of food and cleanliness (Acts 10:10–20). The communal meal was very important for the Jews in both a religious and a societal sense. It marked them as a people apart,[17] but engendered anti-Semitic feeling among Greeks and Romans who, mainly for reasons of sociality and camaraderie, engaged respectively in the *symposium* and the *convivium*. The Roman historian Tacitus described the Jews as a people that felt hatred and hostility toward others, because they dined separately.[18] This issue of "table fellowship," as observed in the communal meals of early Christians, may have been the single greatest instance of Judaizers' efforts to impose Jewish ways on the entire Christian community.

The tenets of contemporary Judaism had exerted influence over the growth of the Church and relations between members from the earliest days. Dispute between "Grecian" and "Hebrew" members over the fair distribution of welfare assistance to widows had resulted in the appointment by the Twelve of seven presiding officials whose immediate task was to supervise this process of daily ministration, but who are also found to have been engaged in the proselyting of Hellenists, as might be expected since the individual names of the seven were of Greek derivation.[19] One of the seven, Stephen, was not only responsible that "the number of the disciples multiplied in Jerusalem greatly" through his performance of "great wonders and miracles among the people" (Acts 6:7–8), but for open declaration that the law of Moses had seen its fulfillment with the advent of the Savior. This same Stephen was stoned to death under the Sanhedrin's authority to execute Jews in Judea.[20] Another of the seven, Philip, opened missionary activity in Samaria. Moreover, the seven ultimately were also responsible for extending the Church to Antioch.[21]

With a substantial proportion of the Christian movement beginning to consist of Hellenized Jews or Greek converts to Judaism, Peter received revelation to extend the gospel directly to Gentiles who had not previously converted to Judaism. The vision of the Roman centurion Cornelius and Peter's accompanying dream and revelation of the Spirit, later reported to the Apostles and other brethren at Jerusalem, established Church policy that Gentiles who had not previously converted to Judaism could be baptized as Christians (Acts 10–11).[22] Apparently, what had not been determined to the satisfaction of everyone was whether Gentile converts must observe the law of Moses. The issue was addressed in the Jerusalem conference presided over by Peter and the Twelve. The final decision was that Gentiles were admitted to full and complete fellowship by no less than the enactment of a "definitive break of the Christian church from its Jewish matrix."[23]

The development and progression of these problems at Antioch were outlined by Paul and Barnabas[24] before Peter, John, and James in a preliminary meeting or series of meetings. Acts 15:4–6 alludes to this process, noting that Paul and Barnabas were welcomed by the Apostles and elders who subsequently investigated demands from Pharisees who had become believers that all must be circumcised and obey the law of Moses. Paul's recounting of the events was more precise (Gal. 2:1–9). He revealed the identity of the small group who participated in the preliminary meetings, and described the success of his ministry of the past fourteen years in carrying the gospel message to Gentiles in Cyprus, Asia Minor, and, of course, Antioch. In respect to the clamoring of the "false brethren," Paul significantly characterized the attitude of those attending as not even for a moment yielding to the demands that Gentiles be encumbered with Mosaic law.

> The meaning is clear and simple: not at any time during the conference— whether in the private interview or at the public meeting; whether at the beginning, in the middle, or at the close—was there any yielding to the wishes of the enemies of the one and only true gospel. It was one and the same gospel, whether proclaimed by Paul or Barnabas; by Cephas, James, or John.[25]

Peter, John, and James were united with Paul and Barnabas. They extended to them the right hand of fellowship and commissioned them to proclaim the gospel among the uncircumcised. For the three pillars, as for the fourth, this decision had been made long before, when the Lord gave to Peter, the presiding officer, revelation that Gentiles should be accepted in baptism. If the Messiah who declared that He had come to fulfil the law of Moses (Matt 5:17) had not directed any Christians to be placed under that archaic law (Rom. 6:14), then who were these Pharisees, despite their affiliation with the Church, to determine the correct doctrine of Jesus Christ? The Apostles made this point very clear in the ensuing conference.

Peter presided over the Jerusalem Council. "It was Peter who spoke first, an act of presidency, for he held the keys of the kingdom."[26] Peter pronounced the decision of the presiding Apostles, John, James, Paul, Barnabas, and others of the Quorum of the Twelve who had no doubt also been in attendance at the preliminary meetings. At this point any discussion or debate was brought to an end by Peter's words, for he reminded all gathered that:

> A good while ago God made choice among us, that the Gentiles by my mouth should hear the word of the gospel, and believe. And God, which knoweth the hearts, bare them witness, giving them the Holy Ghost, even as he did unto us; And put no difference between us and them, purifying their hearts by faith. Now therefore why tempt ye God, to put a yoke upon the neck of the disciples, which neither our fathers nor we were able to bear? But we believe that through the grace of the Lord Jesus Christ we shall be saved, even as they (Acts 15:7–11).

For Peter and the Apostles, God made the decision: the Gentiles should receive the gospel. This was confirmed when Gentile members received the Holy Spirit. Peter explained to everyone present that, purification through faith, not the law of Moses, was the refining process that followers of Christ must pursue, and in that there was no difference for Jew or Gentile. The conclusion of the matter was clear. If God had chosen not to impose on Gentile converts the yoke that neither the Jews nor their fathers had successfully borne, who were they to demand what God had not? Rather, let all—Jew and Gentile—believe that salvation to any person would come only through the blessing of the Lord Jesus Christ.

Peter's pronouncement of this basic doctrine of the early Church clarifies several important aspects of the religion. The Church was Jesus Christ's. He still directed it through revelation to His chosen leaders, Peter and the Apostles. This was a religion distinct from Judaism, which had found its own way, departing from the old teachings of the prophets, and accepting the principle of continuing revelation. If any doubted that the Church would follow the route of revelation, all they needed to do was look upon Peter, who with calm majesty announced the decision of the Brethren and explained how it accorded with the Lord's will. Calm, but filled with immovable determination to see his Master's plan carried out, Peter stood as a rock of priesthood power and stability. Nor was he alone, for his brethren of the apostleship stood unitedly with him.

Paul spoke next. The Acts account is succinct in its description of Paul's address. It states simply that they (Paul and Barnabas) declared "what miracles and wonders God had wrought among the Gentiles by them" (Acts 15:12). We can easily imagine Paul recounting with great enthusiasm the stories of conversion throughout his journeys in Cyprus, Cilicia, Galatia, and Syria, testifying of how the Lord's power was manifest as he declared the truthfulness of the gospel. The faith and dedication of new Gentile members would have undoubtedly been detailed so that all in Jerusalem might know they were truly brethren in their commitment to Jesus Christ. When Paul sat down, everyone of open mind would have seen in his fourteen years of labor proof of the correctness of the revelation Peter had received so many years before.

Finally, James rose. The brother of the Savior was one known for observing the law scrupulously and frequently attending the temple.

He was unquestionably well respected among that very group who had sought to impose Jewish law upon the whole Church.[27] However, if they expected James's support in this matter, they were disappointed. James endorsed Peter's pronounced decision fully. The presiding Brethren were of one accord. James made the case for the acceptance of this revealed doctrine by demonstrating how it was consistent with the words of the prophet Amos that when the tabernacle of David was in ruins it would be built up again by the Gentiles, since the gospel might then be given to all men (Acts 15:14–17; Amos 9:11–12). To James it was clear that God had known centuries before that He would allow the gospel to go to the Gentiles, just as revealed to Peter. Therefore, he gave the admonishment that "we trouble not them, which from among the Gentiles are turned to God" (Acts 15:19). James announced the plan[28] to send letters to the branches of the Church clarifying that Gentile converts were not required to be circumcised or observe the law. Rather, they needed only to abstain from food polluted by being offered to idols, from fornication, from things strangled, and from partaking of blood (Acts 15:29). The restrictions were minimal and may have been required for centuries of Gentiles residing in a Jewish community. These are four of the seven requirements of the so-called Noachic regulations "traditionally binding on any 'stranger within the gate' in Judaism."[29] Some hold that the origin of the proscription was based on Genesis 9:8–17 and, therefore, outside the purview of Mosaic law, but others believe that its origin was rabbinic and recent.[30]

The Acts account concludes with mention of the content of the letter as both clarifying doctrine and disavowing any attribution to Church leaders of statements designed to compel practice of the Mosaic law. More importantly, as Richard Anderson aptly explains:

> The apostles' letter to Antioch underlined not only the decision, but how the decision was reached: "It seemed good to the Holy Ghost, and to us, to lay upon you no greater burden than these necessary things" (Acts 15:28). Few Christians today see the implications of this powerful ruling of the Twelve. Conservatives today search the Bible for answers, but had the apostles done this, they would have required circumcision for the Gentiles, since it is commanded in the Bible. The apostles were inspired to

go beyond the Bible, to reverse the lesser law given earlier and to extend the higher law through Christ. In other words not past scripture, but new revelation was the foundation of the Church of Christ.[31]

Little has been said of John because the Acts account of the Jerusalem Council makes no specific mention of him, and Paul's own report of the proceeding only provides a single reference to John as one of the three pillars. However, that mention not only reflects John's high standing in the Church, but suggests a significant role in the events of the council, albeit behind the scene in the private preliminary meetings. Of course, John's steadfast companioning of Peter in the early days of establishing Christianity leaves little doubt that he would have remained firm in sustaining Peter in his presiding role.

The Four Pillars

The resolution of this crisis in the doctrine and practice of the early Church, settled at the Jerusalem Council, was arrived at and implemented by these four pillars. Their collaboration on this occasion assured that Christianity would be organized in accordance with the will of the Lord, revealed to His chosen leaders, the Apostles. While the events of the Jerusalem Council provide the only scriptural attestation of interaction between all four of the pillars, there are many instances of several laboring in tandem. Nevertheless, it is their individual lifelong devotion to the work of the Lord that inspires disciples of Christ even today. It may well be that the Jerusalem Council was the last occasion that the Twelve met together. At its conclusion they separated to carry the glad tidings of the gospel to different corners of the world they knew. The same held true for the Four Pillars. Peter went to Antioch, no doubt, to assure the implementation of the new Gentile policy, and to meet with the members of the Church, now more numerous in Antioch than in Jerusalem. He was very likely accompanied by John. When Peter departed Antioch to bring his strength to the branches of the Church at Rome, John moved to Ephesus in Asia Minor, where Paul's efforts had produced a large, vibrant, and still-expanding Christian community. After Peter sealed his testimony with his death in Rome, John presided over the whole Church from Ephesus. There, John's labor of love among his "little children" would witness the composition of profound words designed to acquaint all with the Master he knew so well and provide assurance that Jesus would come again. James, the brother of the Lord, remained in Jerusalem. His name became inextricable from the Christian community in the Holy City as he labored tirelessly to serve them in his own pragmatic way. Paul, the great lion of God, fearlessly proclaimed the message of Jesus Christ throughout Asia, Greece, Italy, and finally the distant provinces of the far west. His labor established the gospel in a seemingly endless number of locales, and his letters of exhortation to the Saints preserve his faithful testimony for the modern era.

Endnotes

1. "Glad tidings" or "good news" is the literal translation of the Greek εὐαγγέλιον, a word found throughout the New Testament and usually rendered in English as "gospel." Gerhard Kittle, ed., *Theological Dictionary of the New Testament,* 2:707–37.

2. The entire account of Acts follows the work of the Apostles as they fulfil the Lord's injunction, spreading the gospel message in Judea and Samaria (chapters 8–11), and throughout the Roman world via Paul's missions to Cyprus (chapter 11), the Roman provinces of Syria, Cilicia, Galatia, and Asia (chapters 13–16), the provinces of Macedonia and Achaea in Greece (chapters 16–19), and at Rome (chapter 27–28). See Joseph A. Fitzmyer, *The Acts of the Apostles* (1998), 201.

3. The Greek verb for "witness" is μαρτυρέω. It ultimately came to connote a testimony sealed with the sacrifice of life. See Kittle, *Theological Dictionary,* 4:474–514.

4. The chronology of this era remains uncertain. The year 48 or 49 is usually offered as the date of this Jerusalem Council. For chronologies of both the New Testament era and Paul's life and ministry, see John W. Welch and John F. Hall, *Charting the New Testament* (2002). Also see Richard L. Anderson, *Understanding Paul* (1983), 390–98.

5. The recognition of an apostasy of the Jews and the need it occasioned for a new dispensation is found in Joseph Smith's writings related to dispensations. See Joseph Smith, *History of the Church,* vol. 4, 207–09, 610; and vol. 6, 478–79. In discussing the mission of John the Baptist, the Prophet Joseph wrote "The Jews, as a nation, departed from the Law of God and the Gospel of the Lord" (Ibid., vol. 5, 257). This doctrine accords with Christ's teaching that in Him, the law of Moses was fulfilled (3 Ne. 9:17).

6. Ancient references to the size and importance of Antioch are Strabo, 16.2.5, and Josephus, *Bellum Judaicum,* 3.2.4. The best modern consideration of Christianity at Antioch is Raymond E. Brown and John P. Meier, *Antioch and Rome* (1983), discussing the nature of the city (22–24, 30) and the origin of its Christian community (32–44).

7. A variety of critics accept the troublemakers at Antioch as belonging to that group of Pharisees who had affiliated with the movement of Christ's followers, known at Antioch as *Christianoi* (Acts 11:1), but in Jerusalem as *Nazarenoi.* For a summary of scholarly opinion, see Fitzmyer, *Acts of the Apostles,* 541–45. See also F. F. Bruce, *The Epistle to the Galatians* (1982), 114–16.

8. The Greek verb ἀνατίθημι implies a recognition of the authority to make a final determination on the part of the persons before whom a matter is laid. A fuller discussion of its usage is found in Anderson, *Understanding Paul,* 157.

9. Whether this extension of fellowship constituted the admission of Paul, already an Apostle, and perhaps also Barnabas (Acts 14:4, 14), into the Quorum of the Twelve is discussed below in section 5, chapter 4.

10. Many commentators recognize the inner circle of three. A summary of information about them can be found in F. F. Bruce, *Peter, Stephen, James, & John* (1979), 15–23. See James E. Talmage, *Jesus the Christ* (1972), 362 for Peter's presidency; 370–76, 611–17 for the activities of the inner circle of the three; 219, 768 for the restoration of Melchizedek Priesthood keys. Also see John F. Hall, "Peter," *Encyclopedia of Mormonism,* ed. Daniel H. Ludlow, (1991), 3:1077–79.

11. The confusion of the Jameses is addressed in Welch and Hall, *Charting the New Testament,* chart 13-10. A summary of information is provided in Donald A. Hagner, "James," *Anchor Bible Dictionary,* ed. David Noel Freedman, (1992), 3:616–18.

12. Anderson, *Understanding Paul,* 52. Summary discussions of the debate over what Acts account parallels Galatians 2 are provided by Charles B. Cousar, "Council of Jerusalem," *Anchor Bible Dictionary,* vol. 3, 766–68; Fitzmyer, *Acts of the Apostles,* 539–40; and Bruce, *Galatians,* 69–76.

13. A sound treatment of this process is found in L. H. Feldman, *Jew and Gentile in the Ancient World* (1993), 288–341, in a section regarding the success of proselytism by Jews in the Hellenistic and Roman eras.

14. For the process of change in Judaism and the origin of diverse groups of Jews see Helmut Koester, *Introduction to the New Testament,* vol. 1, *History, Culture and Religion of the Hellenistic Age,* 2nd ed., (1995), 197–271. For an inclusive summary of Zealot groups see Kent P. Jackson, "Revolutionaries in the First Century," *Masada and the World of the New Testament,* ed. John F. Hall and John W. Welch, (1997), 129–40.

15. William Hendriksen, *A Commentary on Galatians* (London: 1969), 51.

16. Dennis E. Smith, "Table Fellowship," *Anchor Bible Dictionary,* vol. 6, 302–03, suggests that early Christian communal meals were "imbued with ritual meaning" since "eating together was often utilized to symbolize the ratification of a covenant between parties" as in Genesis 26:26–31.

17. Ibid. "In Judaism, the food laws ("*Kashruth*") functioned as a means to define boundaries between the Jewish community and the rest of the world."

18. Tacitus, *Historiae* 5.5.2. *adversus omnes alius hostile odium separati epulis discreti cubilibus.*

19. Acts 6:1–6 reports the complaint of "Grecians" against "Hebrews." The King James Version renders the Greek *Hellenistai* as "Grecian." Scholarly opinion is divided as to whether this group consisted of Greek members of the Church who had presumably converted to Judaism at some past time and later became Christian, or whether the distinction is between two groups of Jews, one that had become Hellenized and were, therefore, speakers of only Greek, and another group which consisted of those who spoke Aramaic, with or without knowledge of Greek as a secondary language. Summary of the issues, evidence, and scholarly opinion is presented by Fitzmyer, *Acts of the Apostles,* 347–49. Although at present the majority of scholars opt for the difference between the two groups as a linguistic distinction alone, it seems unlikely that this could account for the severity of the complaint and the scope of the Twelve's resolution of the problem. A more deep-seated ethnic division seems a greater likelihood for the apparent magnitude of the concern.

20. "The Coming of Jesus, Stephen maintained, involved the abrogation of the Mosaic customs and the cessation of sacrificial worship," Bruce, *Peter, Stephen, James, & John,* 52. Also see M. Boismard, "Stephen," *Anchor Bible Dictionary,* 6:207–11. On the role of the Sanhedrin in capital cases see Fitzmyer, *Acts of the Apostles,* 390–91; and Raymond E. Brown, *The Death of the Messiah* (1994), 363–72.

21. Bruce, *Peter, Stephen, James, & John,* 50, asserts that the seven as a group were "foremost in propagating the Christian message throughout Judea and the neighboring regions; it eventually launched the Greek mission, and in particular was responsible for founding the Church at Antioch." For Philip see J. F. Watson, "Philip," *Anchor Bible Dictionary,* 5:311–12.

22. See Fitzmyer, *Acts of the Apostles,* 446–73; and Pheme Perkins, *Peter, Apostle for the Whole Church* (1999), 92–94.

23. Fitzmyer, *Acts of the Apostles,* 538.

24. Like Paul, Barnabas was a Jew of the diaspora. A Levite from Cyprus, sent to Antioch to teach Gentiles, Barnabas requested Paul's assistance in that labor (Acts 9:27). The two were companions in carrying the gospel message throughout Cyprus and Asia Minor. An apostle, Barnabas may have been received into the Quorum of the Twelve, along with Paul on the very occasion

of the Jerusalem Council. See also J. B. Daniels, "Barnabas," *Anchor Bible Dictionary*, 1:610–11.

25. Hendriksen, *Epistle to the Galatians,* 80.

26. Anderson, *Understanding Paul,* 52. In recent years it has become popular among scholars to portray James as presiding over the conference since he spoke last, and pronounced his opinion on the matter, and from that to opine that it was James, rather than Peter, who led the Church at Jerusalem. See W. H. C. Frend, *The Rise of Christianity* (1984), 88–92. Also see John Painter, *Just James, the Brother of Jesus in History and Tradition* (1999), 48–49. A more balanced approach that recognizes Peter's place in the meeting is Fitzmyer, *Acts of the Apostles,* 542–67. Anderson, *Understanding Paul,* 52, is quite right in demonstrating that in the prior sections of Acts James' name appears only once, while Peter's occurs 57 times, and in concluding "commentators have tunnel vision who see James as council president." It is Peter who presides at the council, for it is Peter who presides over the Church of Jesus Christ, as commissioned by Jesus Christ Himself. (John 21:15–17). This view accords with Bruce R. McConkie, *Doctrinal New Testament Commentary* (1971), vol. 2, 143.

27. Bruce, *Peter, Stephen, James, & John,* 86–101 assesses James as having strong appeal to the Judaizers because of his own practice of the law, but wrongly concludes James has surpassed Peter as leader of the Church at Jerusalem.

28. That James makes this announcement is interpreted by many scholars as corroboration of his presidency of the council. See Bruce, *Peter, Stephen, James, & John,* 91; J. Painter, *Just James* (1999), 49; J. B. Adamson, *James: The Man and His Message* (1989), 22–23. This stance ignores entirely the occurrence of the preliminary meetings where the decision of the chief brethren had been made. James's role is to announce one aspect of that decision: how the doctrine would be disseminated.

29. Frend, *Rise of Christianity,* 92.

30. Fitzmyer, *Acts of the Apostles,* 556–57, outlines questions and issues relating to the Noachic covenant. Moreover, an alternate manuscript tradition is explored, in which a fifth proscription—observance of the *Golden Rule*—is added to the four familiar prohibitions.

31. Anderson, *Understanding Paul,* 53.

CHAPTER TWO

———❧———————————————————————————————❧———

The Apostolic Foundation

The power and authority exercised by the Four Pillars was derived from Jesus Christ through their apostolic calling and as members of the presiding Quorum of the Twelve Apostles. For so long as those apostolic priesthood keys functioned, the Church was directed according to the will of their Master. When men no longer remained to whom the Savior had directly delegated His authority, the Church faltered. Great churchmen of the time recognized the impact of the withdrawal of apostolic keys. Polycarp, bishop of Smyrna and famed disciple of the Apostle John, lamented that throughout Asia these great sources of knowledge departed in the sleep of death. Hugh Nibley has liberally but succinctly translated Polycarp's statement to signify, "the lights went out."[1]

The Twelve

During the period of His Galilean ministry, the Savior called twelve of His leading disciples to perform a special mission and sent them by twos to declare the gospel to the lost sheep of the House of Israel (Mark 6:7). Matthew's account (Matt. 9:35–11:1) amplifies the Lord's instructions to the Twelve by prophesying of opposition and persecution by Jew and Gentile, but instructing them to rely on the Holy Spirit as they exercised their newly received authority to heal the sick, raise the dead, and cast out demons.

Upon their return from their missionary experience, this special group of disciples, endowed with priesthood power unique to their calling, were thereafter referred to as the Twelve (ʹοι δώδεκα) or simply as the Apostles (ʹοι απόστολοι). In ancient classical Greek, among other meanings, ἀπόστολος signified one delegated or one sent as a delegate. The word's use as a title in the *Koine*, or common Greek, of early Christianity must be understood primarily as having reference to the delegation by Christ of special power and authority, just as noted in the scriptural account of His organization of the Twelve.

That the Twelve were viewed as a distinct group is clear from the repeated use of ὁι δώδεκα in the gospel accounts (twelve times in Mark, six in Matthew, six in Luke, and four in John). This does not escape the understanding of the eminent historian of the early Church, Kirsopp Lake, in his observation that the Twelve acted as "inspired and miraculously powerful heads of a new society—the Church—endowed with power to confer the gift of the Holy Spirit, which they themselves had received from the risen and glorified Jesus."[2] This body of the Twelve, by virtue of their endowed power, exercised both spiritual leadership and administrative authority over the Church belonging to Jesus Christ. There was no question, as Eduard Meyer declared, that the highest authority was held by the Twelve, and at their head was Peter.[3]

Again, that the Twelve was conceived of as a single quorum is made clear by the urgency to fill the vacancy brought about by the betrayal and suicide of Judas Iscariot (Acts 1:15–26). Moreover, the charge of the Savior to carry the glad tidings of the gospel throughout the world was given specifically to the Twelve (Acts 1:8–11). Talmage concluded that this event "indicates the authority of the Apostles to administer the affairs of the Church after the ascension of the resurrected Messiah. That Peter, the senior member of the apostolic council, was given a position of presidency appears from the Savior's special admonition and charge on the shores of the Tiberian Sea."[4]

Apostolic Authority

Not only Peter but all of the Four Pillars fulfilled their role of spiritual leadership of the Church by virtue of apostolic authority. The Prophet Joseph Smith declared the nature of this authority as restored to the present dispensation to be to "preside over the churches of the Saints, hold the keys of the ministry to unlock the door of the Kingdom of Heaven unto all nations, and to preach the Gospel to every creature."[5] The work of presiding over the Church and preaching the gospel is not only the calling of latter-day Apostles, but was clearly manifest in the activities of the original Apostles of the first century. In conjunction with the apostolic role of presiding over the Church is the bestowal of the keys that Christ first conferred on His Apostles as a mode of delegating His own authority to His chosen Twelve. Brigham Young explained that these "keys of the eternal priesthood, which is after the order of the Son of God, are comprehended by being an apostle."[6] Through the exercise of these keys, the Four Pillars accessed the powers of heaven and functioned in their apostolic calling. Two of the four, first Peter and afterward John, presided over the whole Church as Senior Apostle.

The Twelve understood that the authorization the Savior had given to the Church to operate in accordance with the directions of the Holy Spirit, exercising gifts of that same Spirit, depended on the apostolic keys that linked the earthly Church with the heavenly. This connection made through the Apostles is what Paul alludes to in his declaration that the Church is "built upon the foundation of the Apostles and prophets, Jesus Christ himself being the chief corner stone" (Eph. 2:20). In other words, without the Apostles there could be no authorized Church, no legitimate earthly body corresponding with the assembly of the faithful in heaven, which could access, even in this world, the very powers of heaven.[7]

The special charge of the Savior to His Apostles, to preach the gospel and preside over the Church, was carried out by virtue of the exercise of apostolic keys. Through those same keys the Apostles organized local branches of the Church, appointed local officers, *episcopoi* (ἐπίσκοποι), to oversee the work of churches in individual locales, along with members of local councils to advise them, *presbyteroi* (πρεσβύτεροι), and others, *diakonoi* (διάκονοι), to minister to the needs of members in their separate congregations or house churches.[8] Local Church organization was created under the direction of the Apostles, and without apostolic delegation of authority no local churches could function properly or legitimately exist.

Missions of Individual Apostles

Before turning attention to the monumental work of the Four Pillars, it may be beneficial to examine the other Apostles' efforts. The scant evidence of surviving sources and the morass of tradition and legend concerning the missions of the Apostles allows comparison of the magnitude of the labors of Peter, John, James, and Paul, for a comprehensive, though incomplete, understanding of the nature and scope of the Church in the apostolic era.

An intriguing passage in apocryphal scripture, *The Acts of Thomas*, links the distribution of mission territories among the Apostles to the Jerusalem Council of A.D. 49.[9] If this was, in fact, the last assemblage of the Twelve before separating to proclaim the glad tidings of the gospel to the four corners of the world, it makes sense that it also provided the occasion for determining areas of supervision. It is very important to recognize the poor communications that prevailed in this age, and the difficulty such communications imposed upon the Apostles in coordinating their efforts. For those laboring within the boundaries of the Roman Empire, the situation was somewhat better, since the extensive and well-maintained Roman road system and the transportational advantage of the centrally located Mediterranean Sea provided superior communication and the opportunity for an occasional meeting of two Apostles.

James, son of Zebedee and brother of John, as noted earlier, comprised with Peter and John the inner circle of three Apostles who were the Savior's companions at the raising of Jairus's daughter, the Transfiguration, and Gethsemane. James was martyred before the Jerusalem Council, but surely the Apostle labored to advance the Christian movement for many years in Jerusalem and Judea before he was put to death by Herod Agrippa. For most of his life this Herod, grandson of King Herod, had governed Galilee as *tetrarch*, but had been elevated in 41 B.C. by his boyhood friend, the emperor Claudius, to rule as king over the reconstituted Judean kingdom. Herod Agrippa died in A.D. 44, before which date James would of necessity have been killed. It is, however, unknown whether James was proselyting in Galilee or Judea when Herod, to please his subjects, chose to execute the Apostle. These circumstances that Acts reports in connection with James's death suggest great success in converting to Christianity the Jews of Judea and/or Galilee. Eusebius claims that Clement of Alexandria taught that James's prison guard was converted as the Apostle awaited execution and, rather than take part in James's death, chose to be killed along with the man who had brought him the gospel. Tradition, probably dating no earlier than the sixth century, attributes to James a mission to the three Roman provinces in Spain. Although it is not impossible that James departed Judea for several years before returning to meet his death, the tradition may have developed as an explanation for James's role as patron saint of Spain.[10]

Andrew, Peter's brother, is said to have introduced Christianity to the area on both sides of the Black Sea, the Roman provinces of Bithynia and Pontus in modern day northern Turkey, and to the lands of the Scythians in the area that is today Ukraine. After Constantinople became one of the great Christian patriarchates in the fourth century, Andrew was claimed as the apostolic founder of the Church there. Modern scholars assume that to compete with other great Christian centers claiming apostolic foundation, such as Rome, Ephesus, and Antioch, Andrew was appropriated because of the manifold traditions of his Black Sea missions. Not only was Constantinople situated near the Black Sea but, as chief city of Greece, it also capitalized on the story of Andrew's martyrdom in the Roman province of Achaea in southern Greece. The apocryphal *Acts of Andrew* reports that a local ruler, one Aegeates, whose wife Maxmilla had been converted by Andrew, crucified the Apostle on an X-shaped cross. Andrew's missionary labors are said to have borne much fruit as the Apostle's miraculous healings, exorcisms, and raisings from the dead were witnessed by the people of Greece.[11]

The Apostle Thomas was a major force in the spread of Christianity to areas east of the Roman Empire. However, Thomas is a figure made complex by a great many legends and traditions about him, as well as a number of apocryphal works whose composition is attributed to him. Thomas's identity is still unresolved by scholarship. His name derives from the Aramaic *te'oma*, which signifies "twin." Indeed, in Greek texts Thomas is referred to as Didymus, the Greek word for twin. Early Christian tradition holds that he was a brother of Christ who so resembled Jesus that he was identified as His twin. Suggestion has been offered that Thomas Didymus was, in fact, Jude, author of the epistle that bears that name and identifies its composer as the brother of James, considered to be James, the brother of the Lord. A manuscript of the Syriac version of the New Testament provides a variant reading of John 14:22 to say that Thomas's given name was Jude.[12] Thomas is associated with the evangelization of Mesopotamia, Parthia (Iran), and India, where tradition holds he met his death. Because these are areas where the Syriac-speaking Church developed, Thomas is very important in the traditions of that strain of Christianity and was "revered in the early Syriac church as an Apostle and twin brother of Jesus."[13] Highly valued writings for the early Christians in the East and in Egypt were the *Acts of Thomas* and especially the *Gospel of Thomas*, whose format of recording sayings of Jesus by simply listing them one after another, largely devoid of the context of events, lends an air of authenticity.[14]

Eusebius quotes Papias as saying that Matthew also compiled the sayings of Jesus into the Hebrew dialect.[15] This may have been a strictly Jewish oriented precursor to the gospel that took form later.[16] Little information survives regarding Matthew's activities after the Apostles departed Judea. Legends merely suggest the area of his continued efforts, since they provide a multiplicity of deaths and locations. One tradition holds that Matthew was beheaded in Ethiopia, another that he was killed in Persia, and yet another that he died in Pontus on the shore of the Black Sea from natural causes. A passage in the *Babylonian Talmud* claims that Matthew was executed in Judea by the Jewish Sanhedrin.[17]

Nathanael, often identified by his patronymic Bartholomew (son of Thalomaeus), is said to have preached the gospel throughout Armenia, Mesopotamia, and Persia. Tradition holds that he was flayed and beheaded, a mode of execution typical of the Parthians within whose empire Bartholomew would have spent his ministry, no doubt teaching in the many communities of Jews who chose not to return from their Babylonian captivity, but to remain in the Mesopotamian region. To Bartholomew are attributed three apocryphal works: a *Gospel of Bartholomew*, which has not survived, a *Questions of Bartholomew*, for which both Greek and Latin manuscripts exist, and the *Book of the Resurrection of Jesus Christ by Bartholomew the Apostle*, known in a Coptic version which details the Lord's visit to the world of the dead and His deliverance of Adam.[18]

Because of his name, the Apostle Philip is generally thought to have been a Hellenized Jew or a Greek converted to Judaism, who served, therefore, as an intermediary between Christ and believing Greeks (John 12:20–22). For this reason Philip is thought to have labored among the Gentiles in Asia Minor. Tradition connects him with Hierapolis, 100 miles east of Ephesus, where it is believed he was martyred and buried along with his daughters. Philip's tomb was an important pilgrimage site for the Christians of Asia Minor for centuries. Nevertheless, the tradition may be inaccurate and the Philip buried at Hierapolis may be Philip the evangelist, chosen by the Apostles as one of seven who subsequently carried the gospel to the Samaritans. The evidence of Acts 21:8–9 that mentions Paul remaining with Philip the evangelist and his four prophetic daughters suggests as much.[19]

The Apostle Thaddeus seems to have been directed eastward in his labors. He is much connected with the city of Edessa, midway between Syria and Mesopotamia. There Thaddeus is said to have testified, converted, and performed miracles of healing. Also connected with his apparently lengthy residence in Edessa is the composition of an *Acts of Thaddeus,* of which both Greek and Syriac versions survive.[20]

Of Simon the Zealot or James, son of Alphaeus, beyond their original inclusion into the Twelve, no information—even by way of legend or tradition—exists today. It is not impossible that they had passed away before the time of the Jerusalem Council, resulting in the induction of Paul and Barnabas into the Twelve.

This discursus on the work of the other Apostles has been brief, made so necessarily by the lack of reliable evidence. This, however, in nowise suggests that the efforts of the others were insignificant, but rather that their missions, especially those beyond the confines of the Roman Empire, in which setting the traditions of western Christianity were preserved, left a legacy in writings that did not receive canonization in a later era. Nevertheless, just as Paul observed, there were pillars in the Church, and their work was directed westward, where their acts and words have continued to exert influence through the centuries up to the modern era.

Endnotes

1.   Eusebius, *Historia Ecclesiastica*, 5.24.2 quotes Polycarp as follows: καὶ γὰρ κατὰ τὴν Ασίαν μεγάλα στοιχεῖα κεκοίμηται. See also Nibley, *When the Lights Went Out* (1970).

2. Foakes Jackson and Kirsopp Lake, *The Beginnings of Christianity: The Acts of the Apostles* (1933), 5:39.

3. "Die höchste Autorität aber bilden die Zwölf, un an ihrer Spitze Petrus," Eduard Meyer, *Ursprung und Anfange des Christentums* (1962), 3:263–64.

4. James E. Talmage, *The Great Apostasy* (repr. 1968), 7.

5. Joseph Smith, *History of the Church*, 2:200.

6. *Journal of Discourses* (repr. 1967), 1:134–35.

7. The word used by the early Christians for "assembly" is the Greek ἐκκλησία. The citizen assemblies of the various Greek city-states had been for centuries named by this word. However, in English versions of the New Testament, the original ἐκκλησία is invariably rendered "church." For the early Christians, the Church was, therefore, an earthly extension of the heavenly assembly. See Kittel, *Theological Dictionary*, 3:501–36.

8. For the structure and work of local churches in the apostolic and post-apostolic eras, see B.H. Streeter, *The Primitive Church* (1929); Raymond E. Brown, *The Churches the Apostles Left Behind* (1984). Perhaps the best work on the topic is Hugh Nibley, *Apostles and Bishops in Early Christianity*, ed. John W. Welch and John F. Hall (forthcoming).

9. Harold Attridge, "The Acts of Thomas," *Anchor Bible Dictionary*, 6:531.

10. Hagner, "James," *Anchor Bible Dictionary*, 617.

11. Jeffrey T. Tucker, "Andrew," *Eerdman's Dictionary of the Bible* (2000), 62; J. Christian Wilson, "Acts of Andrew," *Eerdman's Dictionary of the Bible*, 62; Dennis R. MacDonald, "Andrew," *Anchor Bible Dictionary* (1992), 242–43.

12. Raymond F. Collins, "Thomas," *Anchor Bible Dictionary*, 6:528–29.

13. Ron Cameron, "Gospel of Thomas," *Anchor Bible Dictionary*, 6:535.

14. Ibid.

15. Eusebius, *Historia Ecclesiastica*, 3.39.16.

16. Scholarship too extensive to list here offers a wide variety of theory regarding the date, occasion, and place of the composition of Matthew's gospel. A sound summary of scholarly views is found in John P. Meier, "Gospel of Matthew," *Anchor Bible Dictionary*, 4:622–41.

17. Kent Newport, "Martyrdom of Matthew," *Anchor Bible Dictionary*, 4:643.

18. Michael J. Wilkins, "Bartholomew," *Anchor Bible Dictionary*, 1:615; Jon B. Daniels, "Gospel of Bartholomew," *Anchor Bible Dictionary*, 1:615–16.

19. JoAnn Ford Watson, "Philip," *Anchor Bible Dictionary*, 5:311.

20. JoAnn Ford Watson, "Thaddeus," *Anchor Bible Dictionary*, 6:435.

CHAPTER THREE

The Jewish Background of Early Christianity

Christ was the long-prophesied Messiah of the Jews. Therefore, the Jewish origin of the first Christians is obvious. Moreover, that Christianity spread by proselyting in the farflung communities of the Jewish *diaspora*, the scattering and subsequent settling of the Jews outside of Palestine, is apparent to anyone who, through even a cursory perusal of Acts, may be familiar with Paul's missionary methodology. However, the very extensive spread of Jews in the diaspora and the resultant facility of Christianity's phenomenal growth remain largely unrecognized. Even more astounding is the misperception that the Judaism of the time of Christ was the same as the law codified by Moses and inculcated by Old Testament prophets. The nearly five hundred years between the end of the Old Testament and the beginning of the New Testament not only witnessed the creation of the diaspora, but also the transformation of the religion of the Hebrews into a new Judaism, myriad in its forms and apostate in all its diversities.

Exile, Return, and Diaspora

In 722 B.C., Samaria, capital city of the kingdom of Israel, fell after a three-year siege by Assyrian armies. The city was sacked and burned; the kingdom of Israel ceased to exist, its territory annexed to Assyria and its people led away to be settled initially in the northern reaches of Assyrian-controlled territory and finally disappearing to history as the lost ten tribes.

A scene similar in many ways was reenacted with the fall of Jerusalem and the kingdom of Judah when, in 597 B.C., Babylonian armies of Nebuchadnezzar carried away Judah's rebellious monarch and many of Jerusalem's leading families. Afterward, Zedekiah reigned over Judah as a vassal king for nine years until his own rebellion brought an end to the Jewish state. In 587 B.C. most of the inhabitants of Judah were deported to Babylon. They were not lost to history but are known to have been placed in settlements throughout Babylonia, with particular concentration along the Chebar River near the city of Nippur, southeast of Babylon.[1]

With these events began the *diaspora*, or dispersion of the Jews. The removal to Babylonia was obviously forced, but other migrations dating to the early sixth century B.C., as well as later movements, were far from compulsory and represented voluntary relocation of Jews in search of better opportunities. Indeed, when Cyrus the Persian permitted the return of Jews to their homeland, many preferred the fertile lands along the Euphrates to the stony, often barren ground of the Judean hills and valleys. This Babylonian Jewish community ultimately achieved wealth and prestige, with some of their number, such as Daniel, serving as government officials, first of Babylonia, and, after Cyrus's 538 B.C. conquest, of Persia. It was partly a result of the influence exerted by the Babylonian Jewish community on the Jews who returned to Jerusalem, that new language (Aramaic) and new religion (the Talmudic Judaism of the rabbis) came to Judea.

Babylonia was not the only place of Jewish dispersion. Since nine years intervened between the first and second capture of Jerusalem by the Babylonians and the taking captive of the Jewish population, many of Judea's inhabitants were, no doubt, able to depart. Strong evidence survives to indicate Jewish migrations to Egypt,[2] that began the almost continual influx of Jews over the next several centuries, culminating in the extremely populous Jewish community located in Alexandria, capital of Ptolemaic Egypt. Political ties of the kingdom of Judah to Egypt influenced the rebellions against Babylonia that brought about the Babylonian captivity. It is, therefore, not surprising that Jews fleeing Babylonian overlordship would seek refuge in Egypt. Ties to Egypt are demonstrated in the story of the merchant-become-prophet, Lehi, whose own flight from Jerusalem corresponded chronologically to the events of the time period.[3]

Claiming descent from both Medes and Persians, Cyrus was the architect of an empire that, under his successors, extended westward to northern Greece, eastward to the borders of India, encompassing western continental Asia, and even including Egypt. Within the boundaries of that vast dominion, loyal subjects were allowed free movement. Accordingly, not only with Cyrus's acquiescence, but even with his urgence, Jews returned to rebuild Jerusalem. For the Jews of the time, Cyrus's reversal of Assyrian and Babylonian policy of keeping subjugated peoples captive at the center of the empire, instead encouraging return to homelands, was of monumental significance, so much so that it marked the close of Old Testament history.

> Since the Hebrew order of the Old Testament books places Chronicles last, the Jewish Bible closes with Cyrus' proclamation of 538/537 allowing the Jews to go up to Jerusalem to rebuild the temple (2 Chron 36:22–23; cf. Ezra 1:1–4). Although the decree has no extrabiblical attestation, it accords with Cyrus' general claim to be the servant of the gods of his conquered peoples.[4]

The return of the Jews first under Zerubbabel, as well as later in a relocation led by Ezra, along with the establishment of the postexilic community and commencement of the era of the second temple, is perhaps less important (at least for the consideration of early Christianity), than the migration of individual or small groups of Jewish families to many locations throughout the Persian domain. Continued immigration into Egypt and, more importantly, the establishment of Jewish groups in the cities and towns not only of Syria but even in Asia Minor, began to establish a broad diaspora where the Persian world, and, more significantly, the later Hellenistic successor empires of the Greeks, would become familiar with the Jews and their beliefs, laying the groundwork for the later expansion of Christianity.[5]

The New Jewish Religion

During the next centuries Judea was a small and unimportant backwater district of the Persian Empire.[6] Few historical sources remain to chart the reestablishment of Jewish community and the development of a reformed religion which appropriated to itself beliefs and practices found in neither the ancient faith of the patriarchs nor the law of Moses.

The Persian period is one of the more obscure periods of Palestinian Jewish history, because of the paucity of extrabiblical source material. Nevertheless, the importance of this period is undoubted for the foundations of postbiblical Judaism were laid during this time. This was the achievement of those Jews who returned to Palestine from their exile in Babylonia under the auspices of their new Persian rulers.[7]

Little direct evidence is available to provide detail for the process of this change. While many sources treat the beginnings of the new Jewish religion, they are restricted so as only to compare the religious beliefs and practices of sixth and fifth century B.C. Judea with the Hebrew religion that preceded this postexilic Judaism.[8]

Although the temple with its purificatory ritual for the people as a whole, as well as for individuals, resumed functioning after its reconstruction, the importance of priests gave way to a new class of religious leader of whom and for whom Ezra was a paradigm. Perhaps more than a century after the initial return of Jews to Jerusalem, Artaxerxes, king of Persia (464–425 B.C.), directed a large group of Jews to depart from the land of Babylon and to return to Judea under Ezra's charge. Ezra is described as "a ready scribe in the law of Moses" (Ezra 7:6). One commentator characterizes the function of Ezra and successive scribes as supplanting priests and substituting scholarly pursuit of the law for absent revelation.

> Previously the religious leaders were the priests, prophets, and wise men; but prophecy was soon to cease, and while there were still priests, they were concerned with the temple ritual and its affairs. A different kind of "wise men" arose—scholars in the sacred writings. Scribes replaced priests as the interpreters of the law and in the absence of prophetic revelation, scribal interpretation became the authority.[9]

In Ezra's profession is discovered the prototype of the rabbi, and Ezra is sometimes held to be the founder of rabbinical Judaism in Palestine. The Torah in its present form is attributed to Ezra, as is the establishment of the synagogue among the Jews of Judea. It is generally assumed that under Ezra's direction the institutions and tenets of religion as practiced by Jews in Babylonia were transplanted to

Judea.[10] Henceforward, purification of the Jewish people through strict observance of the law as interpreted by the scribes and taught in the synagogues would constitute this Judaism's path to individual salvation. And while the written opinions of the rabbis would not appear in codified form until the advent of Mishnah at the end of the second century A.D., the process of *midrash,* or interpretation of the Torah, may possibly date its beginnings from as early as this era.

So fundamental a change in the basic premises of the doctrine and practice of a religion typically result, as they certainly did in this instance, in dissenting divisions and splinter groups claiming to represent the proper mode of religious observance. Jews and other Israelites who had survived the deportations of earlier centuries still remained in the region of Samaria and practiced a form of the religion deriving from that which was followed before the exile. From this period a schism developed between Samaritan and Jew, exacerbated by Ezra's attempts to compel religious reform in Samaria. More significantly, diverse schools of religious practice evolved in Judea, forerunners to a fragmented Judaism in which Pharisees, dedicated to the law as interpreted by rabbinical scribes, disputed with priestly Sadducees and separatist Essenes. The new Judaism was not one religion but many, and "the ingredients of these divisions are already evident in the Persian period," when "the Babylonian Exile supplies the contours of the larger Judaic framework within which the various Judaisms developed."[11]

Judaism in the Hellenistic World

In 332 B.C., after victories in Syria and Phoenicia, Alexander the Great, Macedonian Greek conqueror of the Persian Empire, while en route to Egypt, stopped to offer sacrifice in Jerusalem to the God of the Jews. Alexander envisioned a new kind of empire in which ruler and subject shared the best of their cultures, including respect and accommodation for religions. Alexander's life was short and ended before his multidimensional cultural sphere, or Hellenistic civilization, could fully develop. Instead, Alexander's empire fragmented in war between his generals, each of whose kingdoms aggressively imposed Greek culture and language. Only in Egypt did the Macedonian Ptolemies attempt to blend local culture with their own Greek way of life. By contrast, the Macedonian Seleucid rulers of

Syria, Mesopotamia, and Asia Minor superimposed Greek ways on their subjects by whatever means necessary.

Within a few decades the eastern Mediterranean and its hinterland had been "Hellenized." Greek communities were established within large cities or as separate foundations in proximity to existing towns. Greek schools and academies provided education in Greek literature and philosophy. This greatly affected the thoughts and ideas of local peoples, especially the aristocratic classes who readily embraced Greek ways. The Greek language, learned and used by many, became a force for cultural unity throughout all the lands of the Near East, in many of them filling the role of *lingua franca* that Babylonian-employed Aramaic once held.

The coming of the Greeks complicated the diversity of strains within Judaism, not only in Palestine and Babylonia, but also among *diaspora* Jews in Egypt, Syria, and Asia Minor. The Persian Empire had fallen to Alexander the Great and the Macedonian conqueror had established his policy of Hellenistic *oecumene* (οἰκουμένη), a community of shared cultures, ideas, and ethnicities where things Greek were combined with cultural attributes of their new subject peoples. The successor kingdoms to Alexander's empire either continued to propagate this Hellenistic ideal or, as in the case of the Seleucid monarchs, opted for a more aggressive imposition of Greek culture. While Alexander seemed to understand Jewish distinctiveness, and the Ptolemies of Egypt (under whose rule Judea initially found itself), endeavored to implement Alexander's less severe Hellenistic ideal, the Jews of Judea at first reacted with mixed acceptance of Greek ways, education, and values. However, after Judea became subject to the Seleucid kings, active Hellenization may have been readily embraced by upper classes seeking to emulate the customs of their rulers, but the majority of the populace ultimately rebelled, incited by Maccabee leaders.[12] Nevertheless, after three centuries under Greek rule or Greek cultural domination of one variety or another, even for Judea "extensive Hellenization of the Jews is now undeniable."[13]

By the time of Christ, Greeks lived in the cities of Judea. Samaria, Galilee, and surrounding areas contained whole Greek towns and cities. This close interaction with Greeks ensured the expansion of Greek culture and language. Greek schools could even be found in Jerusalem, and a significant proportion of Greek-speaking Jews existed. The infusion of Greek culture among Jewish Palestinian society is further demonstrated by archaeological evidence, including local coinage with Greek inscriptions, the use of Greek personal names by Jews, numerous inscriptions and papyri in Greek, Greek schools, Greek architecture, etc.[14] It is difficult to measure the effect of Greek thought on intellectual life among the Jews of Judea. Greek words and phrases as well as citations and paraphrases of Greek literature or philosophy, are found variously in writings from the period, even in the words of the rabbis themselves, who often condemned Greek culture in the same compositions where Greek learning was employed.[15]

Judaism increased in its complexity and diversity in the atmosphere of Greek influence. The Judaism of the first century, already highly diversified, was affected even more profoundly by Hellenization, as well as by a seemingly endless variety of local interests and concerns.

Nevertheless, in all its regional forms the Judaism of the *diaspora* was practiced by individuals who were thoroughly imbued with Greek culture and for whom Greek had become their primary language, whether in Alexandria or Antioch, Ephesus or Tarsus. Moreover, the population of Jews living in the *diaspora* was far greater than that of the Jews in Palestine.

Both ancient literary sources, including Josephus in particular, as well as the evidence of archaeology, allow definite conclusions to be reached about the presence and size of Jewish communities in the towns and cities of the hinterland of the eastern Mediterranean. Josephus informs us that most Jews lived in Syria and most of these in Antioch. When the city was founded by Seleucus I as capital of his empire, Jews were invited to settle there. Many came from Babylon and surrounding areas, attracted by the promise of citizen rights. The Seleucid rulers further granted the Jews of Antioch the right to exercise their religion and maintain a synagogue.[16]

Only Alexandria, largest city in the world, exceeded Antioch in the size of its general population and perhaps also in the size of its Jewish community. Under the Ptolemies as well as under Egypt's later Roman overlords, some Alexandrian Jews became locally prominent and many exercised citizen rights. Most were thoroughly Hellenized, so much so that Greek had become their new native language and increasingly large numbers could no longer read Hebrew. Consequently, new scriptures in Greek were prepared by about seventy scholars in Alexandria, and the resultant Septuagint became the religious text of the Jews of the *diaspora*. Centuries later, it would serve as scripture for early Christians, many of whom were drawn from the Jewish *diaspora* communities, for whom Greek was more versatile than the disappearing Hebrew and the Aramaic once utilized by the governments of Babylonia and Persia.[17] Quotations of Old Testament scripture in New Testament writings generally derived not from Hebrew texts but from the Septuagint,[18] the heavy Christian use of which later occasioned a new Greek translation of Hebrew scriptures for use by Jews who preferred not to read the Christian-appropriated Septuagint.[19]

Asia Minor had become a region with Jewish populations in most towns and cities. Some of these communities had their genesis in the migrations at the beginning of the Persian Empire, but "the massive influx of Jewish population into Asia Minor took place at the end of the third century B.C. when Antiochus III settled two thousand Jewish families from Mesopotamia and Babylonia in Lydia and Phrygia."[20] At the time of this relocation, Josephus informs us that the substantial Jewish community in Ephesus was granted Ephesian citizenship by the same Seleucid ruler, Antiochus III.[21] Even though Ephesus has to date been only partially excavated, sufficient epigraphic evidence has been uncovered to corroborate the presence in Ephesus of a large Jewish population.[22]

No doubt, similar situations existed in the other cities of Asia Minor. Ruins of the Jewish synagogue of Sardis survive even today. Miletus, once the greatest city of the region, is known to have been home to many Jews, and is believed to have possessed a synagogue, possibly unearthed in recent excavations. Pergamum, Smyrna, Tarsus, Nicomedia, and a host of other cities are known to have possessed Jewish communities. The book of Acts informs us of Paul's work with congregations of Jews, not only at his home of Tarsus, but in many cities through which he journeyed, both in Asia Minor and in Greece.[23]

The conclusion is patently manifest. Not only in Judea itself, but even more importantly throughout the *diaspora* (that in the first century had extended even to Italy and Rome's western provinces), Jews absorbed some of the Hellenization process that turned the eastern Mediterranean and Near East into the Greek-speaking, culturally influenced *oecumene* envisioned by Alexander in the fourth century B.C. Acts provides certain evidence that in Jerusalem the Church was comprised of Aramaic-speaking Jews, Greek-speaking Jews, Greek proselytes to Judaism who had become Christian, and Greek Gentile converts. Throughout the *diaspora,* as the missionary work of the Four Pillars bore fruit, more Greek-speaking Jews and Greek proselytes to Judaism were converted to Christianity. (There was indeed deliberate design in Paul's missionary method of speaking in the synagogues of Asia Minor and Greece.) Ferguson is very correct in his dictum that "the Jewish matrix of early Christianity was itself already Hellenized."[24] The degree of Hellenization evidenced in the quickly expanding religion increased significantly as more and more new converts were Gentile Greeks and other Hellenized Gentiles who accepted the truths of the gospel. For these reasons it is doubtful whether Christianity can be viewed as an extension of the new Judaism of the rabbis or, for that matter, even as a mere extension of the Hebrew religion of the prophets which preceded rabbinical Judaism. Rather, early Christianity was unique, a fuller unfolding of the eternal gospel of Jesus Christ, and, in a certain sense, a restoration of truths and practices lost through the centuries by the Israelites, and abandoned by the apostate Judaism that developed during and after the Babylonian captivity.

Endnotes

1. Michael Grant, *The History of Ancient Israel* (1984), 142, 163.

2. Everett Ferguson, *Background of Early Christianity,* 2nd ed. (1993), 377.

3. Hugh Nibley, *Lehi in the Desert* (1952), 1–26.

4. Ferguson, *Backgrounds,* 376.

5. Clearly the spread of the greatest numbers of Jews throughout this area occurs during the era of the Seleucid and Ptolemaic Empires. Archaeological evidence and the occasional comment of Josephus nevertheless indicates Jewish presence in such metropolitan areas as Sardis or Damascus during the time of the

Persian Empire. See Irina Levinskaya, *The Book of* Acts *in its First Century Setting*, vol. 5, *Diaspora Setting (1996)*, 138–57; and Paul Trebilco, *The Jewish Communities in Asia Minor* (1991).

6. "Jerusalem was the center of the minuscule district of Yehud, governed by a *pehah* under the viceroy of the enormous region 'across the river,' which extended from the Euphrates to the Mediterranean Sea and had Damascus as its capital." Elias J. Bickerman, *The Jews in the Greek Age* (1988), 26.

7. Ferguson, *Backgrounds,* 376.

8. See, for example: Jacob Neusner, *A History of the Jews in Babylonia*, 5 vols. (1965–1970). W. D. Davies, *Paul and Rabbinic Judaism* (1955). As adequate a summary as any other is found in the *Anchor Bible Dictionary*'s survey in seven articles of Judaism from its reformation in the Babylonian era to the Mishnic era of the second and third centuries A.D. See *Anchor Bible Dictionary*, 3:1037–89.

9. Ferguson, *Backgrounds,* 377.

10. K. Koch, "Ezra and the Origins of Judaism," *Journal of Semitic Studies*, 19 (1974), 173–97. Also see Robert North, "Ezra," *Anchor Bible Dictionary,* 2:725–28.

11. J. A. Overman and W. S. Green, "Judaism (Greco-Roman Period)," *Anchor Bible Dictionary,* 3:1038.

12. By far the best treatment of the history of the Near East from the time of Alexander through the Roman era, and especially the influence of Greek culture on Judaism and Christianity within that context, is F. E. Peters, *The Harvest of Hellenism* (1970). Also see Cecilia Peek, "Alexander the Great Comes to Jerusalem: The Jewish Response to Hellenism," *Masada and the World of the New Testament*, ed. John F. Hall and John W. Welch (1997), 99–112.

13. Tessa Rajak "The Location of Cultures in Second Temple Palestine: The Evidence of Josephus," *The Book of Acts in its Palestinian Setting,* ed. Richard Bauckham (1993), 7.

14. David Fiensy, "The Composition of the Jerusalem Church," *The Book of Acts in Its Palestinian Setting*, 213, and 230–31. See also T. Rajak, "The Location of Cultures."

15. Louis H. Feldman, *Jew & Gentile in the Ancient World* (1993).

16. Josephus, *Bellum Judaicum*, 7:43–44.

17. Various theories of origin for the Septuagint have been advanced. Most likely is that the Greek translation represented neither directive from the Ptolemies as legend suggests, nor any official effort from the rabbis of Judea. Rather, it originated out of the need of Alexandrian Jews themselves, and was undertaken entirely at the direction of the Jews of Alexandria, by Alexandrian Jewish scholars, and thence was distributed throughout the world of the *diaspora* where existed equally great need for scriptures in the common language of

Greek. Ferguson, *Backgrounds,* 407–91.

18. Welch and Hall, *Charting the New Testament* (2002). See also Roger Beckwith, *The Old Testament Canon of the New Testament Church* (1986).

19. The translation was undertaken in the second century at the time of standardization of rabbinical Judaism under the direction of the Jamnia school and perhaps in connection with that rabbinical academy by Aguila, a Greek proselyte to Judaism from Pontus, who is sometimes identified with Ongelos, author of Aramaic Targums. Ferguson, *Backgrounds,* 411–12.

20. Levinskaya, *Diaspora Setting* (1996), 138. Also see Josephus, *Jewish Antiquities,* 12:149.

21. Josephus, *Jewish Antiquities,* 12:125.

22. Levinskaya, *Diaspora Setting* (1996), 146–48.

23. The evidence for Jewish communities throughout Asia Minor is detailed in Tribilco's *The Jewish Communities in Asia Minor.* For Greek cities with significant Jewish populations see Levinskaya, *Diaspora Setting* (1996), 153–66. Also note A. T. Kraabel, "The Diaspora Synagogues: Archaeological and Epigraphic Evidence," *Aufstieg und Niedergang der Römischen Welt,* vol II. 19.1 (1979), 477–510.

24. Ferguson, *Backgrounds,* 375.

CHAPTER FOUR

The Greek and Roman World of the New Testament

At the time of Christ, a huge part of the world was contained within the borders of Rome's empire. Rome ruled for a thousand years, dominating all to whom her senate, and later, her emperors, directed their attention. Protected by well-trained and exercised legions along the frontiers, *pax romana*, or the Roman peace, guaranteed that prosperity prevailed within. Travel and communication were facilitated by Roman roads, which connected well-developed urban centers with infrastructures maintained by an efficient government, a quality that was identified by the greatest of Roman poets, Vergil, as Rome's special natural gift. Christianity developed and expanded under these conditions. Roman government, law, society, religion, and custom influenced the inhabitants of those large portions of Europe, Asia, and Africa over which Rome exercised dominion. Latin was spoken in the west and Greek in the east. Romans were conversant with the Greek language and admired Greek literature, thought, and other aspects of Greek culture that predominated Rome's eastern provinces and influenced literate life in Italy and the west. Nevertheless, the term Greco-Roman is a modern misnomer. The cultures, religions, and motivations of Greeks and Romans were as different and distinct as were their languages. Greek idealism resulted in political division and Greek cynicism created a societal attitude generally skeptical of things religious. By contrast, the Roman *mos maiorum,* the chief motivating factor for Roman conduct to embrace with honor the religion and customs of their ancestors, produced a pragmatic and energetic people who believed that they were the chosen people of the gods, destined to impose their civilized rule on all nations. It may have been that very devotion to their own religion which engendered respect for the dedication of the Jews to their religious system, and brought special privileges and protections under which Jews and Christians, between whom Romans were normally unable to differentiate, enjoyed the opportunity for growth in the first and second centuries. In short, though both possessed urban-based societies and the Romans admired Greek literary attainments, in spirit and orientation toward religion and family, Romans resembled the Jews and not the Greeks.

Greek Life of the Polis

For much of their history as an independent people, the Greek way of life was that of the *polis,* the city-state which was at the same time both urban center and nation. Paradoxically, devotion to civic life within their individual cities led to political separation and disunity as a people. If not for conquerors like Alexander the Great or his father, Philip of Macedon, Greek power would probably not have been marshaled to overcome Persia and establish the Hellenistic cultural sphere throughout the eastern Mediterranean and Near East.

At the heart of Greek culture was the impetus to contribute to the *polis*. While state religion was practiced, and the old gods sacrificed to for the public good as a custom of civic life, by the first century Greek *paideia* (an educational system encompassing literature, philosophy in its many varieties, and rhetorical discourse), had long since assumed the chief role of determining the values and actions of those residing in Greek-style *polises,* whether in Greece proper or throughout the Hellenistic world.[1] For the Greeks, their traditional polytheistic religion was found wanting, since it had only pertained to assuring safety and prosperity in this world, and through sacrifice and respect had sought to guarantee that supernatural powers and forces were restrained from bringing harm or disadvantage. By the time of the fifth century B.C., confidence in a system of beings unperceivable through the empirical means that constituted the foundation of Greek rationalism was untenable. As religious devotion disappeared in Greece, even the Eleusinian mysteries long celebrated in Attica in honor of Demeter and the promise of salvation after death, lost much of their appeal.[2] Consequently, some inhabitants of Greek-style cities, both the educated and the uneducated, had begun to embrace the new salvatory religious movements, of which the worship of Isis and Mithraism became the prime competitors of Christianity in attracting those searching for real hope of life after death. The new systems of belief offered by these religions advanced values and codes of behavior that variously contrasted or accommodated the traditional elements of Greek culture and *paideia*.[3]

Greek learning and thought acted, therefore, as an independent system of value and actuating principle on the one hand, while on the other hand it exerted an indirect influence upon religions or philosophies through adherents who, having embraced these new belief systems, nevertheless brought with them previous training and frames of reference acquired as a result of their Greek or Hellenistic educations. In this way, aspects of Greek *paideia* influenced or entered into, for example, Judaism and developing Christianity. In the same manner, the distinct system of the Romans admitted Greek influences into some aspects of intellectual life.

Rome, Holy City, and Seat of Empire

The original inhabitants of Rome, drawn from a variety of Latin towns in central Italy, seem to have viewed themselves as especially preferred by their gods. The Romans were particularly devout in assuring that sacrifice and a host of other required religious ceremonies be observed. Their religious system, like that of the Greeks, was polytheistic, but the Romans believed in and respected their gods, more numerous by far than those of the Greeks. The Romans possessed a seemingly unending number of minor gods and divinities associated with individual locations, such as woods, springs, rivers, etc., and functions of life such as marriage, birth, coming of age, entering military service, etc. Similarly, families possessed different sets of familial divinities and household protectors, the *lares* and *penates*. Ancestors were accorded divine honors as well, but were not considered divine.[4]

From the beginning, the Roman monarch ruled by virtue of conferred authority from the gods. Patriarchs of tribes and fathers of families exercised similar powers over their patrimony. Early Rome was very much a sacral state. After Rome admitted kings from the neighboring and technologically more advanced Etruscans, religion was organized and codified. The collection of villages which comprised early Rome was urbanized as the new Etruscan population merged religious systems, societal practices, and civilizational advances with the earlier Latin inhabitants to form a new people, neither Latin nor Etruscan, but Roman. Protected by their chief god, Jupiter Optimus Maximus, who presided from a great temple on the Capitoline Hill in the urban center of the ever-expanding city, Rome's people believed they were destined to exercise Jupiter's authority over all the nations.[5]

In these origins are found a number of features that marked Roman character and civilization for a thousand years. Religion and family were inextricably interwoven and comprised the most central aspect of Roman value. State and religion were originally virtually identical. Roman government officials were the same individuals as religious officials, whether in the era of monarchy, republic, or empire. Roman law originated as the rulings and practices of those acting as officials of both state and religion. Because it derived from the gods, Roman law could extend to all nations as the *ius gentium* (law of nations), which required the guarantee of fair treatment for all men, though Roman citizens exercised higher privileges and received greater prerogatives under that law.[6] However, because Rome had developed into a city when separate peoples merged to become Romans, an innovative concept took form that citizenship was not limited to children born to Roman citizens, but could be extended to whole cities that Rome annexed in Italy, or could be granted even to individuals who by their acts and services merited Roman privileges.[7] Similarly, the favored destiny of Rome and her people, as ordained by Roman gods to civilize and rule all the nations, produced military skills that allowed Roman legions to expand Rome's borders to encompass many nations and peoples.

By the turn of the second century B.C., the Romans had emerged from decades of war to become the greatest power in the known world. They defeated Carthage and organized the western Mediterranean into Roman provinces. The municipalities of Italy enjoyed the same benefits of victory as Rome, and Italian towns began to adopt Roman institutions and customs, with Latin replacing local languages and dialects to affix linguistic unity to political. Unchallenged Roman control in the west permitted Rome's aristocratic leaders to survey the opportunities presented by the already decaying kingdoms of the Hellenistic east, a new theater of operations for Italian businessmen and Roman arms for the next seventy years.[8]

Rome's eyes turned to Greece and the Hellenistic east, but with caution and also with an abiding affection for things Roman. While Romans clearly appreciated and even appropriated aspects of Greek culture, literature, and thought, Roman culture remained, Roman government remained, Roman custom, religion, and spirit remained, and were enshrined in a single phrase that embodies all that was historically Roman—*mos maiorum*. In accordance with the "custom" or "tradition" of the ancestors, the lives of Romans, especially of the ruling families, who were the arbiters of culture and fashioners of Latin letters, were expected to conform. Although it was accorded the awe of religion and observed with the same scruple as the most sacred cultic rite, and, indeed, embraced within its scope the entirety of Roman religion, *mos maiorum* was a living principle encompassing the whole of Roman life and tradition—religious, but also political, legal, governmental, societal, familial, and personal. It served effectively for centuries to preserve a Roman uniqueness of character and spirit, and was the determining quintessence of Rome and of what was Roman. Moreover, it was, in fact, this *mos maiorum* that determined the parameters and methods of Roman rule and which features of Roman government, law, and civilization were imposed upon Rome's subjects. Accordingly, its effect is virtually immeasurable.

Roman Governance

Rome organized the territories acquired outside of Italy into regional divisions called provinces. These areas were assigned to former magistrates of the central government at Rome who received governorships over individual provinces for periods of usually from three to five years. Some provinces subject to threat of internal or external disruption maintained compliments of troops. Frontier provinces were garrisoned by the premier forces of Rome, the legions. Where there was little likelihood of difficulties, as for example the interior provinces bordering the Mediterranean, such as Asia or Judea, the governor was accompanied only by a few troops acting as a ceremonial bodyguard. The provincial system under the emperors witnessed the division of provinces between those whose governors were appointed by and reported to the emperor, and those administered by the Senate. The most strategically important provinces were imperial, possessed garrisons of legions, and were governed by imperial legates. Major senatorial provinces were under the charge of senators who had attained the high rank of *consul*, and governed provinces with the title of *proconsul*. Minor provinces, such as Judea, were governed by lower ranking equestrian officials known as procurators.[9] Some areas of Rome's domain in the eastern reaches of the empire were administered by local dynasts loyal to Rome who ruled over province-sized regions as client kings. While Herod lived, Judea had, for example, been organized under his direct control as a monarch whose rule was supported by Rome.[10]

In the first century A.D., subject to the emperor's *maius imperium,* or greater authority to countermand the authority of governors, the provincial governor was supreme in his province in all spheres administrative, military, or judicial. However, since the governor was accompanied by a small personal staff, his direct involvement in the day-to-day running of provincial life was very limited. In fact, he usually interposed himself only in matters that involved Roman citizens. Otherwise, the affairs of the cities and towns of the provinces and the local populace were directed by local officials to whom the business of government fell. Most of these "were members of the local aristocracies in the towns of the provinces. As members of local governments in Roman provinces they were granted Roman citizenship" in many instances.[11] Such local leaders—for example, the Sanhedrin in Judea—could be counted upon to return Rome's favor with their loyalty and "could be trusted to do Rome's bidding."[12] As long as protection was provided for the interests of Rome and any of her citizens who may have had dealings or involvements in the province, little attention was typically apportioned to issues of provincial towns and cities.

> Roman policy had long adhered to the perspective that local governance was most convenient provided the status quo be maintained, including the preservation of law and order, the collection of assessed revenues, and the support of Roman foreign policy with the supply of troops when necessary. Rome's major

concerns for the provinces were to maintain a peace in which Roman trade and commerce could be conducted, and Romans could come and go in safety. Taxes were collected to support the framework of government, including the army as guardians of internal security and providers of protection from the threats of foreign powers or barbaric enemies outside the empire.[13]

If Rome's interests were not provided for in a clear and orderly manner, the provincial governor or the imperial government acted quickly and decisively to guarantee the resumption of this preferred status quo.

Jews, Christians, and the Roman Empire

Contrary to erroneous popular opinion (usually derived from novels or films, rather than the pages of history), Romans had, in fact, treated the Jews of Judea relatively well until the A.D. 66 rebellion of Zealots. Moreover, Roman relations with the Jews of the *diaspora* were largely unaffected by affairs in Judea and remained quite good. These considerations are important not only to obtain accurate information about Jews in the Roman Empire, but, more importantly, also for studying Roman attitude toward Christians who, since many were of Jewish origin anyway, were hardly distinguishable from the Jews, at least in the understanding of most Romans. For example, the Roman biographer Suetonius recorded the occasion of the emperor Claudius's expulsion of Jews from Rome in A.D. 49, due to a riot between two groups of Jews, one group comprised of followers of a certain Chrestus. The passage is normally interpreted as making reference to Christians by the phrase, "Jews who followed Chrestus," and serves to underscore Roman confusion regarding the difference between Christians and Jews. However, by the early second century when Tacitus wrote his account of the A.D. 64 Great Fire at Rome (actually caused by Nero but blamed on Christians), at least that Roman historian was able to recognize Christians as a group distinct and apart from the Jews.[14]

By 146 B.C., Greece had been brought into the sphere of Roman control and was ultimately organized into the provinces of Achaea and Macedonia. Soon afterward, long-term Roman business concerns in the very rich and productive region of Asia Minor extended to become political interests; in 133 B.C. the last ruler of Rome's traditional ally, Pergamum, died bequeathing to Rome his Pergamene kingdom, located in the western half of Asia Minor. Organized as the Roman province of Asia, control of Pergamum brought Rome into conflict with the decaying empire of the Seleucids. It is not surprising that in order to maintain their hard-won independence from the Seleucids, the Maccabean rulers of Judea approached Rome for aid against a common enemy. Although then at peace with Seleucid Syria, the Roman senate entered into a treaty with Judea, warning the Seleucids that aggression against the Jewish state would constitute aggression against Rome. With Rome as protector, the Hasmonean dynasty of the Maccabees ruled Judea in relative security. Ironically, it was Roman power that made the functioning of a free Jewish state possible.

As the Seleucid monarchy grew weaker, several small kingdoms emerged from its territory and the Parthian Empire arose in Mesopotamia. To counteract attacks against its territory from these petty kings and to ensure the tranquility of the strategically and commercially important sea in the center of its territory, Rome was compelled to take control of the entire coastal area of the eastern Mediterranean. By 63 B.C., what was left of the Seleucid Empire was organized into the Roman province of Syria, directly administered by a Roman governor with a sufficiently large complement of legions to prevent Parthian incursion. Other territories were structured according to the client king pattern of administration that Rome practiced in the eastern reaches of its domain. At that time rival factions of the Jewish ruling Hasmonean family vied for power, producing chaotic conditions and internal conflict that threatened the peace of surrounding territories. This necessitated Roman intervention to maintain law and order, not only in Judea but throughout the immediate region, so Judea was attached directly to the Roman province of Syria, rather than organized into a client kingdom. Nevertheless, by authorizing local administration under a Hasmonean high priest and an assembly of nobles, or *Sanhedrin,* standard Roman practice of preferring local government was still followed. As much as was feasible, the Jews of Judea were left to themselves, and practiced self-rule and administration. Rome could have imposed its direct governance on Judea at any time, but preferred friendly relations with both the Jewish homeland as well as with the Jews of the *diaspora* living throughout many Roman provinces and subject territories.[15]

Increasing rivalry between Jewish factions ultimately brought a new dynasty to power in Judea whose loyalty to Rome was so firm that Julius Caesar himself sanctioned the authority of the Herodians. Because of his friendship with Antipater and his son Herod, Caesar personally extended to them the privilege of Roman citizen status. "Moreover, as undisputed master of Rome, Caesar promulgated laws to protect the religious freedom of Jews throughout the empire, extending to the Jews an unprecedented grant of special privileges."[16] Josephus provides information concerning the content of Caesar's decrees, including such rights as recognition as a *religio licita* (an officially acknowledged sect); exemption from military service (which would require not only fighting and killing, but the taking of oaths and the making of sacrifices to Rome's gods); the right to certain tax exemptions and the privilege of sending monies to the temple at Jerusalem; the permission to register congregations in cities as corporate groups (which brought not only the freedom of assembly but the ability to own property such as buildings for the purpose of assembling); and the right to build and maintain synagogues in the cities of the Roman Empire.[17] Such rights were really quite phenomenal and no doubt engendered on the part of other residents feelings of jealous antipathy toward the privileged Jews, especially in Hellenistic cities where there had been a long tradition of anti-Semitism among Greeks because of Jewish exclusiveness. Indeed, records exist of repeated Roman governmental demand at this time that cities in Asia Minor cease harassment of Jews.[18]

After Caesar's assassination on the Ides of March in 44 B.C., his *acta,* or official decrees, were ratified and given continuing legal status by the Roman government. When Caesar's grand-nephew reigned as Augustus, the first Roman emperor, the policies of Caesar were continued. Accordingly, the extraordinary privileges granted to the Jews persisted through the reigns of Caesar's descendants, Rome's Julio-Claudian emperors. At the end of the reign of Nero, last of these emperors, the Zealots of Judea killed Romans, Greeks, and many of the Jewish leaders and started the so-called Jewish War. However, the uprising did not affect Jews outside of Judea. Vespasian and his son, Titus, quelled the revolt and also rose to imperial honors at Rome, succeeding the Julio-Claudians in a new Flavian dynasty. Vespasian and Titus saw to it that the privileges of diaspora Jews, who had been overwhelmingly loyal to Rome during the Jewish War, were in nowise adversely affected. During the reign of Vespasian's other son, Domitian, the *fiscus Iudaicus,* relating to tax privileges and regulations regarding the temple tax, was somewhat altered; but in general, throughout the first and second centuries, Jewish privilege remained an attribute of life in the Roman Empire.[19] In many ways, only Roman citizens themselves exercised greater rights and privileges.

At first, since Christians were viewed as a Jewish separatist sect, they too benefitted from the privileges established by Caesar's acts. Around the time of the revolt in Judea, it became common knowledge that Christians were a group apart from the Jews and, despite the Jewish ancestry of some Christians, Jewish privileges were denied to them. By the time of Nerva's emperorship, an imperial edict made clarification that the legally recognized definition of a Jew would be thenceforth based on religious affiliation and not ethnicity. A Christian of Jewish parentage could not be counted Jewish, but a Gentile proselyte to Judaism was for legal purposes considered a Jew.[20] With the loss of Jewish privilege, Christians no longer possessed the right of being a *religio licita,* neither could they organize corporately, nor own property. Consequently, Christianity under Roman law could not qualify as a *religio* or *societas.* It was, therefore, a group without legal recognition or justification for existence.[21]

Romans were appreciated in their own time for their religious toleration. Their treatment of the Jews demonstrates their patience with other religions.[22] Their attitude toward Christians was also without rancor. Contrary to modern images created largely by Hollywood, Christian persecution by Romans did not develop, per se, until the early fourth century as part of the political struggle for the control of the empire waged by Constantine and his rivals. The killing of Christians in A.D. 64, while heinous, was nevertheless locally restricted to Rome as an exercise of the emperor's *coercitio* (magisterial authority) when Nero used Christians as scapegoats for the great fire and preemptorily executed them as criminal arsonists.[23]

The first century is a period treated by many surviving literary and historical sources, and documented by an abundance of inscriptions and surviving papyrological texts. Nowhere is there mention of any further governmental action against Christians. Quite to the contrary, the Church at Rome at the end of the first century, at least as delineated in *First Clement,* was a Church loyal to the empire and expecting to live in peace with it. Clement held up Roman law and order for admiration, the discipline of Roman legions to be emulated (*1 Clement* 37), and encouraged Roman rulers to be included in prayers (*1 Clement* 61). A plethora of Christian sources survive from the first century, and even more from the second century. New Testament writings seem not to indict Rome for killing Christians, but correspond with Roman second-century documents that reveal Rome as something of a protector of Christians, even if merely because Roman law was precise in insisting that crimes be proven.

It is abundantly clear from Acts that in the first century the persecutors of Christians were not Romans but Jews, the former brethren of so many Christians converted from Judaism. Who does not recall the many times Paul's successful proselyting of local Jewish congregations resulted in angry synagogue leaders demanding action against Paul from town administrators? While it cannot be denied that Paul's status as a natural-born Roman citizen furnished the Apostle great protection, it is also clear that even the non-citizen was accorded certain legal rights under Rome's concept of *ius gentium.*

The disposition by Jewish authority condemning Christians as apostates from Judaism, the great antagonism toward Christians, who refused to support the Jewish rebellion in A.D. 66 and fled to Pella or Antioch to escape the Zealots (for whom Christians were as favored a target as Greeks or Romans), and the later concerted efforts to discredit Christians in the writings of the rabbinical school at Jamnia are important considerations that induce Frend to conclude that most of the persecutions of individual Christians at this time appear to be "the direct result of Jewish hostility, far greater toward Christians than even toward pagans."[24] For our purposes, let it suffice to affirm that Jewish action against Christians was seldom "en masse." The martyrdom of Polycarp, bishop of Smyrna in A.D. 150 is the best known exception.[25] For the most part, however, individuals were accused of crimes and greater atrocities before local legal authority, whether Roman or the magistrates of "free cities" in the provinces. Moreover, such individual accusation was not limited to Jews, but extended to individuals of all or any persuasion who would find in

Christians easy targets to accuse out of personal enmity or the possibility of personal gain.

Such activity did not abate in the second century, and a most accurate document about the position of the Roman government vis-a-vis the Christians reflects precisely this kind of individual prosecution on charges, often anonymously alleged. When Pliny, governor of Bithynia-Pontus, corresponded with the emperor Trajan, he demonstrated that trials of Christians were commonplace, especially in the provinces of Asia Minor where the Christian population was burgeoning. Pliny was himself unfamiliar with the procedure of such trials and inquired whether being Christian itself was cause for condemnation. "Should the name, if free from crime, be punished, or only the crimes attached to the name." Trajan's response was telling. "They are not to be sought out; if they are denounced and proven guilty they must be punished, provided only this—that a man who denies he is a Christian and proves it . . . by praying to our gods, may obtain forgiveness."[26] Trajan concluded with an admonition against anonymous documents figuring in any charge, calling it a "vile precedent." The policy of Trajan persisted throughout the second century. It was reaffirmed formally by both Hadrian and Marcus Aurelius, while Antoninus Pius issued edicts forbidding mob violence directed toward Christians. In this era, the persecution of Christians was not an object of Rome's imperial administrations. Mattingly closes his study of Christian relations with Rome by concluding that "persecution, then, was intermittent and to some extent accidental," asserting that "early Christians attracted little attention from the Roman government, were not persecuted, might even be protected against their enemies the Jews."[27]

In conclusion, the Roman Empire provided a safe and prosperous location conducive to the rapid spread of Christianity. Roman government and Roman law, at least during the first and second centuries, guaranteed individual protection of rights, according to class and status. Without these protections, the history of early Christianity may have been very different, indeed.

Endnotes

1. The most thorough treatment of the subject is Werner Jaeger, *Paideia: The Ideals of Greek Culture,* 3 vols. (repr. 1957–1965).

2. This process and its ramifications are elucidated in Hugh Nibley, *The World and the Prophets* (1987).

3. A recent summary of the doctrines and practices of the oriental mystery religions is Robert Turcan, *The Cults of the Roman Empire* (1989). Also see John Ferguson, *The Religions of the Roman Empire* (1989).

4. Mary Beard, John North, and Simon Price, *Religions of Rome,* 2 vols. (1998); and G. Dumezil, *Archaic Roman Religion,* 2 vols. (1970).

5. For Etruscan influences at Rome, see *Etruscan Italy,* ed. John F. Hall (1996).

6. Religiously based principles pervasive through the development of Roman law are emphasized in two works of Alan Watson, *The State, Law, and Religion: Pagan Rome* (1992); and *The Spirit of Roman Law* (1995).

7. A. N. Sherwin-White, *The Roman Citizenship* (1973).

8. The consolidation of Roman power in the western Mediterranean is summarized in H. H. Scullard, *A History of the Roman World 753–146 B.C.,* 4th ed. (1980). The contact of Rome with the Greek east is analyzed in Erich S. Gruen, *The Hellenistic World and the Coming of Rome* (1984).

9. Welch and Hall, *Charting the New Testament* (2002), chart 4–5.

10. Richard Holzapfel, "King Herod," *Masada and the World of the New Testament,* ed. Hall and Welch (1997), 35–73.

11. James S. Jeffers, *The Greco-Roman World of the New Testament Era* (1999), 115.

12. Ibid.

13. John F. Hall, "The Roman Province of Judea: A Historical Overview" *Masada and the World of the New Testament,* ed. Hall and Welch (1997), 321.

14. Suetonius, *Claudius,* 25.4; Tacitus, *Annals,* 15.44. The Suetonius account was actually composed later. However, Suetonius was far less critical and precise than Tacitus and displayed a proclivity for uncritically using earlier sources which may account for his reflecting the lack of knowledge among Romans that Christians were anything but another Jewish sect. See G. B. Townsend, "Suetonius," *The Oxford Classical Dictionary,* 2nd ed. (1970). See also Ralph M. Novak, *Christianity and the Roman Empire* (2001), 20, 27–30; Harold Mattingly, *Christianity in the Roman Empire* (1967), 29–40. A valuable contribution to the topic of Roman perception of the Christians is Robert L. Wilken, *The Christians as the Romans Saw Them* (1984).

15. For detailed treatment of these events, see Peters, *Harvest of Hellenism,* 261–349.

16. Hall, "The Roman Province of Judea," *Masada and the World of the New Testament*, ed. Hall and Welch, (1997), 324. Also see Peters, *Harvest of Hellenism*, 380–82.

17. *Jewish Antiquities*, 18.81–84.

18. Feldman, *Jew & Gentile*, 92–94.

19. Ibid., 98–100.

20. Levinskaya, *Diaspora Setting*, 3–6.

21. Christian envy of Jewish status as an official religion is expressed by Tertullian, *Apologeticum*, 21.1.

22. Jeffers, *The Greco-Roman World*, 105–11.

23. Tacitus, *Annals*, 15.44. See also Mattingly, *Christianity*, 29–40, and A. N. Sherwin-White, *Roman Society and Roman Law in the New Testament* (1963), 1–23. *Coercitio* is the authority of a magistrate to compel citizens to act in accordance with his judicial rulings.

24. W. H. C. Frend, *Martyrdom and Persecution in the Early Church* (1968), 185.

25. Novak, *Christianity*, 56–64. Mobs of Jews seldom attacked Christians. Rather, Jewish action against Christian individuals or groups utilized government organs of city administration or the courts to prosecute Christians on trumped-up charges. The killing of Polycarp by a mob of Jews is quite the exception to the normal *modus operandi* of local Jewish leaders.

26. Pliny, *Epistulae*, 10.96 and 97; see Mattingly, *Christianity*, 36–39.

27. Ibid., 41 and 39.

SECTION TWO
Peter

CHAPTER ONE

The Impetuous Disciple

> Simon bar-Jona, later known as Cephas or Peter, became the senior and chief Apostle of Jesus Christ. . . . The New Testament contains more information about Peter than about any of the other Apostles. This provides some indication of his ministry, his character, and his relationship to the Savior. In contrast to the sometimes impetuous younger Peter portrayed in the Gospels, the Apostle's later ministry and epistles bespeak a mature leader of patient faith whose sincere concern is for the spiritual well-being of the flock that Jesus entrusted to him. (Jn 21:15–17).[1]

Modern characterization of Simon Peter often depicts an impetuous disciple who, at moments of crisis, was found wanting. Such interpretation ignores the achievements and accomplishments of a man of energy and determination already successful before his calling to follow the Christ. Moreover, such a portrayal misunderstands that Peter's impetuosity was born of confidence in the Savior and that, though sometimes insufficient, it was this disciple's faith that enabled him to dare what others did not.

Simon bar-Jona

Peter's given name was Simon, and his patronymic was bar-Jonah. "Most Christians know Simon as 'Peter' or 'Simon Peter.' The double form is most common in the Fourth Gospel. Otherwise it appears only in Luke 5:8, Matthew 16:16 and 2 Peter 1:1."[2] Simon and Andrew (Andreas), his brother, both have names that are of Greek derivation. Three of the Twelve Apostles, Peter, Andrew, and Philip, are said to have originally come from Bethsaida (John 1:40–44), on the north end of the Sea of Galilee. Philip is also a Greek name. Apparently Bethsaida was located in an area of considerable Hellenization, not merely because three of its Jewish native sons had been given Greek names, but because archaeological evidence has revealed Greek inscriptions in the region. Historical sources indicate that Herod Philip, son of Herod and tetrarch of the Gaulanitis region within which Bethsaida lay, had made grand improvements to the town, encouraged population increase by non-Jewish settlement, and finally raised Bethsaida to the status of a city, renaming it Bethsaida-Julias, in honor of the Julian family of the Roman Caesars.[3] Jews born and raised in Bethsaida could not only be expected to bear Greek names, but to speak Greek and be familiar with Greek ways.

Simon Peter's father's name is given as bar-Jonah. While this would point to Peter's father as a Jonah, the form of the patronymic given in Matthew 16:17, bar-Jona, may suggest the name to have been simply John. "'Jona' (*Yōnā*) may well be an abridged form of *Yōhānān*, 'John,' rather than the equivalent of the Hebrew name Jonah (*Yōnāh*)."[4] Peter, of course, is the Greek (*Petros*) rendering of the Aramaic *Kepha,* sometimes Hellenized as Cephas, the special name given by the Savior to Peter. Paul, for example, often refers to Peter by the name of Cephas.[5]

In addition to his father's name being Jonah or John, his brother being named Andrew, and his place of origin as the Hellenized Bethsaida-Julias, it is also known that Peter was married before his call to the apostolate and remained married afterward. At the time Jesus called Peter to follow Him as a disciple, Peter resided in the town of Capernaum (Mark 1:21, 29) and had living with him his wife's mother, who was later healed by the Savior (Mark 1:29–31; Matt. 8:14–15; Luke 4:38–39). Paul makes reference to Peter being accompanied by his wife as he journeyed teaching and presiding over the Church (1 Cor. 9:5). First Corinthians was written from Ephesus during Paul's three-year stay there (A.D. 54–56), nearly thirty years after the time Peter would have been called as a disciple. Peter had not put aside his wife for the ministry, as later suggested upon of the advent of celibacy. Further detail about Peter's family, information about children or other relatives, is absent from the sources. From the size of his house, discussed below, inference might be made that he had a rather large household, whether children, family members, or servants.

Peter resided in Capernaum. Archaeology reveals the town to have been structured in the normal Roman orthogonal plan, with rectilinear streets platted from a north-south main street, the *cardo,* and an east-west main street, the *decumanus,* crossing in a main square, the *forum.* This indicates that Capernaum was a Hellenized site with a significant non-Jewish population. Relations between ethnic groups seem to have been peaceable and Luke even informs us that the local Jewish synagogue had been built under the sponsorship of the faithful Roman centurion who later petitioned Jesus to heal his servant (Luke 7:2–10). From scriptural reference and the evidence of archaeological excavation, the site of Peter's house can be ascertained. Its north side, in fact, lay under the balcony of this very synagogue. On the south the house extended to the *decumanus,* while on the east it opened onto an open area adjoining the *cardo,* in perhaps an extension of Capernaum's *forum.* The scriptures refer to large crowds gathering in this open area, and Jesus taught from the door of Peter's house (Mark 1:33, 2:2). The house was situated in one of the prime locations of the town, in its very center, adjoining on one side the town square and on the other, the synagogue. The structure itself was rather large, with three interior courtyards, paved floors covered with the same type of expensive lime plaster found in the palace of Herod at Machaerus.[6]

Obviously such a house, in such a prime location, did not belong to a poor Galilean peasant-fisherman. Rather, it was the home of a well-to-do, successful businessman of some local prominence, who owned fishing boats in a partnership with Zebedee and his sons, James and John, and who had sufficient means to pay special taxes to the tetrarch of Galilee to continue his right to exercise a fishing franchise on the Sea of Galilee. It is very likely that the collector of this *tributum* for Herod Agrippa, Galilee's ruler, had been none other than the collector of such fees, Matthew, also called as one of Jesus' Apostles.[7] Capernaum maintained an industry for production and export of salted fish and the fish sauce so widely used as a condiment throughout the Roman world. It was a place where the fishing industry would have been a profitable business.[8] Scriptural evidence also demonstrates the prosperity of Peter's fishing business partner Zebedee, who was sufficiently wealthy to have servants (Mark 1:20). It was not therefore, as some have erroneously claimed, because Peter was in economic need that he easily dropped his affairs to follow the Christ. Rather, it was because of his belief in the Savior's teaching, that for him justified any sacrifice as he consecrated himself to the Lord's work. Indeed, "John and Luke provide a religious context for understanding why Peter and the others were willing to drop everything to follow Jesus. Archaeological evidence weighs against those modern theories which appeal to economic or social deprivation."[9]

When Peter, with John, was summoned before the Sanhedrin to be forbidden to perform any further miraculous healings or to continue to testify that Jesus was the resurrected Messiah, he fearlessly rebuked those rulers of the Jews who had put his beloved Savior to death (Acts 4:8–10). Luke describes the Sanhedrin's reaction as follows:

> Now when they saw the boldness of Peter and John, and perceived that they were unlearned and ignorant men, they marvelled; and they took knowledge of them, that they had been with Jesus. And beholding the man which was healed standing with them, they could say nothing against it (Acts 4:13–14).

This expressed collective perception of the Sanhedrin that Peter and John were unlearned and ignorant men has contributed to the false image of Christ's chief followers not only being poor, but also illiterate peasants. To understand the intent of the Sanhedrin's assessment, which may or may not have been accurate, it is necessary to go beyond the language of the King James Version. The original Greek word rendered as "unlearned" was *agrammatoi,* and as "ignorant" was *idiotai.* The former term actually indicates that Peter and John were without the education of the Hellenistic *gymnasium* where, among other subjects, rhetoric and logic were taught to prepare patternistic arguments and speeches in accordance with accepted Hellenistic form and practice. The latter term has been explained by one critic to mean "amateur" or "nonspecialist" with both Josephus (*Jewish Antiquities,* 2.12.2) and Paul (2 Cor. 11:6) cited as using the word "to describe those unskilled in speaking."[10] Members of the Sanhedrin, including the nobility and leading clerics of the new Judaism, would have been well-educated men, trained in either the *paideia* of the Hellenistic *oikoumene,* or under the tutelage of rabbinical groups or leading rabbis, such as Paul's teacher Gamaliel (Acts 5:34–40; 22:3), forerunners of the later formalized rabbinical schools.

Surely Peter and John were without either of those kinds of education. Their speeches may not have followed standard rhetorical patterns but, instead, were made powerful by the Spirit. Nevertheless, they were effective and may well have displayed a knowledge of religion that the Sanhedrin found amazing in those who were not rabbinically trained. Moreover, they very likely were, in fact, able to speak Greek, even if not learned in the Greek rhetorical tradition. Certainly, their background in the Hellenized towns of Galilee with mixed populations including Greeks suggests as much, thus explaining the ability both displayed in utilizing Greek to write the messages to the Christian flock which bear their names as author.

> Living in a region where, in addition to the native Aramaic, Greek was widely used as a language of business and trade, Peter may have been conversant with the tongue in which his scriptural writings were later penned . . . and despite the description of Peter and John by the elders of the Sanhedrin as being without learning, the Galilean Apostles were literate men, probably without normal rabbinical training, but with broad general understanding and capability.[11]

Such skills enabled Peter to conduct a ministry of teaching, testifying, and presiding among Christians of diverse background. "We later see Peter dealing with both Aramaic-speaking and Greek-speaking Christians within the Jerusalem community (Acts 6:1) and preaching in churches like those in Antioch, Corinth, and Rome where Greek was the common language."[12] Clearly, in the modern sense of the words, Peter was neither ignorant nor unlearned, nor, for that matter, unlettered in Aramaic or Greek.

The Calling of Simon Peter

Several varying accounts of the calling by Christ of Peter as disciple can be found in the scriptures. The accounts of the synoptic Gospels are generally in accord, but John's account is distinct and may contain information to provide better understanding of Peter's primacy among the Apostles.

Matthew and Mark provide almost identical accounts that when Jesus walked along the shore near Capernaum, he came upon Peter and Andrew casting nets into the sea. Jesus then issued to the brothers His great invitation to follow Him with the promise that He would make them fishers of men (Matt. 4:18–19; Mark 1:16–17). Luke's account is similar, though more detailed (Luke 5:1–11). Luke also places Christ at the Sea of Galilee, although he employs its alternate name, Lake Gennesaret. In this narrative we learn specifically that two fishing boats, belonging to Peter and Andrew, and to Zebedee and his sons, had fished through the night without success. Christ entered Peter's boat to speak to the crowd on shore and after finishing His discourse instructed Simon Peter to cast his net in a particular spot. Peter obeyed and pulled up a net full of such a catch of fish that he was obliged to call his partners in the other boat to assist in hauling in the load. John and James were as astonished as Peter at the event, so much so that Jesus comforted them with the encouragement to fear not and the assurance that thenceforth they would be catchers of men.

The three synoptic accounts are by no means contradictory. Luke's version simply provides more detail. The disciples were fishing in boats; Christ used Peter's boat as a platform to address the crowd on the shore; John and James were Peter's partners and were also present. On the other hand, Andrew is mentioned by Mark and Matthew, but ignored by Luke.

John chronicled the circumstance of Peter's calling very differently, however. He provides some background information that Andrew and John himself, the disciple whom Jesus loved, had been followers of John the Baptist, who left the Baptist to follow Christ (John 1:34–42). The Lord turned to speak to them, asking what they sought of Him. The two addressed Christ as Rabbi (Master) and inquired where He dwelt. The question may have been posed on several levels and possessed many implications beyond Christ's place of residence. Similarly, the Lord's response is perhaps multifaceted as well, signifying more than the mild imperative directed to His two future Apostles to "come and see." Indeed, it is as timeless an invitation to come to know Christ as the invitation to serve that lays at the core of the Savior's promise to make certain of His disciples "fishers of men."

According to John's account, after this experience, which no doubt entailed instruction by the Savior during the time they abode with Him, it was Andrew who went to find his brother Simon Peter and excitedly explained that he and John had found the Messiah, the Christ. When

Andrew brought Peter to Jesus, John reports the Savior as declaring, "Thou art Simon the son of Jona: thou shalt be called Cephas, which is by interpretation, A stone" (John 1:42). This final stage of the events as unfolded by John differs from the synoptic Gospels. In John, Peter's new name is bestowed and is referred to in the context of Peter's meeting with the Savior after John and Andrew's recognition that He was the Christ. It is apparently not connected by John with the profession of Peter's own faith in Jesus, a prominent feature of Peter's story in the synoptic chronicles. Rather, that event is associated by John with departure of many of Christ's followers after the Bread of Life sermon (John 6). The episode of the calling of the two sets of brothers to be fishers of men is also not found in John's story.

Modern critics resort to literary analysis and redaction criticism[13] to dismiss the accounts of Mark and Matthew in favor of those of Luke or John because "the more complex circumstances which the stories in Luke and John suggest for the calling of Peter have a plausibility that the brief Markan account lacks."[14] Nevertheless, for those who accept the historicity of all accounts, there is no reason to reject any of the treatments. Although they are not identical, they are likewise not mutually exclusive, but compatible and complementary, open to synthesis.

What emerges from such synthesizing efforts is the story of four friends and business associates. Their two well-to-do families have apparently become involved with the religious reform movement of John the Baptist, through which John and Andrew became acquainted with Jesus and were convinced of His Messiahship. Peter and James came to know Jesus through their brothers. It is entirely plausible that upon meeting Simon, Jesus referred to him as Cephas, though, as alluded to in the synoptic accounts, He may again have later emphasized the importance of the name in connection with Peter's priesthood assignment. John no doubt reports the initial meetings of the friends with the Savior, while Luke offers the fullest account of their calling as disciples. Indeed, that Peter allowed Christ to use his boat with such apparent readiness suggests a prior relationship between the two. The incident on the shore was not their first meeting, but it was the day when Peter's life changed as he accepted the Savior's call to become a fisher of men. Moreover, this incident prefigures the calling of all four of the Galilean fishermen to become Apostles. Matthew lists the four first, presenting their names as two pairs of brothers, Peter and Andrew, and James and John (Matt. 10:2), and Luke lists the Apostles in pairs of two, combining the brothers Peter and Andrew, James and John (Luke 6:13–16). In his account of the ordination of the Twelve, Mark names the first of the Twelve as Simon surnamed Peter, James the son of Zebedee, and John, brother of James, surnamed the *Boanerges*, or sons of thunder, and Andrew (Mark 3:14–18). There is little question of the preeminence of these four as friends and followers of Jesus.

The Inner Circle of Three

Peter, James, and John are often described as forming an inner circle of three within the Twelve. They alone were permitted by the Savior to experience certain events and to have knowledge of particular acts and doctrines. Three of these special events to which they alone were privy are recounted in the scriptural account of the Savior's ministry: the raising of the daughter of Jairus (Matt. 9:18–26; Mark 5:35–43), the Transfiguration (Mark 9:2–10; Luke 9:28–36), and the Savior's act of atonement in the Garden of Gethsemane (Matt. 26:33–35; Mark 14:32–42; Luke 22:40–46). In all three events Jesus was revealed in His true character as the Son of God. This is obviously information the Savior did not wish known until the right time. It went beyond the "Messianic secret" the Twelve were charged to keep when Peter confessed in behalf of all that Jesus was the Christ (Mark 8:29–30). John portrays a similar incident at the aftermath of the Bread of Life sermon in which the Savior clarified that He was not the bringer of political revolution so many Jews expected in the role of their Messiah, but the sacrificial flesh sent from heaven. By this time, at least, Peter understood the divine implications of Christ's mission, for which he had previously been rebuked in private for misconstruing (Mark 8:32–33), and confessed that Jesus was not only the Christ, but the Son of the living God (John 6:69).

Although specific details of the raising from death of Jairus's daughter are not provided, it is clear that Jesus was firm in allowing no one to be present except Peter, James, and John (Mark 5:37). Only the chosen three were allowed to witness that demonstration of the Lord's true power.

Similarly, the glory of the Lord was manifest at the Transfiguration when, "the fashion of his countenance was altered, and his raiment was white and glistering" (Luke 9:29), "shining, exceeding white as snow" (Mark 9:3). Moses and Elijah spoke to the Savior about the act of atonement He would soon accomplish. Clearly, the Lord was revealed to the three privileged witnesses in His glory as the Son of God. Peter spoke for his awestruck companions, offering to build tabernacles for the heavenly beings to "retire for devotion" and delay "the departure of the visitants."[15] At that moment the climax of the experience transpired as all were overshadowed by a bright cloud from which a voice declared, "This is my beloved Son: hear him" (Mark 9:7; Luke 9:35). "It was Elohim, the Eternal Father, who spake; and at the sound of that voice of supreme Majesty, the Apostles fell prostrate. Jesus came and touched them, saying, 'Arise, and be not afraid.' When they looked they saw that again they were alone with Him."[16] Upon departure Jesus charged them to "tell no man what things they had seen, till the Son of man were risen from the dead" (Mark 9:9). As with the raising of Jairus's daughter, the secret needed to be kept until the right time arrived to reveal it.

The final occasion for which we know that the three Apostles were alone permitted to be present was in the Garden of Gethsemane, where the Savior brought to pass the fulfillment of His Father's plan of salvation in the Atonement. As His three friends repeatedly dozed and slept, the Son of God, alone, drank the bitter cup. What the three Apostles witnessed of that process in their intermittent sleep is not revealed in the scriptures. But how privileged were Peter, James, and John to be at hand during this act of the greatest eternal significance!

Latter-day Saint doctrine maintains that Peter, James, and John functioned in a special role of presidency over the other Apostles and the Church. The inner circle of three was, in fact, a First Presidency, upon whom were bestowed keys of priesthood authority to preside. Joseph Smith taught that "the Savior, Moses, and Elias, gave the keys to Peter, James, and John, on the mount, when they were transfigured before him."[17] For this reason it was the three ancient presidents who returned to restore those same Melchizedek Priesthood keys in this modern dispensation.[18]

> Latter-day Saints believe that the New Testament Apostles, Peter, James, and John comprised a First Presidency with Peter as the presiding officer and with James and John as counselors. As an ancient First Presidency, they functioned in a manner similar to the First Presidency today. For instance, the Bible describes occasions when Jesus dealt with Peter alone (Mt 18:19; Lk 24:34), and others when the three Apostles were involved (Mt 17:1–3; 26:37–39; Mk 5:37–42). These passages suggest that the roles of these three men were different from the roles of other Apostles.[19]

The gospel accounts provide sufficient evidence of a special role for these three Galilean Apostles. It is intriguing to speculate that there may have been other instances when the three functioned together and apart from the rest of the Twelve, under the Savior's direction. Clearly, Peter and John are often associated as acting in tandem; at the Last Supper (John 13:23–26), in the courtyard of the high priest (John 18:15–16), and at the empty tomb of Jesus (John 20:2–10). A special place is accorded both in the post-resurrection narrative of John 21. Similarly, it is Peter and John who figure so prominently in establishing the Church in Jerusalem after the Savior's resurrection (Acts 1–4).

In addition to witnessing the most sacred actions of the Savior, along with James and John, Peter is privileged to have had certain experiences alone in the presence of the Lord. Notable are private dialogues with the Savior (Matt. 18:21) and the very intriguing post-resurrectional appearance of Christ to Peter alone (Luke 24:34). Of this experience, beyond Luke's information of its occurrence, nothing more is known, though Paul may refer to it in 1 Corinthians 15:5. Peter's private conversation with his resurrected Lord in John 21 qualifies as an indication of Peter's role as the Apostle most often singled out, and is discussed later in the context of Peter's presidency. Though Peter was joined to John and James in the inner circle of three, Peter was himself in a special position of seniority vis-a-vis the Lord.

Impetuous Disciple or Man of Faith

In works that treat Peter, it is not uncommon to find sections that attribute to him an unparalleled impetuosity, or to encounter even longer discussions about whether Mark deliberately sought to criticize him or John as a rival. Since the Gospels, for which modern critics variously consider Mark and John authors or at least sources, both recount episodes in which Peter's impetuous acts and failings are noted, source-critical techniques are applied to those writings in particular. Matthew and Luke are usually considered to have followed Markan source material and are for that reason excluded from such authorial intent-oriented analyses by scholarly critics. Similarly, the same events in which Peter seems to have failed or been rebuked are cited as evidence of Peter's impetuosity. They typically include his failure to walk on water, his removal by sword of the servant's ear at Gethsemane, and, of course, his three-time denial of Christ.[20]

The Gospel of Mark is sometimes described as offering a significantly harsher portrait of Peter than Matthew or Luke.[21] And yet Mark is specifically characterized by Eusebius as being Peter's particular follower, whom tradition portrays as recording the recollections of Peter and later basing the gospel he wrote upon them (*Historia Ecclesiastica*, 3.39.15).[22] The seeming inconsistency is really not inconsistent at all. If Peter was the source of Mark's information, it is not at all unlikely that Peter would have been harsher on himself than anyone else would have been. No doubt Peter would have made use of his own deficiencies to show how the teachings of Christ, when applied with faith, would produce a spiritual fortitude sufficient to accomplish the life of service and guidance that Peter had provided for the Church. Similarly, the portrait of Peter in John ought to be construed as the telling of actions of a friend who through years grew and progressed in his faith and devotion. The Acts chronicle leaves no room for doubt that Peter and John, far from being rivals, were the closest of friends and associates who labored together, as both dedicated themselves to the service of their Master. Nevertheless, episodes found in the Gospels that are misconstrued by the critics as indicative of weakness are, in fact, revealing of another quality: faith. Mark and John composed their respective narratives in that vein.

Most telling in this regard is the episode of Peter walking on water. It is Matthew who alone of the Gospel accounts reports this incident. As the Apostles were distressed by a storm in the midst of the Sea of Galilee, Christ appeared, walking on the sea, comforting them with His greeting, "Be of good cheer; it is I; be not afraid" (Mark 6:50; Matt. 14:27; John 6:20).

Then the Savior bid Peter to come to Him,

> And when Peter was come down out of the ship, he walked on the water,
> to go to Jesus. But when he saw the wind boisterous, he was afraid; and
> beginning to sink, he cried, saying, Lord, save me. And immediately Jesus
> stretched forth his hand, and caught him, and said unto him, O thou of
> little faith, wherefore didst thou doubt? (Matt. 14:29–31).

The criticism directed at Peter for his failure to make it across the tossing waves to Christ probably derives from the Savior's appellation of Peter as "one of little faith," and from His questioning of His disciple as to why he had allowed doubt to enter in. Perhaps these are not words of criticism, but words of love and encouragement. Yes, Jesus knew Peter had doubted at the crucial moment, but He must also have been tremendously proud of the faith enabling Peter to trust that if Jesus bid, Peter could accomplish, even if it meant walking on water. Indeed, when the Savior stretched forth His hand, Peter's faith was restored and he walked with his Master to the boat. It is possible that Peter's faith in his own ability to stay upright on the tossing and wind-blown waves was more at issue than his faith in the Savior. Intervention from Christ redirected focus and faith to Christ, and Peter stood upright. Christ's remark converted the incident into a lesson for Peter and his fellow Apostles, as well as for all readers of the Gospel account. It neither mocked nor embarrassed Peter. There is little doubt that when the Savior and Peter were back in the boat, and the tempest had been stilled by the Master of even the elements, He turned and gave Peter an embrace of love. After all, Peter had shown more faith than any other man of the time; he had walked across a storm-tossed sea. Of what other man can the same be said, even today? Peter's act was not born of impetuosity, but derived from great faith, which would become greater yet as the Lord utilized the occasion to instill faith.

All four Gospel records mention the smiting of the high priest's servant and the excision of his ear (Matt. 26:51; Mark 14:47; Luke 22:50), but only John attributes the act to Peter (John 18:10). Is John's mention made by way of condemning Peter's impetuosity, or admiring his courage? We must remember that of the four evangelists, only John had actually been present when Jesus and His three companions had been surrounded by the Jewish militia, the guards of the high priest, and when the "officers of the Jews took Jesus, and bound him" (John 18:12). For Peter to have drawn his sword and sprung to the defense of the Savior, in face of such overwhelming armed opposition, unhesitatingly and boldly striking, is less an instance of impetuosity than a display of magnificent courage. It is plausible that Peter, James, and John had possessed from the time of the Transfiguration some understanding of what Christ must endure, but it is also likely that they did not realize that the process had already begun at Gethsemane. Christ communicated this as He commanded Peter to sheath his sword, reminding him, "The cup which my Father hath given me, shall I not drink it?" (John 18:11). Probably only then did Peter and the others realize what was occurring and submit as their Master was carried away, with the traitor Judas leading the Jewish soldiers of the high priest and Sanhedrin. To show restraint in that situation also required a different and perhaps greater kind of courage.

Peter's greatest moment thus far came when he continued that restraint, even though he experienced the galling irony of seeing his own words bitterly invalidated. When the Lord had informed the eleven who remained with Him to finish the Last Supper that they would soon be scattered, Peter protested that he would never abandon the Savior, but sooner go to his death. Tradition portrays Christ as then prophesying of the three-time denial of Peter to come that very night (Matt. 26:31–35; Mark 14:27–31; Luke 22:31–34; John 13:36–38). However, close examination of the original Greek of John's account (John 13:38) reveals that the phrase "till thou hast denied me thrice" is structured around the verb ἀρνήσῃ, a second person singular future indicative verb form. Virtually the same verb ἀπαρνήσῃ, in the same second person singular future indicative form, appears in Matthew (26:34) Mark (14:30), and Luke (22:34). Although the tense is future, and may accurately be construed as indicating a prediction or prophecy of Peter's future behavior, it is possible that such a rendering is not at all the meaning of Christ's statement. In Greek, a future tense verb in the second person can also be construed to express a command, just as if it were an imperative form of the verb. This usage is given the grammatical term of the "jussive future." It occurs not infrequently in both classical and *koine* Greek.[23]

Accordingly, if the future in these passages is interpreted as a jussive future, then Christ would seem actually to be giving Peter a command to deny knowing Him, and Peter's protestation would seem to reflect his dissatisfaction about such an instruction. This rendering appears very much in keeping with Peter's natural courage. Restraint would test Peter's faith so much more, for he was being refused permission to expose himself to the tribulations that Christ must undertake alone. Luke's account is especially insightful, and suggestive of Peter's need for self-preservation. There the Savior presented Peter's coming test of faith: "Simon, Simon, behold, Satan hath desired to have you, that he may sift the children of the kingdom as wheat: but I have prayed for thee, that thy faith fail not: and when thou art converted, strengthen thy brethren" (JST, Luke 22:31–32). It is in the context of the Savior's words and as a test of faith that Peter's experience must be understood.

It is likely that Peter already realized he had been given the charge to provide the necessary leadership for the Twelve and the Church after the Savior had completed His mission, the underlying meaning of Christ's instruction to "strengthen thy brethren." When Christ was taken, instead of acting impulsively, Peter did demonstrate great restraint both in not trying to interfere in the process of Jesus' death and in protecting himself that he might live to fulfil his mission. How he must have wanted to wield his sword and free the Savior! How he must have desired to proclaim Jesus as the Christ to those assembled in the courtyard! Although Peter never denied the divinity of Christ, he must have been in tremendous turmoil not to be able to admit to his friendship with Jesus, and could even have felt as if this practically constituted a denial of his friend. Each time Peter was questioned as to his association with Jesus and compelled to deny it, seemingly contradicting his own pledge of loyalty unto death, what faith was put into the charge Christ had given him for the future! Peter was neither impetuous, nor did he lack faith. Quite the opposite. The man who had fearlessly struck with his sword at Gethsemane, was the same man who evidenced fearless and faithful restraint in the court-yard of the high priest. John's telling of the event shows Peter's faith, not his fear. President Spencer W. Kimball provides insight into this incident as he asks:

Is it possible that there might have been some other reason for Peter's triple denial? Could he have felt that circumstances justified expediency? When he bore a strong testimony in Caesarea Philippi, he had been told that "they should tell no man that he was Jesus the Christ." (Matthew 16:20.) When the three Apostles came down from the Mount of Transfiguration they were again charged implicitly, "Tell the vision to no man, until the Son of man be risen again from the dead." (Matthew 17:9.) Could Peter have felt this was not the time to tell of Christ? . . . Surely Peter did not think of escape as cowardice but as a wise expediency. Christ's time was not come.[24]

By conducting himself in this manner Peter had passed the test of faith. He triumphed in the face of Satan's temptation, just as the Savior's willing submission to the Sanhedrin's condemnation and crucifixion would constitute not defeat, but the triumph of the Father's plan. President Kimball again portrays Peter not as the forlorn coward, but as the brave follower of the Lord who withstood Satan's temptation and grew greater in faith.

Peter was under fire; all the hosts of hell were against him. The die had been cast for the Savior's crucifixion. If Satan could destroy Simon now, what a victory he would score. *Here was the greatest of all living men.* Lucifer wanted to confuse him, frustrate him, limit his prestige, and totally destroy him. However, this was not to be, for he was chosen for and ordained to a high purpose in heaven. . . . Peter was full of faith. He never faltered. From the day he forsook his nets and boats, his feet never turned away. Even in his denial, he was as near to his Lord as he could be.[25]

Endnotes

1. Hall, "Peter," 1077.
2. Perkins, *Peter*, 40.
3. James F. Strange, "Bethsaida," *Anchor Bible Dictionary*, 1:692–93.
4. Bruce, *Peter, Stephen, James, & John*, 16. For John 1:42 variants see R. F. Collins, "John," *Anchor Bible Dictionary*, 3:886–87.
5. Detail on the origin and significance of the name is provided in the next chapter.

6. Virgilio C. Corbo, "Capernaum," *Anchor Bible Dictionary,* 1:866–69, for a summary site report for the Capernaum excavations with particular attention to the house of Peter.

7. Richard A. Horsley, *Archaeology History and Society in Galilee* (1996), 73–83. Also see R. Alan Culpeper, *John the Son of Zebedee* (2000), 14.

8. For an economic survey of the Galilee, see Sean Freyne, *Galilee, Jesus and the Gospels: Literary and Historical Approaches* (1988); and for Capernaum's fish industry, 154–60.

9. Perkins, *Peter,* 39.

10. Fitzmeyer, *Acts of the Apostles,* 302–03.

11. Hall, "Peter," 43.

12. Perkins, "Peter," 43.

13. Redaction criticism contends that the Gospels represent less accurate accounting of historical events than interpretation and presentation of those former events as perceived at the later period when the writings were composed.

14. Perkins, *Peter,* 28.

15. Talmage, *Jesus the Christ,* 371.

16. Ibid.

17. *Teachings of the Prophet Joseph Smith,* ed. Joseph Fielding Smith (1938), 158.

18. Jae R. Ballif, "Restoration of the Melchizedek Priesthood," *Encyclopedia of Mormonism,* 2:885–87.

19. J. Lynn England and W. Keith Warner, "First Presidency," *Encyclopedia of Mormonism,* 2:512–14.

20. *Peter in the New Testament,* eds. Raymond E. Brown, Karl P. Donfried, and John Reumann, (1973); Donfried, "Peter;" and Perkins, *Peter;* all recent standard treatments are organized to accomplish such source critical comparison and all examine the usually adduced incidents identified as examples of impetuosity.

21. *Peter in the New Testament,* 57–58; Perkins, *Peter,* 52–66.

22. Paul J. Achtmeier, "Gospel of Mark," *Anchor Bible Dictionary,* 4:542–43; Perkins, *Peter,* 53.

23. H.W. Smyth, *Greek Grammar* (1920), 428–29.

24. Spencer W. Kimball, "Peter, My Brother," *BYU Speeches of the Year* (1971), 3.

25. Ibid., 3, 6 (Italics added).

CHAPTER TWO

The Rock

The new name Christ bestowed upon Simon, *Petros,* signifies "the rock." While the term had extended meaning beyond the person of Simon Peter, it was, nevertheless, very appropriate, especially in the sense that Peter often stood as a mighty rock in behalf of his Brethren and the entire Church. In fact, it was in large part Peter's strength that helped the followers of Jesus carry on after the Savior's departure. Peter possessed the strength of character necessary to protect and nourish the nascent Church.

Simon's New Name

The synoptic Gospels record that when Jesus taught in the region of Caesarea Philippi in Galilee, He asked His Apostles who the populace believed Him to be, and who the Apostles themselves believed Him to be. Simon answered for all, declaring, "Thou art the Christ" (Matt. 16:16; Mark 8:29; Luke 9:20). Matthew alone records Christ's response to that confession of faith:

> Blessed art thou, Simon Bar-jona: for flesh and blood hath not revealed it unto thee, but my Father which is in heaven. And I say also unto thee, That thou art Peter, and upon this rock I will build my church; and the gates of hell shall not prevail against it (Matt. 16:17–18).

Thenceforth Simon was known as Peter or Simon Peter.

Matthew's account in the Greek of early Christian scripture gives *Petros* as the new name of Simon and the similar Greek word *petra* for the term rock. Though the words are not identical, they derive from the same root, and the play on words is obvious. But Catholics and

Protestants have long debated whether the variation in the words is sufficient to prove or invalidate the Catholic contention that the passage proclaims Peter's presumed papal position.[1]

> A dispute of long duration continues among Catholic and Protestant scholars concerning the definition of *petros,* "a rock or stone" and *petra* "a large mass of rock," as these words pertain to Peter's name and its connection to Christ's word play, "Thou art Peter, and upon this rock I will build my church."[2]

While it is not impossible that Christ made His original declaration of the new name in spoken Greek, it is more likely that on this occasion He used Aramaic. Accordingly, an English paraphrase of the statement would more appropriately be given as "You are *kepha* and upon this *kepha* I will build my church."[3]

> The Aramaic *kepha,* "like its Hebrew counterpart *kph* (Job 30:6; Jer 4:29), means 'rock'; in the Job targum from Qumran Cave 11 it is used twice as the rendering of Hebrew *sela* ('rock' or 'crag'), and it seems to have the same sense in the Aramaic fragments of Enoch from Cave 4. It appears as a personal name in one of the Jewish documents from Elephantine in Egypt."[4]

John provides a different occasion for Christ bestowing the new name on Peter. When Andrew brought Peter to look upon the Messiah, Jesus gave Peter his name: "And he brought him to Jesus. And when Jesus beheld him, he said, Thou art Simon the son of Jona: thou shalt be called Cephas, which is by interpretation, A stone" (John 1:42). Writing in Greek, John supplied "the Aramaic word with the Greek nominative termination, so that *kepha* becomes *kephas* (Cephas in most English versions)."[5] John refers to Simon throughout his gospel narrative as Simon Peter, Peter, or Cephas. Interestingly, Paul is persistent throughout his epistles in his use of *Cephas* to refer to Peter.

The nature of the *kepha* or *petra* referred to and its relations to *Kepha* or *Petros,* as noted above, has often stood at the center of theological controversy. That the words are slightly different in Greek may be insignificant, since the intent of the word play is clear and the name and the rock are the same word in Aramaic. During ancient times, early Christian leaders and commentators (for example, Origen and Ambrose), explained that *petra* does not refer to *Petros* himself, but to Peter uttering the great confession of the Savior's identity, or to Peter when he acts on the things of God.[6] With almost a similar understanding,

> LDS doctrine holds that revelation was the rock denoted by Jesus and that Peter's call to become the prophet to lead the early Church is here foretold. Relevant to this passage, Joseph Smith applied the term "seer" to define cephas (JST John 1:42) and Bruce McConkie (Doctrinal New Testament Commentary I, 133, 380–83) relates this to seership, or power of continuing revelation, which he further connects to the keys of the kingdom (Matt. 16:19) bestowed on Peter, the chief apostle, upon the Mount of Transfiguration, an account of which immediately follows in Matt. 17:1–13.[7]

Of course, the keys Peter would be given were the keys of the Melchizedek Priesthood. This was accomplished at the Transfiguration, as Elder McConkie explained, and as noted in the preceding chapter of this work. At the time of the reception of his name, Peter was promised these "keys of the kingdom of heaven," with the assurance that through the power of this priesthood of the Son of God, "whatsoever thou shalt bind on earth shall be bound in heaven: and whatsoever thou shalt loose on earth shall be loosed in heaven" (Matt. 16:19). Through these apostolic keys bestowed upon Peter, James, and John—and only through those keys—could the earthly Church function with the legitimization of heaven. The man to whom the keys were promised and would be bestowed had to be a man of the greatest strength, of the greatest faith, and of the greatest devotion to Jesus Christ. That man was Simon, renamed by Jesus, Peter, "the rock."

The Forty Days and Peter's Commitment

"The forty days" is employed in early Christian literature to refer to that period between the Resurrection and Ascension of the Lord. For Peter, these few weeks must have been a time of spiritual renewal, strengthening of commitment, and instruction at the feet of his glorified Master. He emerged from these experiences, more than ever before, "the rock" whose strength was so sorely needed by his brethren and all the followers of the Savior.

When Mary Magdalene announced that the stone had been moved from the tomb, who else but Peter and John would have run as fast as they could to the sepulchre? Fearless, full of faith, they ran to meet their Master. There was surely no doubt in the mind of either of the two Apostles that the Lord would return as promised. These two had not abandoned Him on that terrible Thursday night and Friday morning when they were compelled to witness His suffering and degradation. They would stand by Him now that there was no secret of His identity to be kept. Peter's strength was as the rock, and John's perfect love cast out all fear.

What indescribable joy Peter must have experienced when his beloved Master appeared to him in resurrected glory! All we know of that event is that it transpired and that Peter revealed to the Brethren that, like Mary Magdalene, he had seen the Lord (Luke 24:33–35; 1 Cor. 15:5). Can we suppose that Peter was then commended for the strength he had displayed in the days just past? Can we consider it likely that at that time the Savior clarified to Peter what was entailed in his role, responsibility, and calling to lead Jesus' followers and preside over the Church? Surely Peter departed from the presence of the Lord a strengthened man, and with a vigor equal to the task that had been given him.

The events recounted by John at the shore in Galilee demonstrate the tremendous joy Peter still felt in his Master's company (John 21:1–23). How revealing of Peter's affection for Jesus that when John recognized Jesus standing on the shore, Peter leapt into the sea and swam to land, in order to arrive before the boat could be brought in. At this point in his narrative John places the Savior's thrice-asked question of Peter, "lovest thou me?" and the thrice-given charge to "feed my sheep." Just as Peter had to show restraint with three questioners in the high priest's courtyard to conceal his connection to Christ, three times the same question was posed and three times Peter was given the opportunity to declare his love and loyalty. This confirmed his connection to Christ through his willingness to care for the flock in the same manner as the Savior would.

President Spencer W. Kimball characterized Peter as "a man who had grown perfect through his experiences and sufferings—a man with vision, a man of revelations, a man fully trusted by his Lord Jesus Christ."[8] It is the last line of this apt characterization that is of greatest impact. By the time of the events of John 21, very possibly the last occasion for meeting with the Lord before the moment of His Ascension, and certainly the final episode of John's record, Peter stands revealed as a man fully trusted by his Lord Jesus Christ. On this occasion Christ entrusts to Peter the care, teaching, and continued salvation of His dearly loved followers. What a tremendous expression of confidence by no less than the Savior of worlds! As humble a man as Peter may have been, clearly he realized the weight of the responsibility Jesus was placing on his shoulders and with it recognized that his Master trusted him. The Lord was satisfied that, of all men, Peter had learned the lessons Jesus taught and possessed sufficient spiritual strength to live up to the name Christ had bestowed upon him.

The Rock of Jerusalem

After the Lord's ascension, through the authority of the keys of the Melchizedek Priesthood received at the Transfiguration,

> Peter, James, and John directed the Church in the name of Jesus Christ. Peter presided over the selection of a new apostle to replace Judas (Acts 1:15–26) and over the ministry on the day of Pentecost (Acts 2). Peter confronted the Sanhedrin, performed miracles, and preached the gospel of Christ (Acts 3–4). In many of these activities John was Peter's companion, but Peter took the lead.[9]

In our view, the companionship of Peter and John functioned not only for many years in Jerusalem, but long afterward as well. Peter, however, was the chief Apostle, the presiding officer. John acted as his trusted and dependable counselor. This position stems from the familiar Church doctrine that Peter and John functioned together in a quorum of the First Presidency.

In contrast, modern critics see the two brethren as rivals. One commentator who seems less compelled to accept such a rivalry explains in the context of the special charges Jesus gave to both John and Peter by the shore of the Sea of Galilee (John 21) that,

> Many modern commentators see an ancient rivalry between "those of Peter" and "those of John," the Petrine supremacy being challenged. But the chapter as it stands shows Peter and the other disciple together by the lake. The Lord gave his instructions to one and tacitly confirmed the role of the other, in the hearing of them both. Different as they are, both are

the disciples of the Lord and they belong together. The beloved disciple, it would seem, is the theologian, Peter the Church leader. Not from Peter would come the profundities of the Fourth Gospel. Yet it was the rough and ready Peter who had to love Jesus by feeding his sheep. Peter's function was practical rather than speculative.[10]

It was Peter who would raise a mighty voice of testimony as he proclaimed with power that Jesus was the Christ, and so conducted the Church's mission to convert members of the House of Israel.

In the Jewish liturgical calendar, the fiftieth day from the sabbath of Passover is celebrated as the Feast of New Grain, or Pentecost.[11] In other words, nine days after the ending of "the forty days" with the Lord's Ascension, the Holy Spirit came as Jesus Himself had foretold at His Ascension (Acts 1:8). The Jerusalem Christian community was gathered together when this great spiritual manifestation transpired. The noise of a rushing wind filled the city and holy fire rested upon the heads of many Christians without harm. All were filled with the Spirit and began to speak in tongues (Acts 2:1–4). The city was heavily occupied for the feast with Jews from all parts of the *diaspora*, who witnessed these events in amazement, with the result that some believed and some mocked (Acts 2:5–13).

This directed the attention of those assembled to the missionary effort of Christ's Apostles. Peter spoke on behalf of the Twelve.

> Peter's speech is closely linked to the symbolic event that has preceded; it is, indeed, its complement, explaining the theological meaning of the event. . . .
> It is the first of the missionary speeches in Acts, an address delivered to Jews, kerygmatic and Christological in content. It is benevolent in its thrust, ending with an appeal for repentance and conversion. It proclaims the Christian message . . . and identifies Jesus as "Lord" and "Messiah."[12]

Peter's message was simple but powerful. The Jews had crucified Jesus, but God had resurrected Him, of which they and this manifestation of the Spirit, were both witnesses. God has made Jesus of Nazareth Messiah and Lord. Therefore, repent and be converted. A few excerpts show the power of Peter's words:

Ye men of Israel, hear these words; Jesus of Nazareth, a man approved of God among you by miracles and wonders and signs . . . ye have taken, and by wicked hands have crucified and slain . . . This Jesus hath God raised up, whereof we all are witnesses. Therefore being by the right hand of God exalted, and having received of the Father the promise of the Holy Ghost, he hath shed forth this, which ye now see and hear. . . . Therefore let all the house of Israel know assuredly, that God hath made that same Jesus, whom ye have crucified, both Lord and Christ (Acts 2:22–36).

Many did repent, were baptized, and received the Holy Spirit. Since a great number present were Jews from throughout the spread of the *diaspora*, the glad tidings were carried far and wide.

In the days that followed the events of the Pentecost, "many wonders and signs were done by the apostles" (Acts 2:43). Acts 3 records a great miracle wrought by Peter which came to be known throughout Jerusalem, since the recipient of the Apostle's blessing was a man widely recognized, who had been lame from birth and regularly sat at the gate of temple complex, seeking alms from all who entered. In response to his petition to Peter and John, Peter, of course, replied in words now famous, "Silver and gold have I none; but such as I have give I thee: In the name of Jesus Christ of Nazareth rise up and walk" (Acts 3:6).

To those who witnessed the miracle, Peter addressed a powerful discourse similar in content to the one he had delivered on the day of Pentecost. He accused the people of Jerusalem of killing "the Prince of life, whom God hath raised from the dead; whereof we are witnesses" (Acts 3:15). Peter explained that the miracle had been wrought in the name of that same Jesus of Nazareth whom they had sentenced to death.

The miracle performed in the name of Jesus became so widely known, and the reaction of the populace so positive, that Peter and John were arrested and brought before a worried Sanhedrin, the very body whose leaders had arrested and condemned Christ, and, according to John (John 19:15–18), had been given the Savior by Pontius Pilate, to do with as they wished. Before these murderers of their Master, Peter and John were arraigned, but they conducted themselves boldly. Peter and John withstood the threats of the high priest and Sanhedrin, leaders of the new and apostate Judaism. Peter, filled with the Spirit, declared to the very men who had hated, feared, and killed the Lord:

> Be it known unto you all, and to all the people of Israel that by the name
> of Jesus Christ of Nazareth, whom ye crucified, whom God raised from
> the dead, even by him doth this man stand here before you whole. . . .
> Neither is there salvation in any other: for there is none other name under
> heaven given among men, whereby we must be saved (Acts 4:10, 12).

Neither Peter nor John feared what the Sanhedrin had power to inflict, even their own deaths, and when commanded not to speak of Jesus, their response questioned the presumed religious experts as to "whether it be right in the sight of God to hearken unto you more than unto God" (Acts 4:19). They were released and returned to their Brethren, who joined with them in a prayer of praise that God had performed miracles to witness the divine mission of His Son (Acts 4:23–31). One commentator observes that "this passage serves as a climax of the narrative that began at 3:1 and conveys Luke's real intention: Peter and John have not been acting on their own, but rather as God's agents on behalf of the rest of the Jerusalem Christians."[13]

Peter's strength in the weeks and months after Jesus' death assured that the Church would grow and prosper. Through Peter, the Lord could exercise His power to the performing of miracles. John and the other Apostles possessed similar faith, and the Lord's power was manifest in the signs and wonders accomplished by all. But Peter was the rock.

Endnotes

1.   A. Burt Horsley, *Peter and the Popes* (1989); Michael M. Winter, *Saint Peter and the Popes* (1960). The Latin version of the scripture is gilded in huge letters that surround the interior base of the Vatican dome and are of great theological import to worshipers there: *Tu es Petrus et super hanc petram aedificabo ecclesiam meam.*

2.   Hall, "Peter," 514.

3.   Donfried, "Peter," 257.

4.   Bruce, *Peter, Stephen, James, & John,* 17.

5.   Ibid., 17–18.

6.   Donfried, "Peter," 257.

7.   Hall, "Peter," 514.

8. Kimball, "Peter, my Brother," 1.

9. Hall, "Peter," 515.

10. John de Satge, *Peter and the Single Church* (1981), 21.

11. Fitzmyer, *Acts of the Apostles,* 237–38.

12. Ibid., 248.

13. Ibid., 306.

CHAPTER THREE

Presiding Apostle

As presiding authority in the Church of Jesus Christ, Peter directed not only the founding of a permanent Christian community in Jerusalem as discussed earlier, but gave the necessary leadership to expand the glad tidings throughout surrounding areas. This was in accordance with the instructions given at the Lord's ascension that the gospel be established "in Jerusalem, and in all Judæa, and in Samaria, and unto the uttermost part of the earth" (Acts 1:8). As Hall states,

> Through important revelations pertaining to the extension of the gospel to the Gentiles (Acts 10), Peter's calling as prophet, seer, and revelator is evident. Although modern revelation provides much clarification of information in this regard, Peter's role of presiding over Church councils and directing general apostolic effort is patently demonstrable through examination of the New Testament and other early Christian sources.[1]

In addition to overseeing the expansion of the Church into many new areas, Peter's work as presiding Apostle directly involved extension of the gospel to Gentiles, personal supervision of the rapidly growing Christian community at Antioch, and similar direct involvement with the Christian branches at Rome.

Peter in Judea

Peter is presented in Acts as dynamically directing the growth and development of the Christian community at Jerusalem in the years following the Savior's Crucifixion and Resurrection. Peter functioned as presiding officer at the selection of Matthias to fill the vacancy among the Twelve (Acts 1:15–26) and at the events of Pentecost (Acts 2). When Ananias and Sapphira violated the *koinonia*, or rules of community conduct in sharing together, Peter presided in judicial fashion over the inquiry into their deceitful practice (Acts 5:1–11). Peter's activities as presiding officer extended to acting as the chief ministering servant of the community. Peter's healing of the lame man at the temple gate, combined with his being called before the Sanhedrin to answer for this act, which in turn resulted in his rebuking of the Sanhedrin for putting the Savior to death, seem to have become widely known—so much so that Peter was sought after as a healer, and multitudes of men and women became believers (Acts 5:14). The Acts chronicle provides notice that:

> They brought forth the sick into the streets, and laid them on beds and couches, that at the least the shadow of Peter passing by might overshadow some of them. There came also a multitude out of the cities round about unto Jerusalem, bringing sick folks, and them which were vexed with unclean spirits: and they were healed every one (Acts 5:15–16).

As previously noted, Peter was the chief spokesman of the Christian community and its leadership. It was Peter who delivered the great discourses at Pentecost, after the healing of the lame man at the temple, and before the Sanhedrin, condemning the Jews for having put to death their Messiah and calling for their repentance. Finally, the success of Peter and the other Apostles elicited retribution from a jealous and fearful Sanhedrin. Thrown into prison and beaten for their defiance of the high priest and his minions, nevertheless Peter and the Apostles taught "daily in the temple, and in every house, they ceased not to teach and preach Jesus Christ" (Acts 5:42).

After Philip's initial success in converting men and women in Samaria, Peter and John proceeded into the region, bringing with them the gift of the Holy Ghost, bestowed by their laying on of hands upon those who had been baptized by Philip. On this occasion Peter is first known to have encountered Simon Magus, recently baptized, but who is portrayed at various times as the originator of gnosticism, or as the self-proclaimed successor of John the Baptist. Peter rebuked Simon's efforts to buy the priesthood powers of the

Apostles for money and, according to tradition, would repeatedly expose the charlatan activities of this man.[2] Peter and John continued their ministry to the Samaritans, preaching in many villages before returning to Jerusalem (Acts 8:25).

Later Peter seems to have been much involved with preaching the gospel and performing miraculous acts throughout Judea, Galilee, and Samaria (Acts 9:31–32). Two healings are specifically noted in the record presented in Acts: that of Aeneas, bedridden with palsy for eight years; and, in Joppa, of the disciple Tabitha, also called Dorcas, who was raised from the dead at Peter's command (Acts 9:33–43). Many believed because of Peter's exercise of priesthood power. Moreover, Peter was unique from the other Apostles in that he performed miracles of the sort the Savior had performed, including the raising of the dead. His ministry of teaching and service had extended beyond Jerusalem, throughout the entire region, with spectacular results.

In terms of making decisions of Church policy, Peter is very clearly portrayed in the Acts account as the one and only person to whom the Lord delivered guidance to effect churchwide change. The decision to extend the ordinances of the gospel to Gentiles was wrought under heavenly direction to Peter. The account of the angelic visitation to the Roman centurion Cornelius, a Gentile of Italian origin, and the dreams sent to Peter regarding the termination of Mosaic table fellowship, accompanied by voice-direction from heaven that Peter should visit Cornelius and his righteous Gentile friends in Caesarea, led to the extension of Christian fellowship to Gentiles (Acts 10).

The direction had been given Peter, who, when he observed "that on the Gentiles also was poured out the gift of the Holy Ghost . . . answered . . . Can any man forbid water that these should not be baptized, which have received the Holy Ghost as well as we? And he commanded them to be baptized in the name of the Lord" (Acts 10:45–48). Peter's action in altering standing doctrine appears to have been questioned by some Jewish Christians at Jerusalem when Peter returned to the city. Nevertheless, Peter's recounting of events (Acts 11:2–17), combined with his personal authority, had such effect upon them with the result that "when they heard these things, they held their peace, and glorified God, saying, Then hath God also to the Gentiles granted repentance unto life" (Acts 11:18).

When the issue was raised years later as to what aspect of Jewish laws and practice Gentile converts to Christianity should be required to observe, Peter once again took the lead in resolving the crisis at the Jerusalem Council. As noted previously, Peter spoke first at the public meeting of the conference, an indication of presidency; Peter pronounced the decision that had been reached in private meetings by the presiding Brethren; and finally Peter most acted as presiding officer of the Church when he reminded all present that the extension of the gospel to Gentiles had been a decision implemented by Peter years before, but revealed by God through the intervention of the Holy Ghost (Acts 15: 7–11). Peter was well aware that it was not his church over which he had been appointed to preside, but rather that of Jesus Christ.

As Peter's personal strength of faith and character had preserved the fledgling community of Jesus' followers in the early days at Jerusalem, so as the years passed was Peter effective as missionary, teacher, performer of miracles, chief provider of service to his flock, and presiding Apostle of the Church, not only at Jerusalem, but throughout Judea and into Samaria and Galilee. Peter personally brought multitudes into the faith and directed the expansion of Church branches throughout the land. Peter, as befitted his calling of presidency, received revelatory direction from heaven to extend the blessings of the gospel beyond the House of Israel to all men.

Peter in Antioch

The second of the three important Christian centers with which Peter was associated is Antioch. Some time after the conclusion of the Jerusalem Council in A.D. 49, Peter took up residence in Antioch, and may have remained in the city for as long as ten years. This residency during the decade of the 50s does not appear to have been the first occasion of Peter's coming to the Syrian metropolis. Nevertheless, since Peter departed Jerusalem, never to return, and established a long-standing home at Antioch, it is perhaps appropriate to characterize Antioch as the new headquarters of the Christian Church. The presiding Apostle was in residence at the location where the greatest number of Church members lived. Other Apostles, including Peter's frequent companion John, and Matthew, may also have left Jerusalem at the same time, accompanying Peter to Antioch. Antioch is also the likely location for the composition of Matthew's gospel.[3]

In the first century, Antioch still remained one of the most populous cities of the Mediterranean world. Jews had constituted a significant component of the city's population since the time of its founding. Many enjoyed full political rights in the city and, to judge from the significant contributions of temple money to Jerusalem, many had acquired considerable wealth. Estimates of the number of Jews at Antioch in the first century range from a high estimate of 45,000 to a low estimate of 22,000.[4] So cosmopolitan a center as Antioch, with the movement of trade and travelers from north to south, and also from Mesopotamia and other areas of the Parthian kingdom to the east, experienced the sharing of ideas, including religious beliefs.

> Antioch saw the coming and going of peoples of all sorts bringing news of religious movements everywhere in the Roman world. Another local factor of prime importance was the presence of a large and ancient Jewish community which seems to have felt no great hostility toward the Gentiles, and, in turn, appears not to have been worked upon with any degree of disfavor by the Gentiles as a whole, at this time. As was the case elsewhere in the Graeco-Roman world, the Jewish community in Antioch attracted to its ceremonies and teachings a number of Gentiles who found in Jewish monotheism and ethics a form of religion which was more satisfying than the pagan beliefs. The fact that they were able to read the Jewish Scriptures in Greek translation undoubtedly promoted the interest that these inquirers felt in the Jewish teachings.[5]

Josephus takes special notice of the significant interest in Judaism by the Greeks of Antioch.[6] We can surmise that many became proselytes to Judaism and that the Jewish community at Antioch had long accepted Gentiles in their number.

The apparent beginnings of Christianity in Antioch are referred to in Acts 11:19–21. The chronology of Acts places these events after the narrative of Peter's revelation to extend the gospel to Gentiles, but associates them chronologically with a persecution of Christians by the Jews of Jerusalem after the martyrdom of Stephen (Acts 8). The latter event precedes the extension of the gospel to the Gentiles (Acts 20). The account of the introduction of the gospel at Antioch specifies the "preaching the word to none but unto the Jews only" (Acts 11: 19), but goes on to attribute to "men of Cyprus and Cyrene" the preaching at Antioch to the "Grecians" (Acts 11:20). These missionaries could have been Hellenized Jews or Greek Jewish proselytes and could have taken the gospel to either Hellenized Greek-speaking Jews or Greek proselytes to Judaism at Antioch, or they could have preached directly to the Greek population of the city. Critics debate the point in an endless variety of explanations, but most telling seems to be the point that Luke established a deliberate contrast between "Jews" in verse 19 and "Grecians" in verse 20.[7] In any case, the gospel was preached early on among the Greek Gentile inhabitants of Antioch and "a great number believed, and turned unto the Lord" (Acts 11:21). So successful was this unofficial mission that when notice of the many conversions reached Peter and the other Apostles in Jerusalem, they sent Barnabas to Antioch to coordinate and oversee the work of the Church there. It was Barnabas who went to nearby Tarsus to engage Paul in the efforts at Antioch (Acts 11: 22–26).

Paul and Barnabas continued to preach and gather new converts with great success.

> Practical reasons for the success of the early mission at Antioch may have been that in this city the missionaries had not to fear Jewish fanatics such as they encountered in Jerusalem; also that the city, as the capital of Syria, was governed by a legate, and so enjoyed a greater degree of public order, with less opportunity for mob violence such as had occurred in Jerusalem.[8]

For the same reasons that Christianity flourished at Antioch in respect to new converts, it became all the more likely for Christians from Judea to immigrate to this city, which was recognized as more stable because of greater Roman presence, and more pacific even in terms of the community of *diaspora* Jews located there. It is not surprising that, with such migrations and so much growth through proselyting at Antioch, Peter felt the need to become personally acquainted with the situation. Two early Christian sources of third century date assert that Peter made a visit to Antioch immediately after overcoming Simon Magus in Samaria. During this visit, Peter is described as healing the sick and directing the affairs of the Church.[9]

The episode recounted by Paul in Galatians 2:11–14 when Peter varied his custom of personal table fellowship at Antioch, certainly happened after A.D. 49, and therefore cannot be set at the time of these early visits of Peter to Antioch, but may reflect occurrences at a later visit or be chronologically placed after Peter's change of residence. The latter seems more likely, since brethren from Jerusalem had been sent to consult with Peter. Such a delegation may have been dispatched if Peter was only visiting, but could, of necessity, have been sent if Peter was no longer resident in Jerusalem. For this reason, the passage in Galatians can be construed as an indication of the accuracy of later sources concerning Peter's move to Antioch.

A number of early Christian sources from the third and fourth centuries, most likely preserving information contained in earlier sources nearer to the time of Peter, confirm that Peter was either the founder or the head of the Church at Antioch.[10] A few later sources anachronistically describe Peter as bishop at Antioch,[11] providing cause for the Antiochene church to vie with the Roman church in a contest for episcopal primacy based on Peter's presumed bishopric at Antioch being earlier than his presumed bishopric at Rome.[12] Origen "in his sixth homily on Luke speaks of Ignatius as 'the second bishop of Antioch after Peter.'"[13] The implication is not that Origen, usually a reliable source, implies Peter was himself bishop, but that Ignatius was second bishop after Peter directly presided not over just the Church at Antioch but over the whole Church from Antioch. It is well known that the first bishop at Antioch was Evodius. Modern commentaries become confused at references like Eusebius's (*Historia Ecclesiastica,* 3.22.1) that Evodius was first bishop and Ignatius second, without mention of Peter, or even more perplexed that Peter is attributed by some sources as having appointed and consecrated first Evodius, and later Ignatius, as bishop during Peter's own sojourn at Antioch.[14] Concern is raised as to why other men would be appointed bishop, if Peter were already Antioch's bishop. There is no reason for confusion if only Peter is viewed as an Apostle and not as a bishop. In the apostolic era, Apostles appointed and ordained bishops. Only later, in the absence of Apostles, were bishops elected by their congregants. The early Christian writers demonstrate historical accuracy when they associate Peter with Antioch, but not as its bishop, and name Peter as the source of the authority of those bishops whom he, as Apostle, called to service. One commentator very much at home with the tradition of bishops as heads of individual churches is, as an honest scholar, compelled to offer the following synthesis of the ancient commentaries and sources concerning Peter at Antioch:

> So, whether or not Peter could be said to be literally the founder of the church at Antioch and its first "bishop," it is plain that in local opinion he became a principal figure in the early history of the community. As for his supposed episcopate, the tradition, again, could easily arise from local patriotism; to Jerome, the first writer who actually calls Peter bishop of the city, the term, though it may have been an anachronism, was one that would describe the importance of Peter's activity in the city. Actually of course his work there would most likely have been in the nature of an apostolate, rather than an episcopate. The title of bishop in the apostolic period was a designation of function, indicating the head of a local church, rather than a title of rank and it seems likely that Peter was later spoken of as first bishop of Antioch simply because, it was supposed, he had acted as the head of the community there and also, probably, because he was one of the Twelve.[15]

Understanding that Peter was presiding officer of the whole Church sheds light on what kinds of activities he pursued at Antioch. In addition to being of service to the large community of Jesus' followers at Antioch, who were by then known as Christians, at least in Antioch (Acts 11:26), Peter would have directed the work of the whole Church, in its various locations, as far as the communications of the day allowed. That Brethren came from Jerusalem to confer with Peter at Antioch shows continued cooperation between the two principal Christian centers. Peter is presumed to have traveled to Corinth by those who interpret 1 Corinthians 1:12 as indicating his presence in Corinth because a group of Corinthian Christians claimed to be "of Cephas."[16] Similarly, though the place from which Peter penned his first general epistle is traditionally thought not to be Babylon as stated in the epistle (1 Pet. 5:13), but in reality Rome, a spiritual Babylon,[17] it is not impossible that Peter journeyed to Mesopotamia, visited Babylon, where an important Jewish community made its home and where several Apostles were known to have carried the gospel, and from there wrote an epistle back to the Christians at Antioch and to the Church in general. The dating of the epistle would need to be moved to the mid-50s, earlier than the traditional dating, but such a chronological reconsideration actually makes a great deal of sense as it relates to the context of Peter's themes in the epistle. Some have suggested that Peter also made a number of visits to Rome from Antioch. The argument for this theorized visitation involves efforts to have Peter function as bishop of both Antioch and Rome simultaneously. Since he acted as bishop of neither, the justification for the visits disappears. It is more likely that when Peter left Antioch for Rome, he remained in the imperial city.

Just as Peter may have traveled to locations where important Christian communities were found, visits were surely made to Peter at Antioch. Already noted were the Brethren sent by James in Jerusalem (Gal. 2). It is to be expected that representatives from other communities of Christians also would have journeyed to Antioch to meet with Peter and other Church leaders, such as John or Matthew. Similarly, other Apostles may have from time to time returned to Antioch to join with the members of the Twelve located there. Evidence is scant for such matters and shows returns to Antioch only for Paul and Barnabas. The former, after his long years of teaching throughout Asia Minor and Greece, came back to Antioch probably in the year 53 (Acts 15: 41; 18: 22). The latter traveled through his native Cyprus and Asia Minor as well, but remained closely connected to Antioch, where Peter had sent him to organize the Christian community in its early days.[18]

Antioch's larger community of Christians, its proximity to areas of Gentile proselyting in Asia Minor and Greece, and even to Mesopotamia and other eastern reaches of Christian expansion, and finally its setting of freedom from Jewish persecution and the political influence of the Sanhedrin, combined to make Antioch a better location for the headquarters of the Christian movement, and explained Peter's connections to the city.

Peter at Rome

Traditional interpretations of Peter's removal to Rome portray the senior Apostle's change of residence as the culmination of an evolution of Christian thought and practice and the logical transference of Christian headquarters to the seat of imperial government and the capital of the empire. Peter's office is, of course, recast by tradition to be bishop of Rome, acquiring primacy over other bishops because of

Rome's power as a city, and lending primacy to his future successors, because of Peter's apostolic keys. The interpretation obviously belongs to the Roman church, and has never been without disputation, either by other important Christian centers of antiquity, or by other Christians holding to different theologies of authority down to the modern era.

Rome's tenure as Christian headquarters, however, was merely coincident with Peter's residence in the city. When Peter's life ended, apostolic keys remained with Peter's friend, companion, next senior Apostle, and member of the First Presidency, John, who from his new residence in Ephesus would exercise presidency over the Church from that location rather than from Rome. It is perhaps not too speculative to suppose that Peter was aware of what awaited him at Rome and directed John to Ephesus, a major Christian center by A.D. 60, thanks in large part to Paul's efforts. Peter and John both seem to have arrived in Rome and Ephesus at approximately the same time, separating for perhaps the first period of long duration since the Savior had called both by the shores of Galilee to become fishers of men. Undoubtedly Peter remembered the resurrected Lord's differing changes to this two faithful followers as all three stood together for the last time by the shore of the Sea of Galilee: for Peter, "when thou shalt be old, thou shalt stretch forth thy hands, and another shall gird thee, and carry thee whither thou wouldest not. . . . Follow thou me" (John 21:18, 22); for John, "If I will that he tarry till I come, what is that to thee?" (John 21:22). Peter, as presiding Apostle of the Church, followed the directions he received to take himself to Rome and to send John to Ephesus, for the latter to continue to serve and finally preside in Peter's place.

No absolute evidence exists to definitively link Peter to Rome as bishop, martyr, or even visiting Apostle. Tradition is so strong, however, it seems improbable that Peter did not take up residence at Rome. The best that can be provided by way of even pertinent circumstantial information in late first or early second century sources is Ignatius's (Romans 4:3) reference to Peter and Paul giving direction to the Church at Rome and the implication of Clement that the two Apostles died at Rome, either by martyrdom or simply of natural causes. By the third and fourth century, however, the proposition of Peter's bishopric and martyrdom had been accepted *a priori*, and appears in both Irenaeus (*Adversus Haereses,* 3.1.1) and Eusebius (*Historia Ecclesiastica,* 2.25).[19] Based on

Peter's supposed tenure of ten years at Antioch, a tenuous assumption founded on Antiochene traditions presented in sixth century sources,[20] conjecture could be made that Peter departed Antioch approximately in A.D. 60 or 61. It is by no means certain that Peter proceeded directly from Antioch to Rome. Eusebius (*Historia Ecclesiastica*, 3.1.1–2) notes Peter's preaching in various areas of Asia Minor. Whether this mission ever actually transpired, or whether it occurred while Peter was resident at Antioch, or after his departure from Antioch and before his arrival at Rome, is impossible to determine. Nevertheless, the paucity of evidence cautions us to agree that in reality,

> As for Peter, we have no knowledge at all of when he came to Rome and what he did there before he was martyred. Certainly he was not the original missionary who brought Christianity to Rome (and therefore not the founder of the church of Rome in that sense). There is no serious proof that he was the bishop (or local ecclesiastical officer) of the Roman church, a claim not made till the third century. Most likely he did not spend any major time at Rome before 58 when Paul wrote to the Romans, and so it may have been only in the 60's and relatively shortly before his martyrdom that Peter came to the capital.[21]

Without a historical record, traditions grew up at Rome around the activities of Peter in the city. Some of these were included in the *Acts of Peter*, an apocryphal work, probably of late second century date. They linked Peter with the final defeat of Simon Magus, depicted as flying above the Roman Forum and caused to crash by Peter, who in this manner freed many of the followers of Jesus from Simon's false teachings and seductions. Peter is portrayed as teaching and converting many, including wives of prominent Romans, whose angry husbands formed a conspiracy to bring Peter to execution. When warned of the impending danger, Peter departed Rome, only to be met by the Savior on the *Via Appia*, who asked Peter the famous question of legend, *quo vadis*, "Whither goest thou?" Peter is said to have returned to be crucified upside down. During that ordeal, the faithful Apostle is described as having preached a magnificent discourse concluding with a prayer of thanksgiving, the text of which claims to be preserved in the apocryphal work.[22]

The martyrdom here depicted differs in circumstance from the association of Peter's death with the emperor Nero that is consistently portrayed in later Christian tradition by fourth century sources familiar with the later era of persecutions and martyrdom. It is, of course, historical fact that in A.D. 64 much of Rome was destroyed by a nine-day-long fire, for which Nero himself may have ultimately been responsible. Early second century Roman authors, the historian Tacitus (*Annales*, 15.44) and the biographer Suetonius (*Nero*, 16.2), report that the fire began in a riot between Christians and Jews, and the Christians were blamed for the fire. The death of those Christians executed by being burned upon poles to illumine a banquet of Nero was condemned by Tacitus as ruthless and brutal. General scholarly opinion is cautious as to whether this act qualified even as a brief persecution, or included crucifixion of the sort associated with Peter's traditional mode of death. While scholars may continue to debate whether this was indeed a persecution against the *nomen Christianum,* that is, simply being a Christian, or a police action undertaken to restore order by virtue of the emperor's basic magisterial power of *coercitio,* it is difficult to overlook Tacitus' references to charges of arson, or to ignore the context of the Great Fire. Moreover, even the later Christian martyrologies linking Peter and Paul in death, to the execution of A.D. 67 under Nero, agree in portraying the action as both localized and short-lived. By the fourth century, however, the event had grown in proportion and was depicted as a full-blown persecution of the kind familiar to that later era. Clement of Alexandria (Stromateis 7.11.63–64), even tells of Peter enthusiastically shouting encouragement to his wife as he was led off to martyrdom.[23] Such a Peter is not the presiding Apostle of the New Testament. Accordingly, in relation to all claims of knowing about the death of Peter, extreme caution needs to be exercised in light of the silence in contemporary Christian sources. Later legend or romance must give way to legitimate history.

> Where early tradition is largely silent, the early second century material remains silent as well. Consequently, we do not hear of Peter's preaching and healing in Asia Minor or Rome. We know that Peter was martyred but have only vague hints that he died at Rome. No account is given of the event or even of circumstances surrounding Peter's death. Indeed, the identification of time and place are so vague in the sources that some have questioned whether or not Peter died at Rome.[24]

By the third century a martyr cult for Peter had developed on Vatican Hill at the supposed site of his interment, over which Constantine later built the proto-basilica given Peter's name. By this period, aspects of the ancient Roman cult had been incorporated in Christian ceremony. Christians celebrated *refrigeria,* the meals in honor of the dead, which formed a part of the pagan Roman festival of *Parentalia.* For a time, these meals became eucharistic among Christians who thus celebrated the sacral meal, symbolically incorporating as participants the dead whom they honored. The martyr cult of Peter became central to this localized feature of Christian worship at Rome. It was in this same time period that the legendary accounts of Peter's acts and martyrdom at Rome were created.[25] Similarly, in this same era the notion developed that Peter had been Rome's first bishop. Scholars increasingly accept the notion that men like Linus or Clement, whom tradition assigns as successors to Peter's episcopal chair, were in fact bishops of local congregations, perhaps appointed by Peter as had been Evodius and Ignatius in Antioch. "Those mentioned as bishops prior to the middle of the second century A.D. in Rome probably presided over particular house churches. Anicetus (A.D. 154–165) appears to have been the first bishop of the whole city."[26]

We possess no specific knowledge of Peter's activities at Rome, neither of the manner nor of the place of his death. What can be surmised with confidence is that Peter continued to conduct himself as a faithful follower of the Christ, who provided strength to all members of the Church with whom he may have had contact. He was the presiding Apostle of the whole Church, directing its activities as instructed by the Lord, whether at Jerusalem, Antioch, or Rome.

Endnotes

1. Hall, "Peter," 515.

2. Robert Stoops, "Simon Magus," *Anchor Bible Dictionary,* 6:29–31.

3. The evidence for Matthew's presence in Antioch and, indeed, Antioch as the site of composition of the Gospel of Matthew is compelling. See Brown and Meier, *Antioch and Rome,* 15–27. The evidence for John at Antioch is very circumstantial. Ignatius, second bishop of Antioch, characterizes himself as a disciple of the Apostle John. This suggests John's presence in Antioch to have formed a teacher-student

relation to Ignatius. However, the source for Ignatius's remark is his Epistle to the Virgin Mary, a document generally viewed by critics as of a composition to be too late to have been written by Ignatius, despite its attribution to him. See Alexander Roberts and James Donaldson, *The Ante-Nicene Fathers* (repr. 1996), 1:45–48, 126. Nevertheless, the Latter-day Saint view that Peter and John acted as president and counselor in a First Presidency, provides the logical necessity for the continuation of their association. About the time Peter departs for Rome, John proceeds to Ephesus. This coincidence suggests their association prior to these final movements. Antioch is the only place available for such association.

4. Brown and Meier, *Antioch and Rome,* 30–31.

5. Glanville Downey, *A History of Antioch in Syria* (1961), 272–73.

6. Josephus, *Bellum Judaicum,* 7. 45.

7. Fitzmyer, *Acts of the Apostles,* 476.

8. Downey, *History of Antioch,* 274.

9. *Recognitiones,* 10.68–71=*Patrologia Graeca,* 1:1452–53; *Homily,* 20.23; *Patrologia Graeca,* 2:468.

10. Eusebius stated in his *Chronicle,* published around A.D. 300 and preserved in fragmentary form by Syncellus, *Chronographia,* 1.627, that Peter founded the church at Antioch. An Armenian translation of the work, "adds that Peter founded the Church of Antioch in the third year of Gaius (A.D. 39/40)." Downey, *History of Antioch,* 584. Other sources that make mention of Peter's connection with Antioch are Eusebius, *Historia Ecclesiastica,* 3.36.2; Chrysostam, *Homily on St. Ignatius = Patrologia Graeca,* 50:591.

11. Jerome, *Chronicle,* ed. Helm, 179; *Liber Pontificalis,* ed. Duchesne, 51. See Downey, *History of Antioch,* 584–85.

12. Malalas, 242–52, casts Peter in the guise of patriarch at Antioch, first head of the Antiochene church.

13. Downey, *History of Antioch,* 584.

14. *Apostolic Constitutions* 7.26; Theodoret of Cyprus, *Homily I, Immutabilis* = *Patrologia Graeca* 83.81.

15. Downey, *History of Antioch,* 283–84.

16. Perkins, *Peter,* 111–14.

17. Brown, Donfried, and Reumann, *Peter in the New Testament,* 150–52.

18. Daniels, "Barnabas," 611.

19. Perkins, *Peter,* 168–70.

20. Downey, *History of Antioch,* 284–87, 585.

21. Brown and Meier, *Rome and Antioch,* 98.

22. Robert F. Stoops, "Acts of Peter," *Anchor Bible Dictionary,* 5:267–68; Perkins,

Peter, 140–44.

23. Perkins, *Peter*, 144.

24. Ibid., 146.

25. Grayden F. Snyder, "Survey and New Thesis on the Bones of Peter," *Biblical Archaeologist*, 32 (1969): 2–24.

26. Perkins, *Peter*, 168–69.

CHAPTER FOUR

Feed My Sheep: Peter's Teachings to the Flock

When, by the shore at Galilee, the Savior charged Peter with the life-long responsibility of presiding over His Church, he enjoined him with the words "feed my sheep." Each of the three times this instruction was given, it followed immediately upon Peter's profession of love for the Savior (John 21:15–17). There seems to be a clear connection between loving the Lord and demonstrating that love by directing it to the service of the Lord's flock. Peter's continuing concern that the flock be properly cared for undoubtedly derived from the Savior's charge. It imbued Peter's teachings and communications to the flock in all of his writings.

A large number of gospel writings are attributed to Peter. The two New Testament Epistles of Peter have, at least until recent times, when a few scholars questioned their authenticity, been universally accepted as legitimate compositions. For Latter-day Saints there should be no debate of any kind regarding the authorship of these inspiring epistles. Joseph Smith is known to have remarked, "Peter penned the most sublime language of any of these apostles."[1] Moreover, the content of the epistles is doctrinally sound and provides a message as important today as in ancient times.

Throughout 1 and 2 Peter, concern is expressed for the salvation and sanctification of the flock, reminding the faithful that this can be obtained only through the knowledge of Jesus Christ and performances of the ordinances of the priesthood. Peter also provides information about the salvation of the dead, and he exhorts all members of the Church to be holy, to feed the flock, to be humble, and to secure salvation through making their calling and election sure.[2]

The First Epistle of Peter

A recently published commentary on 1 Peter, already considered important and authoritative, thoroughly explores the biblical criticism of the past half century regarding the legitimacy of Peter's authorship of the work, and concludes that:

> 1 Peter bears all the typical features of a genuine letter. In terms of its struc-
> ture, it has the three formal requisites of a genuine letter: a) a personal epis-
> tolary prescript identifying the chief sender and intended recipients (1:1–2),
> b) a letter body (1:3–5:11), and c) a personal epistolary conclusion
> (5:12–14). The latter contains a personal commendation of the letters'
> courier, Silvanus, a reference to the act of writing, greetings from co-senders,
> an urging of familial affection, and a concluding wish for peace. . . . The
> consistency and coherence of its language, style, themes, arrangement, and
> line of argumentation indicate that 1 Peter from the outset was conceived,
> composed, and dispatched as an integral, genuine letter. This conclusion
> represents the position of the vast majority of recent research on 1 Peter.[3]

The majority of scholarly opinion considers 1 Peter to have been legitimately written by the Apostle Peter. As noted above, for a Latter-day Saint audience, the authorship of the epistle is not a matter of further consideration.

More needful of consideration is the origin of the work. Did Peter send it from Babylon, as suggested at the end of the epistle (5:13), or does that phrase in reality signify Rome? Insufficient evidence exists to draw a conclusion. That the letter is addressed to Saints throughout Asia Minor provides little assistance in determining either the provenance or date of the letter. Indeed, the letter could constitute an exhortation following a visit of Peter to the region, either from Antioch in the mid-50s or as he journeyed from Antioch to Rome around A.D. 60. Indeed, even though the Epistle was to be distributed throughout Asia Minor by Silvanus, the words of Peter were valued by the whole Church and applied to all of its members. If the letter's intent is "to encourage soli-darity and cohesion within the Christian community in Asia Minor," the same intent could be applied to the whole Christian family.[4]

The style of the work is marked by excellent use of Greek language, both in grammatical and rhetorical terms. Peter, of course, had probably been conversant with the language since his boyhood in Hellenistic Bethsaida-Julias, but had now had many years of association with Greek-speaking Christians and others at Antioch, and much time to perfect his Greek skills, quite necessary in a Church increasingly composed of Greek speakers.[5] Organization of the epistle provides "the clearest indicators of structure" that "include the composition's epistolary framework, its means of announcing themes, its inclusions, its chiasms," and "its transitions from declarative statement (indicative mood) to exhortation (imperative mood)," all signs of exemplary language skills and ability.[6]

Perhaps the most moving section of Peter's Epistle is its conclusion. Here Peter borrows from the Savior the metaphor of the flock and the shepherd. It is a metaphor Peter had personalized and constructed his life's work around, since Jesus soberly instructed him to "feed my sheep" (John 21:15–17). In turn, Peter exhorts the priesthood of the Church to "feed the flock of God which is among you" (1 Pet. 5:2). Peter further delineates the manner in which Church leadership should be rendered: not by constraint, but willingly; not for money, but with an eager attitude; not as lords over God's heritage, but as examples to the flock (1 Pet. 5:2–3). Those who can thus act as true shepherds of the flock will themselves one day receive a crown of glory from the Chief Shepherd (1 Pet. 5:4). Peter's final exhortation encourages the Brethren to be humble and have their lives centered on the Savior, in whom the strength can be found to endure the trials and sufferings of the world (1 Pet. 5:5–11). The preceding sections of the epistle should be understood as endeavoring to develop faithful members of the flock, who are able to live in peace and harmony with one another and with the world around them.

The Epistle's primary and pervasive theme is that in Jesus Christ is a source of strength and comfort, bestowing the endurance necessary to pass trials of faith and overcome "heaviness," or griefs of this world. In developing this proposition, Peter reveals himself first and foremost as still the faithful disciple of his Master. Secondly, Peter shows how much he cares about the flock that the Savior has entrusted to him. He tries to help the followers of Jesus learn that God raised up the Christ as a source of eternal salvation and the key to overcoming the temptations of the world. He exhorts members to conduct themselves in a godly manner.

Peter begins by urging Christians to celebrate the Father's gift, Jesus Christ, "whom having not seen, ye love; in whom . . . yet believing, ye rejoice with joy unspeakable and full of glory: receiving the end of your faith, even the salvation of your souls" (1 Pet. 1:8–9). Christ's atoning sacrifice is explained as "foreordained before the foundation of the world" and "manifest in these last times" (1 Pet. 1:20), on account of which it is necessary for all to believe in God, to purify their soul by "obeying the truth through the Spirit unto unfeigned love," and to "love one another with a pure heart fervently" (1 Pet. 1:21–22).

Peter instructs the flock that those who pursue the Christian way of living become "a chosen generation, a royal priesthood, an holy nation, a peculiar people" (1 Pet. 2:9). In this world, however, the Lord's flock are "strangers and pilgrims"—not residents, but just visitors passing through; the true residence of Jesus' followers is in the presence of their Master. Nevertheless, they must submit to the rulers of this world, and do no evil, not even to return evil done to them, for Christ "did no sin . . . who, when he was reviled, reviled not again; when he suffered, he threatened not" (1 Pet. 2:22–23). True followers of Jesus, especially husbands and wives, must treat one another with compassion and kindliness. By rejecting evil and doing good, they may so sanctify themselves (1 Pet. 3). This way of righteous living, the prescribed lifestyle for the flock, is so important that Jesus even taught it to the dead so that they too might "live in the spirit according to the will of God" (JST, 1 Pet. 4:6). Of special urgency is that every man, as a good steward of the gifts God has bestowed, should apply them for the good of the flock. Those who speak, should speak as the mouthpieces of God. Those who serve, in whatever way the Lord has made possible for them, should serve "that God in all things may be glorified through Jesus Christ, to whom be praise and dominion for ever and ever" (1 Pet. 4:11).

Such is the message communicated by one who lived the mode of life he advocated to the flock. It accords in all respects with the teachings of Peter's Master. It is delivered in the straightforward style one might expect of Peter, the courageous disciple, but also with great compassion and kindliness. The presiding Apostle had come to love the flock as the Savior loved them.

The Second Epistle of Peter

The Second Epistle of Peter is considered by many modern commentators to be pseudonymous, the work of someone else written after the death of Peter, but claiming Peter as author.[7] Part of the reason for modern rejection relates to the ancient hesitancy in early Christian sources to grant the epistle ready canonicity. This attitude among third and fourth century sources resulted from 2 Peter's treatment of doctrines already rejected in this later period, such as the Apostasy, or from presentation of doctrine believed not to be compatible with the so-called primitive theology of first-century Christians, such as prophesied calamities associated with the *parousia,* or Second Coming.

The apparent intent of the letter, however, does offer good reasons to assert its authenticity. As one commentator explains,

> The letter's double aim was to refute these "false teachers," their theory and praxis, and to reinforce stability and commitment among the faithful through reminder of their divine gifts and calling. . . . To contend effectively in the present and to prepare for the future, it is argued, requires a recalling of the past.[8]

The Epistle cautions about false teachers and the impending Apostasy heralded by their coming. It further warns about coming calamities that are reminiscent of past catastrophes, such as the Flood. All varieties of calamity, whether those past, those threatening the Christians of Peter's day, or those of a future day, can derive from common sources such as apostasy or the wickedness of ambitious men. The examples provided, the cleansing of the world in the era of Noah by the Flood, and the destruction of Sodom and Gomorrah, share those very same common causes. To guard against such dangers, Peter provided his flock with the teaching of godly behavior, which would prevent the falling away of individuals into acceptance of false teachings and abandonment of belief in true doctrines.

His teachings about divine justice are in keeping with Christian doctrine, and therefore do not serve to discredit the claimed authorship of the Epistle or to jeopardize its theological consistency. Quite the contrary. These are precisely the topics that Peter, as shepherd of a flock facing difficult future events related to the Apostasy, could be expected to include in a final message to the people of God. Although the Epistle is addressed to no specific group, the letter builds upon the doctrine of the Christian way of life unfolded in Peter's first epistle, and was probably intended to be distributed not only throughout Asia Minor, but broadly to as many branches of the Church as possible. The important message of warning was for everyone.

Likewise, stylistic considerations are similarly insufficient reason to discredit the writing as belonging to Peter. The Greek syntax is acceptable and, though vocabulary varies considerably from that of 1 Peter, topics and themes are so different that a substantial variance in word use is to be expected. One critic's comment that "with a diction that was exceptionally Hellenistic in its makeup, the letter formulates a message that was remarkably 'primitive' and Jewish in its moral and apocalyptic orientation,"[9] well illustrates the very type of writing Peter might have been expected to produce. His linguistic skills were adequate for acceptable Hellenistic diction; the origin of eschatological and apocalyptic writings with which Christians of Peter's time may have been familiar, was largely Jewish; Peter's straightforward method of presenting truth as simply as possible, could well be improperly characterized by a modern critic as "primitive." Consequently, content, tone, language, and style all seem to point to Peter as the author.

The Second Epistle of Peter (2:1–19), alerts the flock to the immediate danger of false teachers, who propagate incorrect and misleading doctrines, and pursue a mode of life unworthy of a true follower of Jesus. It is this kind who are reserved for the day of judgement to endure their just punishment. Under even greater condemnation are those who have had knowledge of the gospel of Jesus Christ and turned from it to return to wicked pursuits (2: 20–22). In years immediately past, some who claimed to follow Christ had rejected an important doctrine of the early Church, the prophecies of Christ's triumphant return in the *eschaton* ("far off time" or "last days"). This eschatological vision of early Christian doctrine was apocalyptic, or hidden away in secret prophecies of the sort the Savior revealed to the apostles regarding the destruction of Jerusalem (Matt. 24). Such teachings were not foreign to the Christian tradition and John's Apocalypse, the Book of Revelation, became the best representation of the eschatological tradition to which this portion of 2 Peter also belonged (3:1–15). Peter warned his flock of these matters in the hope that foreknowledge of such coming events could assist them to avoid the path to apostasy—if not as a Church, at least as individuals. Indeed, Peter expressed this hope in his concluding verses,

> Ye therefore, beloved, seeing ye know these things before, beware lest ye also, being led away with the error of the wicked, fall from your own stedfastness. But grow in grace, and in the knowledge of our Lord and Saviour Jesus Christ. To him be glory both now and for ever. Amen. (2 Pet. 3: 17–18).

Peter tried to teach all true followers of Christ the virtues of the godly man, or the principles of godliness, because this could fortify them against false teachings and prepare them for the everlasting kingdom of Jesus Christ (2 Pet. 1:8–11). These precepts were built on the Christian way of life taught in 1 Peter, but went beyond it so that individuals could become progressively more Christlike in their personal attributes. Peter made it clear that this kind of progression was made possible as Christ's "divine power hath given unto us all things that pertain to life and godliness" (2 Pet. 1:3). By following the promises of Christ one can escape the corruption of the world and become a partaker of the divine nature by acquiring faith, then virtue, then knowledge, then temperance, then patience, then godliness, then brotherly kindness, then charity, or the true love of Christ (2 Pet. 1: 4–7).

These words comprised Peter's final message as shepherd of the flock and as presiding Apostle of the Church, for the Lord had communicated that his time on earth was drawing to an end.

> I think it meet as long as I am in this tabernacle, to stir you up by putting you in remembrance; Knowing that shortly I must put off this my tabernacle, even as our Lord Jesus Christ hath shewed me. Moreover, I will endeavour that ye may be able after my decease to have these things always in remembrance (2 Pet. 1:13–15).

Other Works Attributed to Peter

Other works less reliably associated with the Apostle include the aforementioned apocryphal *Acts of Peter,* whose late origin has already been established as an effort to create tradition regarding Peter's unknown activities at Rome and to give form to the legend of his death there.[10] Many other works of late origin, similar to the *Acts of Peter,* are linked to the Apostle. They include such titles as *The Passion of Peter and Paul,* and a *Passion of Peter.* Less spurious, perhaps, is a work of earlier date, the *Kerygma Petrou,* or *Preaching of Peter,* a series of sermons, rejected by Origen but accepted by Clement of Alexandria.[11]

The Gospel of Peter is a composition that may actually be a work properly credited to the Apostle. It appears to have been an early gospel written by Peter and used as a source by later gospel writers such as Mark or Matthew, whose works are similar in content and who both had regular contact with Peter. There is evidence of the document's use among early Christian writers who either cite portions of it, or make reference to it. Origen and Eusebius both quote the gospel, though it is not cited at length by them or other patristic authors. Moreover, beyond such citation it has survived to the modern era only in two partial and fragmentary papyrus manuscripts. These seem to preserve a narrative account of Jesus before Pilate, of the crucifixion, and only the very beginning of a post resurrection appearance at the Sea of Galilee, possibly Peter's version of John 21.[12]

The discovery in 1945 of the collection of fourth-century Coptic Christian documents at Nag Hammadi brought to light three tractates associated with the Apostle Peter. They include an Acts of Peter and the Twelve Apostles that probably originated in the second century A.D. The surviving document is twelve pages long and presents an allegory of a merchant who possesses a valuable pearl and, in fact, turns out to be Christ, who then provides instruction to Peter and the other Apostles about forsaking the world.[13] Also found was an *Epistle of Peter to Philip,* an interesting letter that in its first half calls for a meeting of Apostles and goes on to provide a narrative of the subsequent meeting, and that in the second half provides an account of an appearance of the Savior to instruct the Apostles in secret Gnostic doctrines. Accordingly, the tractate, probably composed in the late second or early third century, "legitimates its" Gnostic "message by deriving it from Peter and the Apostles and, ultimately, from Jesus."[14] Finally, an *Apocalypse of Peter,* a poor Coptic translation of a Greek original probably of third-century date, builds upon the theme of false teachers in 2 Peter, and portrays a vision Christ gives Peter in the temple, of the Crucifixion and other events focusing on the Gnostic "dualistic world view for ecclesiology and Christology."[15]

Epilogue

That Peter's name was appealed to as a source of authority centuries later stands as a testament that Simon Peter did his work well, whether as fisher of men, rock of strength, presiding Apostle, or shepherd of the flock. He served the Savior with the effective skills and great faith Christ recognized when He called Peter to follow Him. Truly he was the first of the four great pillars that supported the edifice of early Christianity.

Endnotes

1. Joseph Smith, *Documentary History of the Church,* 5:392.

2. Hall, "Peter," 516.

3. John H. Elliott, *I Peter,* The Anchor Bible (2000), 7, 11. For examination of arguments regarding authorship, 118–130.

4. Ibid., 64.

5. Elliott's (*I Peter,* 41–83) discussion of language, style, and organization is very comprehensive.

6. Ibid., 82.

7. Brown, Donfried, and Reumann, *Peter in the New Testament,* 155.

8. John H. Elliott, "Second Peter," *Anchor Bible Dictionary,* 5:283.

9. Ibid., 284.

10. Stoops, "Acts of Peter," 267–68.

11. Kathleen Corley, "Preaching of Peter," *Anchor Bible Dictionary,* 5:282.

12. Paul Mirecki, "Gospel of Peter," *Anchor Bible Dictionary,* 5:278–81.

13. Douglas Parrot, "The Acts of Peter and the Twelve Apostles," *Anchor Bible Dictionary,* 5:264–65.

14. Marvin Meyer, "Letter of Peter to Philip," *Anchor Bible Dictionary,* 5:265–66.

15. Frederik Wisse, "Apocalypse of Peter," *Anchor Bible Dictionary,* 5:268–69.

SECTION THREE
John

CHAPTER ONE

The Beloved Disciple

John, the Beloved Disciple, the Apostle John, John the Revelator, and John the Evangelist are titles that describe the life and mission of one man, the first and last of Jesus' disciples. Always faithful, John not only accompanied the Savior during the years of His teaching, but at the darkest time refused to abandon his friend. Emboldened by love, John followed Christ within the chambers of the high priest, into Pilate's *praetorium,* and finally to Calvary, where John, the lone man among the small group of women who remained with Jesus, was entrusted by the Savior with the care of His mother, Mary. Throughout his long life among men, John continued to labor with the same bold devotion to bring to pass the purposes of his beloved Lord. As the years passed, the influence that John exerted personally and by means of his writings affected not only individual followers of Jesus, but the entire Christian movement. The Beloved Disciple's emphases were, of course, to propagate the doctrine of the pure love of Christ, and to preserve the knowledge of who Jesus Christ was: Son of God, premortal Creator of worlds, Savior and Redeemer, triumphant agent of the Father's plan of salvation, but also John's own beloved teacher, the Master to whom John devoted his effort for life and beyond. The Lord revealed to the Prophet Joseph Smith the meaning of the cryptic words at the end of John 21: the Beloved Disciple's mission continued beyond the normal bounds of life to permit him to labor faithfully still (D&C 7:1–4).[1]

Identity of the Beloved Disciple

The title of "Beloved Disciple" derives from a recurring phrase in the Gospel of John, "the disciple whom Jesus loved," which, along with the less descriptive term, "the other disciple," the author of the gospel invariably employs to refer to himself (John 13:23; 19:26; 20:2, 8; 21:7, 20). Not once does the modest evangelist even make mention of his own name. Nevertheless, the identity of the writer of the Gospel and, therefore, of the Beloved Disciple was accepted for nineteen centuries of Christian tradition to be John, son of Zebedee and one of the three preeminent Apostles of the Lord.

During recent decades, however, revisionist scholars searching for novel approaches to biblical criticism and Christian history have put forward a variety of candidates for the identity of the Beloved Disciple. In some scenarios the Beloved Disciple is also presented as the evangelist. In others, he is only a character in the Fourth Gospel or the narrator of events later written down by a supposed associate or student who is believed to be the actual author of the Fourth Gospel. The following have been variously supported or opposed in new theories as the Beloved Disciple: Lazarus, John Mark or Mark, Matthias, the "Rich Young Ruler" of parable fame, even Paul.[2] An otherwise unknown John has been theorized into existence, as a young student of John the Apostle at Ephesus, for whom has been appropriated the title of "elder" or "presbyter," before then connected only with the aged Apostle John's own role and activities at Ephesus. The justification for the theory of this second John stems from skepticism that the Apostle John could live so long as to be associated with the actions of the Elder John, dated to Trajan's reign (98–117), and also from the view that the Galilean Apostle was an unlearned man incapable of the profound thought and theology articulated in the Gospel of John.[3] Consequently, scholarly critics wrongly resort to hypothesizing a brand new John.

Despite the revisionist views of some scholars, overwhelming evidence establishes John, son of Zebedee, as the Beloved Disciple and as John the Evangelist, author of the Gospel of John. For Latter-day Saints, the issue is firmly resolved by Doctrine and Covenants 88:141. In this verse the Lord reveals the proper mode of observance of the ordinance of washing of feet with reference to "the thirteenth chapter of John's testimony concerning me." Clearly, the Lord Jesus Christ possesses no doubt that His Beloved Disciple, the Apostle John, was author of the Gospel that bears John's name, and has revealed the same through modern revelation.

A uniform tradition of John as author of the Gospel is also to be found among the early Christians, who believed that the John thought to be the Beloved Disciple, was John the Apostle. "No one in antiquity, as far as we can tell ascribed the Fourth Gospel to this other John, rather than to the son of Zebedee."[4] Several second-century sources are very clear in attributing authorship to John the Beloved. An introduction to an early copy of the Gospel, known as the Latin Prologue to the Gospel of John, explains that the "Gospel of John was published and delivered to the churches by John while he was still in the body, as a man of Hieropolis, Papias, John's dear disciple, has related . . . He wrote down the Gospel at John's direction."[5] The earliest known list of canonical New Testament books is found in the Muratorian Fragment, dated to approximately A.D. 170. Its known author recognized the Apostle John as the author of the Gospel of John, writing that "John, one of the disciples, wrote the Fourth Gospel. . . . saying of himself, 'what we have seen with our eyes and heard with our ears and our hands have touched—this is what we have written.' Thus he claims not to be a spectator and hearer only but also a writer of all the Lord's wonders in due order."[6]

Another important testimony of John is that of Irenaeus, who journeyed from his home near Ephesus to become bishop of Lyon in Roman Gaul (France) in the year 177. Irenaeus asserted that "John the disciple of the Lord, who leaned back on his breast, published the Gospel while he was resident at Ephesus in Asia."[7] For this information, Irenaeus relied on the authority of his own teacher, Polycarp, bishop of Smyrna, a large city of Asia Minor, just up the coast from Ephesus. Polycarp seems to have been the student of the Apostle John himself, and is described as often commenting upon his instruction at the feet of John.[8] In consideration of this authoritative chain of information (Irenaeus to Polycarp, Polycarp to John himself), we can certainly agree with the conclusion that "the Evangelist . . . was the beloved disciple of John 13:23, and his name was John."[9]

The Gospel of John itself serves as evidence for its author, the Beloved Disciple, being the Apostle John. Most important is the fact alluded to above, that John's name is not mentioned in any connection in the Fourth Gospel, while, except for Peter, John is the most frequently mentioned of the Twelve in the three synoptic Gospel accounts. John's reticence to mention his own name also extends to his brother James, whose name is similarly omitted. In place of referring to himself by name, when John must place himself into his account of the Savior's mission, he takes recourse to identifying himself merely as the Beloved Disciple. That this was, in fact, John's practice can be demonstrated. Although the Gospel of John differs in its content from the synoptic accounts, it bears parallel comparison to the other Gospels. Several episodes noted in all four Gospels involve the Apostle John; in the Gospel of John, it mentions instead the one referred to as the disciple whom Jesus loved. Also, pertinent is the companionship of the Beloved Disciple and Andrew, business partner of John, as disciples of John the Baptist who together followed the Savior as His first disciples (John 1). Similarly, the many instances of Peter and his friend and companion, the Beloved Disciple, participating together in activities and events, including the post-resurrection incidents of fishing together and being told the fate of one another by the Lord in the account of John 21, places the Beloved Disciple in a relationship with Peter that would be expected of John, and accords with the companionship of Peter and John portrayed in the Acts chronicle. The episode of the Last Supper, in particular, as well as other aspects of the events leading to the Crucifixion and Resurrection are presented in the Gospel of John as relates to the Beloved Disciple in a manner consistent with John being the Beloved Disciple.[10] Accordingly, the evidence internal to the account chronicled in the Gospel of John corroborates the opinions of early Christian leaders who knew John, that the Beloved Disciple was the Apostle John, the evangelist who authored the Fourth Gospel, accepted in the early Church and subsequent Christian tradition as written by John, son of Zebedee.

John's Family and Background

It is impossible to understand the extremely important role John filled in the early Church without reference to his family background. His origins involve relationships which would orient and inspire the directions of his life's work. As one biographer of John simply puts the matter, "John was the son of Zebedee and his wife Salome, who likely was a sister of the Virgin Mary, which would make him and his brother James cousins of Christ. Other cousins were Andrew and Simon, later known as Peter, sons of Uncle John."[11] John's close personal relationship with the Savior is immediately clarified if John is, in fact, Jesus' first cousin. It is understandable that of the disciples John would naturally have been singled out as the disciple whom Jesus loved.

The scriptures in several locations identify John and his brother James as the sons of Zebedee (Matt. 4:21; 10:2; 26:37; John 21:2), who in the narratives of Matthew (4:21) and Mark (1:19–20) was present when the Savior called his sons as disciples. Zebedee was Peter's partner in the fishing business they conducted at Capernaum. Like Peter, Zebedee seems to have also been a man of some means, having servants and being able to hire men to take his sons' places when they followed the Savior to become fishers of men (Mark 1:20). Salome is scripturally attested as Zebedee's wife (Matt. 27:56; Mark 15:40). On the basis of the records of the synoptic Gospels, some scholars have expressed the opinion that Salome, and indirectly Zebedee, may have made financial contributions to fund the ministry of Jesus and His disciples[12] (Matt. 27:55–56; Mark15:40–41; Luke 8:1–3). That the family may have had at their disposal considerable wealth is in nowise surprising when one considers the lucrative fishing industry on the Sea of Galilee, where pickled and salted fish were produced for export. The Herodian government sold fishing rights to men of means who could afford the initial investment in what generally became a profitable enterprise.[13] On this account, the argument has been offered that Zebedee's family was among the small upper class of Galilee.[14]

Later ancient Christian sources indicate that Zebedee was a member of the tribe of Levi and, therefore, connected to the priestly class.[15] Indeed, Zebedee is reported to have once functioned as a priest at the temple in Jerusalem and owned a house nearby, which Jesus and the Twelve may have made use of. The source for this information is a second-century Christian apocryphal text, *The Acts of John,* whose authorship is attributed to Prochorus, held in Christian tradition to be the scribe to whom John dictated the *Book of Revelation.*[16] This may explain the interpretation of some that Acts 4:6 refers to John as connected to the high priestly family through Zebedee, and the statement of Polycrates, a second-century bishop at Ephesus, that the Apostle John had the right to wear the mitre of the Jewish high priest.[17] If there is validity to these claims, the capability of the Beloved Disciple to accompany the Savior within the inner chambers of the high priest, as is recorded in John 18, is readily explained.

In the Roman world the extended family was more important than it perhaps is in the present era. This was all the more true in the case of Jewish families. Unquestionably, families often endeavored to labor together to maintain their wealth, whether in land, property, or business interests. It was by no means uncommon for relatives to act as business partners.[18] The possibility of a family relationship of Zebedee with Peter and Andrew has been suggested, particularly in view of the commonality of the name John—as that of Zebedee's son and Peter's father. While tenuous, the hypothesis that Peter and Andrew were first cousins to John and James, sons of their uncle Zebedee, is not entirely implausible.[19] Such a familial relationship would help explain the lifelong friendship and efforts of the frequent companions in proclaiming the gospel, Peter and John.

Through his mother, Salome, John appears to have possessed other cousins with whom he would enjoy important lifelong relationships. From the narrative of the Gospels can be extrapolated the information that Salome was sister to Mary, the mother of Jesus. Matthew observes that many women attended Jesus at the Crucifixion but mentions only three as standing by the cross, naming them as Mary, mother of Jesus, Mary Magdalene, and the mother of the sons of Zebedee (Matt. 27:55–56). Mark mentions the same three but refers to Salome by name, and adds a fourth, Mary the mother of James the lesser and Joses (Mark 15:40). In his account, John (John 19:25) names four women also, but does not identify his mother, Salome, by name; instead writing, "there stood by the cross of Jesus his mother, and his mother's sister, Mary the wife of Clopas, and Mary Magdalene." Mary the wife of Clopas seems to be the same woman that Mark calls Mary, mother of James and Joses, while the description "his mother's sister" can only refer to the fourth unnamed woman whom Matthew identifies as "mother of the sons of Zebedee" and Mark as "Salome."[20] It is clear that:

> Attempting to harmonize these lists leads to the inference that the mother of James and John was named Salome and that she was the sister of Mary, the mother of Jesus. That would make James and John the maternal first cousins of Jesus, and also the relatives of John the Baptist. Such relationships might explain why these early disciples were followers of John the

Baptist, if such were the case, and why Jesus gave the keeping of his mother to the Beloved Disciple.[21]

Further direct testimony of Salome's family connection to Mary comes from the apocryphal *Protoevangelium of James,* which gives the parents of Mary as Joachim and Anna and places Salome as present with them at the birth of Jesus. On the basis of this evidence one commentator confidently asserts that "James and John had a close familial link with Jesus. The mothers of James and John, and of Jesus, were the two sisters Salome and Mary, daughters of Joachim and Anna."[22] John's family ties, if they were as the evidence of scriptural parallels suggests, explain much about the Beloved Disciple's role and loyalty. Peter may have been his relative as well as his friend. Jesus could have been not only his teacher and friend, but a cousin as close as an older brother who was much admired and loved, and He may well have looked upon John as a beloved younger brother, always faithful and supportive. To the obvious devotion John felt toward his Savior and Lord could perhaps be added the love of one family member to another.

The Sons of Thunder

Mark 3:17 records that Jesus bestowed on John and James the appellation, *Boanerges,* a transliteration into Greek of an Aramaic word *bone*— "sons of" and *rges,* signifying either "thunder" or "excitement," hence "sons of Thunder," or as one linguist posits, "Sons of the Quaking Heavens."[23] Many explanations have been offered to explain the actual meaning of the term. "Explanations have ranged from the suggestion that James and John spoke with loud voices to the conjecture that as followers of John the Baptist, they had witnessed the voice from heaven, spoken in thunder."[24] Most commentators, however, accept the tradition that the term refers either to the impetuosity or temper the sons of Zebedee could display on occasion. Traditionally, linked to the name is the incident of their urging the Savior to allow them to call fire from heaven down upon the Samaritan village which had refused to hear Jesus' message (Luke 9:54). Some have concluded that *Boanerges* belongs to the earliest Christian tradition and, therefore, could hardly be negative since the Church would not have persisted in employing a denigrating epithet on two of its three presiding officers. Indeed, only upon the Apostles of the privileged inner circle of three are new names known to have been bestowed. As Peter's name Cephas foretold the rocklike strength he would exercise in behalf of the whole Church, so "by the giving of the name *Boanerges,* Jesus announced that James and John would become 'sons of thunder,' mighty witnesses, voices as from heaven."[25] The actions of John's life testify as heavenly thunder to the divine mission of his beloved Teacher and Master. In John's own rendering of events, he and Andrew were the first to follow the Savior. The episode recorded in John 1:37–39 may well be metaphorical as an invitation for everyone to "come and see" who Jesus Christ is. Nevertheless, its reality as an actual event in John's own life is uncompromised. From that day, until the Savior's earthly mission was completed, John followed his friend.

Much of John's activity during the years of Christ's ministry is undifferentiated from that of the other Apostles. As a group they accompanied and assisted the Savior, learned His teachings, and observed the miracles He performed. But John was one of the three Apostles who was able to escort the Savior on the most sacred of occasions. With Peter and John's own brother James, John witnessed the raising of the daughter of Jairus (Mark 5:37; Luke 8:51), the Transfiguration (Matt. 17:1; Mark 9:2; Luke 9:28), and the fulfillment of the Lord's mission of atonement at Gethsemane (Matt. 26:37; Mark 14:33). On these occasions the majesty of the Savior remained hidden no longer, and John was able to behold his friend as Lord and Son of God. The scriptures mention the events but do not reveal them in detail. Only inadequate speculation can reveal what the three chosen Apostles were privileged to know. Whether there were other occasions, unmentioned in the Gospel accounts, when the three were privy to teachings not shared with all the Apostles, cannot be determined. However, at least one instance of Christ imparting special instruction to Peter, John, James, along with Peter's brother, Andrew, is made known by Mark (13:3), as he describes these four learning about the events preceding the Second Coming of the Lord. (See D&C 45.) Through modern revelation it is revealed that Peter, James, and John were entrusted on the Mount of Transfiguration with the keys of the priesthood, and that by virtue of that priesthood authority they functioned as a presiding quorum of three, a First Presidency.

Peter, James, and John, along with Andrew, had been the first called to join the Savior in His ministry. Indeed, they were the only companions of Jesus known to accompany Him in His first tour of Galilee, teaching, healing, and casting out evil spirits (Matt. 4:23–9:8; Mark 1:35–2:12; Luke 4:42–5:26). They were present when the Savior performed His first miracle at Cana (John 2:1–11), when Peter's mother-in-law was healed at Capernaum (Mark 1:29), when He called other disciples and chose who would join His four friends in the Quorum of the Twelve (Mark 3:13–19; Luke 6:12–16).

It appears that Peter and John may have acted as companions in the days of the Savior's ministry, just as they did after His death in the activities described in Acts. Jesus sent them ahead together to Jerusalem to prepare for celebrating the final Passover (Luke 22:8). They had been seated together at the Last Supper, with John seated next to Jesus (John 13:23–24). They raced together to the tomb when told the Lord's body was gone (John 20:3–10). Although others of the Apostles were also present, it was John who at the Sea of Galilee recognized the resurrected Lord and identified Him to Peter, who leapt into the water to swim to shore, and, of course, it was Peter and John together who interacted with Christ to learn the missions and ultimate fates of each other (John 21:15–23).

The Last Disciple

When Jesus hung on the cross, soon to make an end to His mortal ministry, He turned His gaze to those few who stood nearby, their love for Him overcoming their personal grief. He saw the four women—Mary Magdalene, faithful to her Lord, the other Mary, mother of James and Joses, of course His own much loved mother, Mary, and Mary's sister, His Aunt Salome, and with her the sole male, Salome's son, and His own dear friend, cousin, and disciple. John was the last of the disciples of Jesus upon whom the Savior looked in mortality. First called, last present, and last seen, John, Son of Thunder and Beloved Disciple, could not be kept from the side of his Master, even at this time. Many years later the Apostle John, as leader of the Church, instructed the children of God, "there is no fear in love; but perfect love casteth out fear" (1 John 4:18). One cannot but wonder whether the elder Apostle, writing these words, thought back to that occasion when his own fear ceased because of his love for Jesus. We can be certain that the Savior appreciated the strength of

John's love which permitted the Son of Thunder to accompany the Master fearlessly through the travails which preceded Jesus' triumphant completion of His part in the Father's plan of salvation.

From Gethsemane, where Jesus was seized by Judas and the guardsmen of the high priest and Sanhedrin, to the court of the high priest, Caiaphas, to the corrupt pleasure palace of Herod Agrippa, and the tribunal of Pilate, John very likely refused to part from the Savior. John's own account gives the reason that he was able to remain with Jesus while Peter, of necessity, "stood at the door without" (John 18:16). John, calling himself "another disciple," informs us that "that disciple was known unto the high priest, and went in with Jesus into the palace of the high priest" (John 18:15). No doubt John's Levite family connections through Zebedee permitted him access to councils and places where Peter was not allowed to enter. John made use of his priestly rank to accompany Jesus, for he was protected where Peter would not have been.

The Crucifixion would surely have been the most difficult time of all, even for one to whom it had been foretold and who understood its necessity to complete the plan of salvation, the only manner for the Anointed One to fulfil the mission to which He was called before the foundation of worlds. Even so, to witness the suffering of his Master and Lord, John must have looked on with pain and sorrow, but also with admiration and love for the Savior of the Cosmos, whose purpose John describes in that very way at the beginning of his Gospel account (John 1:1–14). Surely the Master had always known that He could rely absolutely on His beloved friend and disciple. John had never failed Him, never abandoned Him, but stood dependably alongside Him. John's presence at the cross served as one more and final proof of the Beloved Disciple's own love and faithfulness. With complete trust, the Savior turned His head to John and demonstrated His love and approbation for His friend, and at the same time His devotion to His mother: "When Jesus therefore saw his mother, and the disciple standing by, whom he loved, he saith unto his mother, Woman, behold thy son! Then saith he to the disciple, Behold thy mother! And from that hour that disciple took her unto his own home. After this, Jesus knowing that all things were now accomplished" (John 19:26–28), could end His atoning mission. Custom had been followed. The Savior had entrusted His mother to a member of the family, her nephew John.

If all of His brothers had not already embraced the Christian faith, they soon would. Why not entrust Mary's care to them, rather than to John? They were not there. John was, and John's trustworthiness and love were exceeded by no one's. Jesus could count on His friend John to care for His mother and do whatever else might be required. How tremendous an indication of approval! The Lord knew John could be depended upon at that time to care for His mother, and later to care for all who belonged to His flock.

Endnotes

1. For a discussion of the doctrine of translation as pertains to John and others, see David B. Marsh, "Give Unto Me Power Over Death," *The Testimony of John the Beloved* (1998), 141–54.

2. A summary of argument and bibliography of critics supporting alternate identities for the Beloved Disciple are offered in R. Alan Culpepper, *John, the Son of Zebedee* (2000), 72–82 and Raymond E. Brown, *The Gospel of John*, Anchor Bible, (1966), 29:xcii–cii. Also see Vernard Eller, *The Beloved Disciple* (1987).

3. Culpepper, *John,* 82–84; Brown, *Gospel of John,* lxxxviii–xc.

4. F. F. Bruce, *The Gospel of John* (1983), 1.

5. Ibid., 9.

6. Ibid., 10. Also see Brown, *Gospel of John,* lxxxviii.

7. Irenaeus, *Against Heresies,* 3.1.2, as cited in Bruce, *Gospel of John,* 11.

8. Eusebius, *Ecclesiastical History,* 5.20.5–6.

9. Bruce, *Gospel of John,* 11.

10. Analyses of internal evidence for John being the Beloved Disciple are offered in Brown, *Gospel of John,* xcii–xciv; Bruce, *Gospel of John,* 3–6; Culpepper, *John,* 72–75.

11. William Dallman, *John, Disciple, Evangelist, Apostle* (1932), 3.

12. J. F. Watson, "Zebedee," *Anchor Bible Dictionary,* 6:1055.

13. A detailed discussion of the Galilean fishing industry in connection with the family wealth of James and John can be found in Culpepper, *John,* 9–17.

14. C. W. Buchanan, "Jesus and the Upper Class," *Novum Testamentum* 7(1964), 206.

15. Culpepper, *John,* 8 and note 4.

16. "Prochorus," *Eerdman's Dictionary of the Bible,* ed. David Noel Freedman (2000), 1085; Culpepper, *John,* 61 and note 15.

17. Bruce, *Peter, Stephen, James, & John,* 126–27.

18. Jeffers, *Greco-Roman World,* 237–58. Also consult *The Family in Ancient Rome: New Perspectives* (1986), ed. Beryl Rawson.

19. Dallman, *John,* 3–4.

20. Some have cast this Mary as sister of Mary, mother of Jesus, so construing John's list as including only three women. Such interpretation of the sister of Mary whom they hold is parenthetically described as mother of James and Joses, if so identified, allows the Catholic theological distinction that the James referred to is but a cousin of Jesus wrongly referred to in Christian tradition as James, the brother of the Lord. Thus, the perpetual virginity of Mary as "mother of God" can be maintained. However, such a position simply ignores the mention of Salome by Mark and Matthew. Moreover, Jewish naming practice typically avoids sisters of the same name. For discussion of these issues see Culpepper, *John,* 8–9.

21. Culpepper, *John,* 9.

22. Ronald Brownrigg, *The Twelve Apostles* (1974), 89. Also see Culpepper, *John,* 9 and note 7.

23. Culpepper, *John,* 38–39 presents a full etymological analysis of the word, citing J.T. Rook's translation "Sons of the Quaking Heavens" as an apt explanation. See Rook, "Boanerges, 'Sons of Thunder' (Mark 3:17)," *Journal of Biblical Literature,* 100 (1981): 94–95.

24. Culpepper, *John,* 39.

25. Culpepper, *John,* 40, who notes the views of Betz (note 42) and Bietenhurd (note 44) in making these suggestions.

CHAPTER TWO

❯❯——————————————————————————————❮❮

The Apostle John

After the departure of the Savior, John labored faithfully and diligently in his apostolic calling for eighty years. While John's age at the time of Jesus' ministry is unknown, it is often presumed that he was the youngest of the Twelve. Even so, he would surely have exceeded a hundred years of age at the time his mortal ministry was brought to a close. This is perhaps the reason that during the long years John presided over the Church from Ephesus, he was referred to as "the Elder." The first decades of John's apostolic calling were accomplished as the frequent companion of Peter. Some of the activities of the two brethren together are chronicled in the account presented in Acts. The New Testament record itself offers no further information about the life of the Beloved Apostle. Nevertheless, writings of Christian leaders of the early second century, some of whom were John's own friends and students, or called by John to episcopal office, provide a wealth of information about John's service in behalf of his beloved "little children." Moreover, John's own writings reveal the concerns and worries of the presiding Apostle as he endeavored to stem the tide of apostasy and turn minds and hearts to the person of Jesus Christ as He truly was, as John knew Him to be.

Companion in the Presidency

As discussed previously,[1] "Latter-day Saints believe that the New Testament Apostles, Peter, James, and John comprised a First Presidency with Peter as the presiding officer and with James and John as counselors."[2] The very sacred occurrences for which they alone of the Twelve were privileged to accompany the Savior and participate in, provide insight into the special prerogatives they possessed. As a quorum they held the keys of the Melchizedek Priesthood and bestowed them upon the Prophet Joseph Smith in this latest dispensation. While James is not mentioned in connection with the events of the first chapters of Acts, it is reasonable to suppose that the many activities engaged in by Peter, along with John, do themselves suggest the functions of a presidency, as Peter and John provided leadership in the earliest days of the Church after Christ's ascension.

By virtue of his office as president, Peter customarily took the lead in preaching, testifying, and performing miracles, but John was invariably present to assist in the laying on of hands, to add his testimony to Peter's, and to boldly proclaim the divinity of Jesus. Indeed, the healing of the lame man at the gate of the temple was pronounced by Peter, but John stood alongside, a strong pillar of faith and love (Acts 3:1–3), and, as a result, the two were taken into custody together to receive the rebuke and warning of the Sanhedrin. The record of Acts describes the boldness before the Sanhedrin not only of Peter but also of John (Acts 4:13). Peter's reply to the men who killed the Savior (Acts 4:10) constituted a courageous declaration of Christ's divine mission (Acts 4:8–12). Whether the boldness attributed to John is the result of a similar response, not recorded in the Acts account, or derived from John's expressions of testimony agreeing with Peter's words, is unknown. But it is clear that John displayed the same courage as his companion, Peter, and that the Sanhedrin marveled at the role played by both Peter and John, though neither was learned in the rabbinical scholarship of the Pharisees (Acts 4:13). Indeed, in response to the Sanhedrin's command "not to speak at all nor teach in the name of Jesus" (Acts 4:18), the record of Acts seems to indicate that both Peter and John answered by asserting it better to hearken unto God than to the Sanhedrin and declaring, "For we cannot but speak the things which we have seen and heard" (Acts 4:20). Peter took the lead, as befitted the presiding Apostle, but John was his companion in receiving the inspiration of the Spirit to declare the glad tidings that Jesus is the Christ. John did not waver, so his faithfulness provided a constant source of strength to Peter and the Church.

Acts suggests that, along with Peter, John reported these events to the Brethren (Acts 4:23–33) and "spake the word of God with boldness" giving "witness of the resurrection of the Lord Jesus" (Acts 4:31, 33). The subsequent outpouring of the Spirit on the small congregation of

Jesus' followers brought to pass marvelous works, healings, and miracles, notice of which finally caused the Sanhedrin to imprison Peter, John, and others of the Apostles. Their release was effected by an angel of God, who instructed them to present themselves at the temple to speak words of life to the people. After great success in this assignment, the Apostles were summoned again before the Sanhedrin. There they were commanded to cease their teaching—not only Peter, but the other Apostles as well. All replied that they would obey God rather than men, indicting the high priest and Sanhedrin for criminal action against "Jesus, whom ye slew and hanged on a tree" (Acts 5:30). Thus the Apostles of the Lord were united in their response and their courageous faith, following the examples of Peter and John.

The works of Peter and John chronicled in Acts may have extended over several years. The lack of chronological reference hinders the establishment of a timeline for Acts. Certainly some time later, Peter and John are still found in one another's company as they labor to bring to pass the purposes of the Lord. Whether a few years or a decade had passed cannot be determined. After Philip had begun to preach the gospel in Samaria, Peter and John left Jerusalem to oversee the establishment of the Church in Samaria. Acts reports the Apostles as bestowing the gift of the Holy Ghost on new members (Acts 8:14–17). It must be supposed that as presiding officers for the whole Church, Peter and John also saw to the organization of branches, the calling and ordaining of local leaders, etc. This was the first major geographical expansion of the Christian community, and it is by no means surprising that Peter and John would direct it. Moreover, it is significant that the two continued to work in tandem, as would be expected of a president and his counselor.

It is also likely that James, John's brother and the other member of the presidency of three chosen Apostles, was associated with Peter and John during these years. Undoubtedly he was among the group of Apostles already mentioned as imprisoned because of their success in proclaiming the gospel. It is possible that when Peter and John journeyed to Samaria James was left behind, perhaps to supervise the work of the group of Apostles recorded as laboring at Jerusalem (Acts 8:14). James was the first of the eleven faithful Apostles who was known to have sacrificed his life in the service of the Master. Acts preserves the account of his execution by sword, at the direction of Herod the king (Acts 12:1–2). As noted in Chapter 2, James's death can be dated to A.D. 41–44, the years of Herod Agrippa's reign. Consequently, when the Jerusalem Council was held in A.D. 49, James had already been killed, but Peter and John continued to preside over the Church. Paul's comment that he met with the pillars of the Church, Peter, John, and James, the Lord's brother, clearly establishes the continued collaboration of Peter and John (Gal. 2:9). Nearly twenty years after the Savior's departure, John continued to act in support of Peter in directing the Master's work. An insightful commentator offers the observation that "the significance of Galatians 2:9 is that it provides unimpeachable evidence of the role of John, son of Zebedee, in the leadership of the early church in Jerusalem."[3]

Contemporary sources provide little information regarding John's activities in the years immediately following the Jerusalem Council. As discussed above, Peter departed Jerusalem for Antioch and resided in the new headquarters city of the Christian movement for approximately a decade. It is quite plausible that John, as Peter's companion in the First Presidency and friend of so many years, accompanied Peter to Antioch.[4] Certainly no further mention is made of John at Jerusalem; but neither do any sources connect John to Antioch. One Antiochene church, probably of fourth century construction, bears John's name, but is not otherwise associated in legend or tradition with John at Antioch. Such evidence is obviously extremely tenuous for forging a link between John and Antioch.[5] Accordingly, no firm conclusion can be drawn about John's residence or activities during this "lost decade" of the 50s. It does seem likely that the Apostle John would have continued in company with Peter, and it is, perhaps, no coincidence that about the time Peter departed Antioch for Rome, John appeared in Ephesus, and perhaps with him, Mary the mother of Jesus. At last the time for separation had come to the two old friends, fellow laborers since the time both had been called by Jesus. The fruitful companionship of more than thirty years had to be set aside in order for Peter and John to fulfil the different destinies the Savior had foretold for each by the shores of Galilee (John 21:15–23): Peter, to follow the Savior in ending his life at Rome; John to Ephesus, soon to assume the role of presiding officer of the Church, but a church that had already begun the great changes that would ultimately result in the removal of apostolic authority and priesthood keys, with the departure of its last Apostle, John.

The Elder Apostle of Ephesus

John's residence at Ephesus is well established in the writings of Christian leaders of the second century and later. That John lived in Ephesus for many, many years until very old age is also firmly documented in early Christian writing. Many of John's actions as the Elder Apostle of Ephesus are described, with the later writers sometimes citing certain well-known men among John's own students or disciples as the source of stories and information about John.

Although earlier authors had associated John with the reception of the Book of Revelation on Patmos near Ephesus, the earliest extant reference that specifically links the Apostle John to long-term residence in Ephesus is found in the writings of Irenaeus, famed as the first systematic Christian theologian. Later bishop of Lyons in Gaul, Irenaeus was originally from Asia Minor where he had been a student of Polycarp, the bishop of Smyrna and disciple of the Apostle John.[6] One modern commentator sums up the information Irenaeus provides concerning the activities of John at Ephesus by asserting that in terms of surviving ancient sources,

> Irenaeus is the first writer to offer a defense of the apostolic authorship of the Gospel and Epistles, the first to claim that the Gospel was written in Ephesus, and the first to report that the apostle John lived to an old age in Ephesus. Irenaeus further contended that John wrote the Gospel to answer the errors of Corinthus and the Nicolaitans.[7]

These people were engaged in heretical reinterpretation of the nature of Christ and His mission, the beginnings of the Apostasy.

Irenaeus reports considerable information about John by way of making mention of his own teacher, Polycarp of Smyrna. Polycarp had not only been chosen and ordained bishop at Smyrna by the Apostle John, but had been John's own student. Irenaeus attributed to Polycarp the teaching that John had remained among the Saints at Ephesus permanently, living with them until the times of Trajan, providing the Christian community in Asia Minor, and particularly at Ephesus, with his true witness of the tradition of the Apostles.[8] Irenaeus also provides information about Papias, bishop of Hieropolis, a city some distance inland from Ephesus and prominent as a religious site for centuries before and after the advent of Christianity. Papias is reported to have also been a student of John's and a companion of Polycarp, both as a disciple of John at Ephesus and as a bishop called and ordained by John.[9] For Irenaeus and Christian leaders of later times the awe and respect with which John was held seemed fitting also to be attached to John's disciples, bishops who were not merely elected to office by the congregations of their cities as had become customary in second century Christianity, but had actually been called and ordained under the hands of an Apostle.

Polycarp's Epistle to the Philippians survives. While the work does not mention John, it is nevertheless written in a style reminiscent of John. The introduction to a standard English translation of Polycarp summarizes the tone of the epistle in terms that demonstrate John's influence on Polycarp and affirms Polycarp's role as the Elder Apostle's disciple.

> It reflects the spirit of St. John, alike in its lamb-like and its aquiline features: he is as loving as the beloved disciple himself when he speaks of Christ and his church, but the "son of thunder" is echoed in his rebukes of threatened corruptions in faith and morals. Nothing can be more clear than his view of the doctrines of grace; he writes like the disciple of St. John.[10]

Several versions of excerpts from a late second or third century composition about Polycarp, known as the *Martyrdom of Polycarp*, are preserved to reiterate the information that Polycarp was a disciple of John, chosen and ordained bishop under the hands of the Apostle John, who is again described as living in Ephesus until he was extremely old, and directing the work of the Church from there.[11] The writings of Papias survive only as individual sections are found quoted in the work of later authors, particularly Eusebius. The relationship of Papias to John is corroborated, as is John's presence at Ephesus.[12]

John's very active leadership of the Church from Ephesus was universally accepted as a historical fact during the first several centuries of the Christian era. Tertullian, writing in Latin rather than Greek, and representing the strain of Christianity of North Africa and the western provinces of Rome, confirms the tradition articulated by Irenaeus regarding John's residence at Ephesus, his leadership of the Church from there, and his composition of Epistles, Apocalypse, and Gospel to continue to testify of his Master.[13] Before Tertullian, Justin Martyr, writing from Rome about his early years in Asia Minor, explicitly names the Apostle John as author of Revelation, thereby placing John in Asia.[14] Clement of Alexandria, learned scholar and first head of the Alexandrian School of Christian theology, similarly placed John at Ephesus. "Like Tertullian, Clement attributed Gospel, Epistles, and Apocalypse to John."[15] Moreover, Clement preserved several vignettes about John's life in the service of the Church members of Asia Minor, apparently having access to sources about John's activities at Ephesus which are now lost. The great Origen, who realized that by the third century the Church had gone through a fundamental alteration, also accepted the tradition both of John as author of the Gospel and the Apocalypse, and of John at Ephesus.[16] Through the late third century, the opinion of Christian leaders and theologians was in agreement that John was the Elder Apostle of Ephesus, living at Ephesus and laboring among the churches of Asia Minor, energetically conducting the work of the Lord.

Writing in the fourth century, Eusebius, a leading bishop and close friend of the Emperor Constantine, revised previous Christian historical traditions in his general treatise, *Ecclesiastical History*. Insofar as John was concerned, Eusebius retained the tradition that John was at Ephesus, but he postulated a second individual, also named John, whom he argued had been confused with the Apostle. Thus Eusebius could offer an explanation he preferred, in order to account for the longevity of the Apostle, his prolific writing, and actions attributed to John that Eusebius doubted could be performed by an aged man. However, based on the witness of Irenaeus and Clement, Eusebius seems to believe that the Apostle John did live at Ephesus as long as the principate of Trajan, at least up to the beginning of that reign in A.D. 98, when, as Eusebius claims,

> That very disciple whom Jesus loved, John, at once Apostle and Evangelist still remained alive in Asia and administered the churches there . . . as fully confirmed by two witnesses...no less persons than Irenaeus and Clement of Alexandria. The former of these writes . . . "and all the presbyters who had been associated with John, the disciple of the Lord, bear witness to his tradition, for John remained with them until the times of Trajan." . . . Clement indicates the same.[17]

Nevertheless, Eusebius construed a particular passage of Papias to mention John among the Apostles, but also to make different and distinct reference to an Elder John or presbyter John. Eusebius's rendering of Papias's text centers on his interpretation of the word for elder, the Greek *presbyter* or *presbyteros*. The Greek term *presbyteros* is used in both a chronological sense to refer to an older person, and with an extended meaning to indicate senior leaders of the community, such as a council of elders. By the late second century *presbyter* had become the title of a priestly office in Christianity. Eusebius interprets *presbyter* with the later meaning it had in his time. Thus a Presbyter John was someone who held the office of presbyter, thereby being differentiated from the Apostle John. For Eusebius, it was obvious that an Apostle John could not be the same man as the Presbyter or Elder John. Commentators after Eusebius, late antique, medieval, and modern, have increasingly accepted the point of view that there were two Johns, and, especially in the modern era, have assigned to this other John of Eusebius many of the achievements uniformly accepted by the early Christians as having been accomplished by the Apostle John, including, in the instance of some critics, the composition of the Gospel of John or the Book of Revelation.

The passage of Papias in question survived only as Eusebius reproduced it in his history: "I inquired about the words of the elders—what Andrew or Peter said, or Philip, or Thomas or James, or John or Matthew, or any other of the Lord's disciples, and whatever Aristion and the elder John, the Lord's disciple, were saying."[18] It should be noted that the word presbyter (elder) is used in reference to all the Apostles. They were the elders of the whole Christian movement, the senior men, the ancients who had known the Christ. Clearly, the term is not used by Papias to signify a particular Church office, but to denote the earliest followers of Jesus, men of the first generation of Christianity. That John is referred to in the list of Apostles and apostolic authors, and also with Aristion, a local bishop of Asia Minor, may mean no more than that John is doubly emphasized, once as an Apostle and once as a churchman residing in Papias's own region, indeed the most important Church leader and one to whom Papias was known to have been a student and personal assistant, the very scribe to whom John dictated his gospel.[19] It is not surprising that Papias would repeat his reference to John, the second time in a local context. Papias does describe John as "elder," just as he did for the whole list of Apostles. Of greater significance is the further description of the John of the second reference as "the Lord's disciple." The phrase undeniably points to the widespread practice of referring to this John as the Beloved Disciple.

Let us then conclude that Eusebius has misconstrued Papias's meaning. We are indebted to Constantine's friend for preserving Papias's account, but not for his faulty interpretation, cast in the mistaken notions of his own era. It is preferable to give heed to the understanding of John's own contemporaries. The Christians who preceded Eusebius by one and two hundred years, as demonstrated above, were uniform in their acceptance of the Apostle John, the Beloved Disciple, as the actual author of the works attributed to him and as one who lived among the saints of Asia Minor to a very old age, performing wondrous deeds and providing inspired leadership as the elder, or aged Apostle of Ephesus.

The Acts of John

Legend attributes a relatively early arrival at Ephesus for John, often thought to have been accompanied by Mary, mother of Jesus, concerning whom there also exists a strong tradition of association with Ephesus. Indeed, one of the popular Christian monuments of Ephesus is the putative House of Mary. Whether Mary lived long enough to come to Ephesus with John and other questions of Christian tradition concerning Mary are beyond the scope of this study. However, that Mary is linked to Ephesus at all surely depends on John's proven presence there and the well-known fact that Jesus entrusted John with the care of His mother. In any case, one modern expert on the traditions of Asia Minor comments regarding John's coming to Ephesus that "John, accompanied or not by the Virgin Mary, was in Ephesus and other cities of Asia certainly by 67, and perhaps a good deal earlier."[20] If, as proposed above, John arrived in Ephesus upon leaving Antioch probably in the late 50s, by the time of the aged Apostle's departure in the final years of Trajan's reign, John would have resided in Ephesus for almost sixty years. During so long a period, the influence which he exerted through his presence on the Christian Community of Ephesus and all of Asia Minor must have been tremendous. A noted scholar of both Johannine and Pauline Christianity comments in reference to the churches of Asia Minor: "Peter's name plays no part in the Christian tradition of that area. Indeed, even the name of Paul plays but a minor part in the Christian tradition of Ephesus and other cities of Asia. The dominant name from the apostolic age which dominates Asian, and especially Ephesian, tradition is that of John."[21] The important place of John as the guiding light of the Christianity of Asia Minor is reflected in the wondrous deeds and acts attributed to the Elder Apostle during his many years at Ephesus. Some are, no doubt, accounts of actual occurrences, or are at least based on events that actually transpired. Some are recounted by known Christian authors of the second or third century. Others appear in compilations such as the *Acts of John,* of unknown authorship, the *Acts of John by Prochorus,* or the *Acts of John at Rome,* highly spurious and of unknown author or compositional date. The stories which comprise these accounts cannot be confirmed as factual and, therefore, should be approached with caution. Several, however, may reflect actual events.

Clement of Alexandria, for example, recounts a vignette that illustrates John's courage and love for his flock. Eusebius preserves Clement's famous story and assesses its value as "fine and edifying."[22] Clement calls his account "not a story, but a true tradition of John the Apostle preserved in memory." John is described on one of his visits to strengthen branches of the Church and select local leaders, as meeting a young man who greatly impressed him and whom he entrusted to the particular care and training of the local bishop. This bishop was diligent at first, but later became lax in watching over the young man. As the years passed, the young man drifted away from the Church community and became involved with dissolute youths, finally becoming the leader of a gang, a robber band. On a subsequent visit, John inquired of the chagrined bishop about the young man. When the aged Apostle learned what had happened, he immediately departed for the robber lair in the nearby mountains and, upon being captured, demanded to be taken to the robber chieftain, the man for whose soul he had such concern. Clement's account of the meeting is as follows:

> The leader waited for him, armed as he was, but when he recognized John on his approach, he turned and fled in shame. But John pursued with all his might, forgetting his age and calling out, "Why do you run away from me, child, your own father, unarmed and old? Pity me, child, do not fear me! You still have hope of life. I will account to Christ for you. If it must

be, I will willingly suffer your death, as the Lord suffered for us; for your life, I will give my own. Stay, believe; Christ sent me."[23]

A repentant young man fell to his knees and was lovingly brought back into the fold by John. The point is made that the bishop was too busy with administering his local Church unit to care about the lost sheep, but the Apostle was not too busy administering the whole Church to go at risk of his own life and redeem the one.

Although of unknown authorship, the work known as the *Acts of John* is generally dated to the third century, and is given a Syrian rather than Asian origin.[24] Because Clement is aware of some of these acts performed by John, some have argued that the *Acts of John* should be given an earlier date. It is likely, however, that both Clement's source and the source of the surviving *Acts of John* was the same and was of early second century date. Such a source does not survive, of course, and no estimation may be made of its similarity or lack of similarity to the extant *Acts of John*. Eusebius was aware of the work called the *Acts of John* and lists it among "the writings which are put forward by heretics under the name of the apostles."[25] The text recounts John's journey from Miletus to Ephesus, teaching, preaching, and healing along the way.[26] The fame of John's actions preceded his arrival at Ephesus. As soon as the Apostle reached the city, he was summoned to the home of one of the city administrators, Lycomedes, who, along with his wife Cleopatra, John raised from the dead. Other healings are mentioned throughout the work, as well as many conversion stories, the most important of which is the raising from the dead and conversion of a chief priest of Artemis, patron goddess of Ephesus. Very interesting is John's recounting his witnessing of the Transfiguration, and then the secret teachings received from the Savior. The well-known story of John commanding the bedbugs in an unclean inn room to remain in a corner so that he could sleep unmolested is also included in this text. Finally, the *Acts of John* concludes strangely with a section where John is described as taking his leave of the Ephesian Saints, followed by a section that seems just tacked on to the rest of the text. In it, John's celibacy is praised and his death is described. The last chapters, as the first chapters of the extant *Acts of John,* seem not to fit and appear more representative of later Christian doctrines unknown in the first century. If there was an original work on which Clement's vignette and the third century *Acts of John* were based, it may well have concluded with John's last sermon and testimony of Christ and his simple departure from his "little children" at Ephesus.

To the *Acts of John,* modern editors have appended as the first seventeen sections readings from a group of independently maintained manuscripts, sometimes called the *Acts of John at Rome.* These texts largely treat John's summons to Rome under Domitian, his condemnation of Jews at Rome, and his attempted execution, first by poisoning and then by boiling in oil, from both of which John emerges unscathed.[27]

The *Acts of John by Prochorus* is probably a fifth-century work presented as the writings of John's assistant Prochorus, an early Christian leader mentioned in Acts 6:5. The stories deal with John's travels from Jerusalem to Ephesus and his activities in Ephesus and on Patmos. They are sometimes so imaginative, exaggerated, and full of pathos and emotion that their basis on fact is dubious.[28] In some ways such work is closely akin to the historical fiction of the modern era. Its purposes for historical information are thoroughly compromised by its lack of reality, even if it is designed to inspire, an object it also seems not to attain. A similar sort of work, though its tone is somewhat more realistic, is the Syriac *History of John,* sometimes identified by the title *History of St. John at Ephesus.* Much of the text is devoted to the theme of John's phenomenal success in making converts. What, if any, of it may be factual cannot be determined.[29]

The Epistles of John

Scholars from late ancient times up to the present day have expressed doubts about the apostolic authorship of all three Epistles bearing the name of John. The author of the second and third Epistles refers to himself as the Elder, or the Presbyter. For this reason many connect these Epistles to Eusebius's theorized Presbyter John. Moreover, modern studies based on stylistic analyses of the original Greek texts of the three Epistles and of the Gospel of John have produced for various scholars at various times, varied results. Some have argued that the style of 1 John differs or does not differ from that of 2 John and 3 John; others, that the styles of 1 John and the Gospel of John are similar; and others that they are dissimilar. In a combination of theories, a variety of suggestions of authorship is based on linguistic and stylistic analyses.[30]

Such stylistic analyses are largely based on the use of vocabulary—for instance, whether the same words are repeatedly used in writings—thus providing an indication of whether the same person has written different passages. The result of such analysis, whether applied to John, Paul, or Peter, is that modern analysts often conclude a lack of vocabulary similarity indicates someone other than the traditional author wrote the work. Whenever such analysis is conducted on a Greek text or, for that matter upon an English text, it is based on a flawed premise which fails to consider that a single author, in writing about different topics, will of necessity resort to different vocabulary. Different themes and subjects require the use of different words.

As regards the use of the term *presbyteros* by the author of 2 John and 3 John, it must be remembered that contemporary or near contemporary authors like Polycarp, Irenaeus, and Clement use the term to refer to men of the generation of Christ, men who knew and witnessed the actions of the Savior. In this sense, "elder" was a term of great respect, possessing a more profound significance than merely one of older age. It has been shown earlier that the term was applied to refer to all the Apostles in the notable Papias passage that was misconstrued by Eusebius to bring Presbyter John to life. Indeed, for the Apostle John to refer to himself as "the elder" seems quite natural. It was a term customarily used as an honorific for Apostles and even others who had known Jesus. Certainly it was employed by Church leaders in Ephesus and Asia Minor as a term of respect for John, so much so that it was particularly attached to John, almost as a title of affection. Indeed, by the time the Epistles were written, John was certainly the last living Apostle and very likely the last surviving of those Christians who had actually followed Jesus. To whom more would this title of honor and affection apply than to John? Perhaps it is for this reason that neither Papias, nor Polycarp, nor even Irenaeus explain the use of the epithet "the elder." Everyone of their time already knew to whom it referred, the one and only John, Apostle, Beloved Disciple, and the single author of the Epistles, Gospel, and Apocalypse that bear the name of John.

F. F. Bruce, in scholarly commentaries on both John's Gospel and Epistles, supports the legitimacy of Johannine authorship. He writes quite simply, "Suffice it to say that here it is accepted that the Epistles were written by this 'John the disciple of the Lord,' and also that he is the Fourth Evangelist."[31] For Bruce, two factors are important for determining John's identity: first, that writers of the early Christian era "who mention him regard him as a companion of our Lord and an eyewitness of His ministry;" second, that John was so very honored since he "lived to a great age, until the time came when he was the sole survivor of those who had been in close contact with Jesus . . . sought out and listened to by people who valued first-hand information about the deeds and words of his Master."[32]

The Epistles of John are brief, but revealing in their message. They provide a glimpse into a time when apostasy was already beginning among many who claimed to be followers of Christ.

The First Epistle of John does not present itself in traditional epistolary form. Contrary to the customary conventions of Greek and Roman letter writing, neither its author nor its audience is declared. "In form and content it is a message of encouragement and reassurance sent to a group of Christians who were perplexed and bewildered by recent happenings in their midst."[33] The author of the letter reveals himself as one who knows the Christ and is, therefore, qualified to recount "that which was from the beginning, which we have heard, which we have seen with our own eyes, which we have looked upon, and our hands have handled, of the Word of Life" (1 John 1:1). Clearly only the Apostle John could meet the description of one who from the beginning of the Savior's ministry had heard, seen, looked upon, and handled. The reference to the Word of Life is, of course, repeated when the Gospel of John was composed at a later time.

The elements are strikingly Johannine, as is the overall theme, that through fellowship "with the Father and with his Son Jesus Christ" (1 John 1:3) the darkness of the world might be overcome. Simple and straightforward in the typical fashion of the Beloved Disciple, John's message to his flock is to acknowledge sin and repent of it, and always remember Christ as our advocate to bring about forgiveness (1 John 1:7–2:1). When repentance is complete, obey the commandments, keep His word and walk as He walked, for in Him the love of God is perfected (1 John 2:3–5). The message recurs throughout all of John's writing, as he declares, "I write . . . the word which ye have heard from the beginning" (1 John 2:7), which was God's commandment that we love one another (1 John 4:21; John 13:34–35). By coming to know Jesus Christ and through Him the love of God, we discover the key to attaining exaltation and becoming like Him: "when he shall appear, we shall be like Him; for we shall see him as he is. And every man that hath this hope in him purifieth himself, even as he is pure" (1 John 3:2–3).

For John, the doctrine of the love of Christ is central to the message of Epistles, Gospel, and Apocalypse. It is, however, perhaps nowhere so simply and eloquently expressed as in 1 John. The Elder writes to his little children that most important of instructions for attaining eternal life: "My little children, let us not love in word, neither in tongue; but in deed and in truth" (1 John 3:18). He repeats the message, explaining that the love of God must be expressed not just to God alone, but to God through loving one another.

> Beloved, let us love one another: for love is of God; and every one that loveth is born of God, and knoweth God. He that loveth not knoweth not God; for God is love. In this was manifested the love of God toward us, because that God sent his only begotten Son into the world, that we might live through him. Herein is love, not that we loved God, but that he loved us, and sent his Son to be the propitiation for our sins. Beloved, if God so loved us, we ought also to love one another (1 John 4:7–11).

The message is profound; we can survive this world through our fellowship with the Father and the Son, and through the practice of Christ's doctrine of the love of God. In the Second Epistle of John, the Elder addresses his message to the elect lady (the Church) and her children (Church members), rejoicing that the little children walk in truth (2 John 1–4). John reminds them all, once again, of the vitally important commandment to love one another (2 John 5–6). A new warning is issued to the Church from its presiding Apostle. Deceivers have entered the fold "who confess not that Jesus Christ is come in the flesh" (2 John 1:7). The earliest stage of the Apostasy had begun. Men changed the doctrine of who Christ was and what His mission was. This loss of understanding about the true person and mission of the Savior seems to be the first stage of all apostasy. Even in the time of John, a group of Christians had begun to teach that Christ did not have a physical body, but only seemed to be in the form of a man. This false doctrine was called Docetism, and its adherents Docetists.

The name derives from the Greek verb *dokeo*, which means "to seem." Christ only *seemed* to have a body, or so taught the Docetists. The heresy apparently spread rapidly and by the mid-second century had become a major problem in parts of Asia and in Syria. John may have had countering the false doctrine in mind when in 1 John he refers to himself as one who had handled. He had touched the Christ. He knew that Jesus had a body—a material body that was real in every way. The Docetists could not expound their lies so long as a real, living witness of the Savior could refute their false claims. John instructs the faithful not to receive nor wish well such false brethren who are transgressors for teaching false doctrine (2 John 1:9–11).

In the Third Epistle of John, the Apostle addresses another problem that manifested itself as the Apostasy took hold. False leaders, motivated by personal ambition and not the humble love of Christ, had seized control of some branches of the Church. One such example was Diotrephes, who, for the sake of his own preeminence, uttered malicious words against John and legitimate Church leaders. He refused to accept communication from John or other brethren, separating his congregation from the larger Church (3 John 1:9–11).

Very little detailed information is provided, but the mention made of these two problems is enough to alert faithful members to the twin problems confronting the Church: false doctrine and false leaders. After John's departure, the men he had selected to act as bishops of the cities of Asia would be hard pressed to stem the tide of growing apostasy, though Asia Minor, where John's beloved little children were to be found, may have preserved true doctrines and practices longer than other regions which had not benefitted from direct personal association with the Elder Apostle of Ephesus.

Endnotes

1. See pages above, 65–68.
2. England and Warner, "First Presidency," 512.
3. Culpepper, *John*, 49.

4. See pages above, 90–95.

5. Downey, *History of Antioch*, 506, 623.

6. Justin Martyr, *Dialogue with Trypho*, 81.

7. Culpepper, *John*, 123.

8. Irenaeus, *Against Heresies*, 3.3.4.

9. Ibid., 5.33.3.

10. Alexander Roberts and James Donaldson, eds., *The Ante-Nicene Fathers* (1885, repr. 1996), 1:31.

11. The most familiar sections of the *Martyrdom of Polycarp* are preserved in Eusebius' *Ecclesiastical History* 4.15.3–45. A discussion of the Pseudo-Pionius version of the work and the recently discovered Sahidic Coptic manuscript of a section of the *Martyrdom of Polycarp*, which affirms much of the tradition of John and Polycarp, now known as the Harris Fragments, are to be found in F. W. Weidmann, *Polycarp and John* (1999) throughout, but especially pages 2–11, and 42–43.

12. The fragments of Papias are collected at the end of J.B. Lightfoot's well known *The Apostolic Fathers* (1891, repr. 1956–1996).

13. Tertullian, *On the Prescription against Heretics*, 32.

14. Culpepper, *John*, 112–14.

15. Culpepper, *John*, 141.

16. Nibley, *When the Lights Went Out*, 5 and note 22; Culpepper, *John*, 144.

17. Eusebius, *Ecclesiastical History*, 3.23.1–19.

18. Ibid., 3.93.3–4.

19. The anti-Marcionite prologue to the Gospel of John claims that "Papias, John's dear disciple, . . . wrote down the Gospel at John's dictation." See F. F. Bruce, *The Gospel of John*, 9.

20. George E. Bean, *Aegean Turkey*, 179.

21. F. F. Bruce, *Peter, Stephen, James, & John*, 20–21.

22. Eusebius, *Ecclesiastical History*, 3.23.6–19.

23. Ibid.

24. Culpepper, *John*, 187–89.

25. Eusebius, *Ecclesiastical History*, 3.23.6–19.

26. An English translation of the text and accompanying discussion can be found in E. Hennecke and W. Schneemelcher, *New Testament Apocrypha* (1964), 2:188–259.

27. Culpepper, *John*, 205–06.

28. Ibid., 206–22.

29. Ibid., 206–30.

30. Raymond E. Brown, *The Epistles of John* (1982), 14–35, provides an excellent summary of such argumentation.

31. F. F. Bruce, *The Epistle of John* (1970), 15.

32. Ibid., 14–15.

33. Ibid., 25.

CHAPTER THREE

Revelator and Evangelist

In his own time and throughout the centuries, the Apostle John's greatest continuing impact on the Christian community has perhaps been through writing the Book of Revelation or Apocalypse, and through his composition of the Gospel *(evangelion)* of John. Because of his connection to these two works, the Apostle John is sometimes also identified by the additional epithets of "Revelator" and "Evangelist."

Both compositions are of sufficiently late date to place them in the period of concern over increasing apostasy within an ever-expanding Church. "The apostasy described in the New Testament is not the *desertion* of the cause, but *perversion* of it, a process by which the righteous are removed, and none perceives it."[1] Perversion derives from the Latin *perverto*—to overturn thoroughly or turn about. During the time of John, just as he warned in his Epistles, doctrines were being overturned and turned about. One of the first great doctrinal changes or misunderstandings related to comprehending the person and nature of Christ. This Christological controversy was dealt with by the Apostle through writing his Gospel to help the Christians of his day come to know the Savior as He was—Son of God, Creator of Worlds, Redeemer, Lord. Another important misunderstanding of the time concerned the Second Coming. John's Apocalypse provides clarifying information about eschatological topics often confused by early Christians.

The Circumstances of John's Revelation

The information that John "was in the isle that is called Patmos, for the word of God, and for the testimony of Jesus Christ" (Rev. 1:9), came directly from John himself as he introduced the profound revelation that he had received. Modern commentaries about the Book of Revelation often extend in sensational ways the circumstances of John being on Patmos. He is sometimes depicted as living in horrendous conditions—enduring beatings or torture as a prisoner in a Roman penal colony, where he was reputed to have been banished by the emperor Domitian. Such information is far from historical and could even be described as bordering on fiction.

Dramatic and creative accounts of this sort ultimately derive from two early fourth-century Christian writers. Eusebius cites Irenaeus as noting that the Apocalypse was revealed at the end of the reign of Domitian. But, without citing a source, Eusebius gives further additional opinion, in part based on his own interpretation of Revelation 1:9, that "the Apostle and Evangelist John was still alive, and was condemned to live in the island of Patmos for his witness of the divine word." The passage is understood by some, even today, to mean John had come to Patmos to teach the gospel and testify of Christ, no more, no less. But after Eusebius assigned it the contrasting meaning that John had been forced to Patmos in punishment of the Apostle's previous work in teaching the gospel, many seemed to follow the new interpretation. The added implication of such an interpretation is that Domitian was responsible for so condemning John.

If Eusebius refused to go further in his speculation about why John may have been on Patmos, Victorinus did not. Victorinus was bishop of Petau and author of an early commentary on the Apocalypse; he lived in a period of government-sponsored persecution of Christians which had not existed in the era of John, and so Victorinus may have been influenced by contemporary events in his conclusions about what happened two hundred years before his time. Victorinus seems to have created the sensationalist circumstances concerning John's presence on Patmos:

> When John said these things he was in the island of Patmos, condemned to the labor of the mines by Caesar Domitian. There, therefore, he saw the Apocalypse; and when grown old, he thought that he should at length receive his quittance by suffering, Domitian being killed, all his judgments were discharged. And John being dismissed from the mines, thus subsequently delivered the same Apocalypse which he had received from God.[2]

The actual circumstance of John's sojourn on Patmos, its cause, or its duration, can never be precisely known. However, sufficient evidence survives from ancient times to point to a more plausible explanation of the Apostle's presence. First, the notion of Roman penal colonies or places of imprisonment is anachronistic, a modern concept applied to an ancient situation. Romans did not imprison as a means of punishment. Exile was employed and isolated islands were, in fact, utilized as places of exile. The exiled person lived among the local populace, however, and not in confinement. One commentator has noted the tremendous "difference between a site being used as an *ad hoc* rather than ongoing place of exile, and . . . the even more profound difference between exile and brutal prison-camp-style punishment."[3]

A list of places used for the practice of exile has been compiled from examination of Roman epigraphical documents and literary sources. Thirteen specific islands of the Aegean Sea can be confirmed as used for exile. Patmos is not included. In fact, it cannot be documented as ever used by the government as a place of exile.[4] Moreover, archaeology has failed to produce the remains of anything vaguely akin to a prison camp with mine or quarry. While it is impossible to exclude as a rare happening that "the island may have occasionally been used for exile purposes, there was nothing approaching an ongoing 'penal colony' or 'prison settlement.' Hence, there would not have been the involuntary manpower available to mine those quarries that is assumed," giving credence to the view of an imprisoned John, though not an enslaved one.[5]

The notion of a sentence of exile being pronounced as a punishment for a Christian of the late first century also seems out of place. The prosecution of Christians that we know about from the correspondence of the emperor Trajan and Pliny, less than twenty years later, is couched in terms of punishment more severe than exile.[6] Moreover, the direct involvement of Domitian in the case of John, as implied by Eusebius, seems unlikely. The widespread persecution of Christians under Domitian, which is asserted by Victorinus in analogy to the Diocletianic and Galerian persecutions of his own later era, is increasingly considered by scholars as having never transpired.

On the basis of the statements of Eusebius and Victorinus, historians of early Christianity once presumed that Domitian engaged in empire-wide persecution of Christians. Today, however, the brief comments of fourth-century writers concerning Domitianic actions against Christians are largely dismissed by modern historical analyses. Domitian's actions seemed confined to the execution of two imperial cousins, husband and wife, Flavius Clemens and Flavia Domitillia, hero and heroine of Roman Christian lore.[7] Indeed, Flavius Clemens is considered by some to have been bishop at Rome and author of 1 Clement. Domitian's traditional unpopularity with Christians probably came not because of persecution, but his restoration of taxation to those of Jewish descent. The exemption prized since the time of Julius Caesar was forfeited not only for Jews, but for Christians of Jewish ethnicity.[8]

To use the term exile is also imprecise. Roman law recognizes two processes which the modern term exile could encompass. The first is *deportatio,* whereby an individual was assigned to live in a particularly designated place as a lifetime punishment. There was no termination or reversal of *deportatio* except by intervention on the part of the emperor. Indeed, the sentence of *deportatio* was also usually dependent on imperial approval. In contrast to *deportatio,* the more common process of *relegatio* entailed mandatory departure from a place. This meant that the person who was punished with *relegatio* could leave their original place of residence and go anywhere else they wished, without subsequent supervision. *Relegatio* simply required that they not return to their original locale, until the term of their *relegatio* was completed. Unlike *deportatio, relegatio* was not of lifetime duration, but normally in effect for a few years, often as little as a single year, since it could be assigned by a provincial governor whose term may have been as little as a year, and whose acts would have become invalid upon his return to Rome. No imperial involvement was required, as only the authority of a governor was necessary to effect *relegatio.*[9]

If John was on Patmos because of exile of any kind, surely it was *relegatio* rather than *deportatio* which would have been pronounced on the Apostle. The need for imperial involvement would be obviated, and a local governor of the province of Asia could have compelled John to leave Ephesus for a temporary time for any of a variety of reasons. John in turn may have chosen to go to Patmos to avoid further conflict with the governor and at the same time remain in close proximity to Ephesus, only a short distance away. The likelihood of such a scenario is increased by Tertullian's statement, almost a century before Eusebius, that John did go into exile for a short time. Tertullian was educated as a Roman lawyer. He knew proper legal terminology. Writing in Latin rather than Greek, Tertullian provides the specific information that John was indeed subjected to *relegatio*.[10] In a detailed scholarly analysis of the circumstances of John's stay on Patmos, Roland Worth arrived at the conclusion that,

> In choosing between relegation and deportation, relegation seems more likely to have been John's punishment. Although it would have required the passive acceptance of the emperor, it was primarily a decision the local governor could implement on his own initiative. It may make for a less dramatic story, but, if anything, that argues for its greater likelihood. It should also be noted that the ancient church writer Tertullian, who was a trained lawyer, actually uses the term in describing John's exile. A lawyer might use the expression in a broader genuine sense, but with Tertullian's specialized background one would naturally anticipate him using it in its correct legal sense.[11]

Patmos is forever famous because John, whether due to his own plans for teaching and preaching, or because he had been subjected to a sentence of *relegatio* and chose the location for a short exile from nearby Ephesus, happened to be on the island at the time the Lord gave him his apocalyptic vision of things that would come to pass at the *parousia,* or Second Coming of the Lord.

The Apocalyptic Message of John

John begins his account by declaring it to be "the Revelation of Jesus Christ, which God gave unto him, to shew . . . unto his servant John" (Rev. 1:1). Although other prophets in various dispensations had been shown the things that John witnessed, they were forbidden to disseminate the visions they received, for this was a task foretold centuries before John's day as belonging to John. Not only had John been specifically designated to convey the Book of Revelation to men, but at the time this message was revealed, John was, in fact, the appropriate person to whom it should be directed. He held the presiding priesthood keys. He was the presiding Apostle of the Church— prophet, seer, and revelator. Accordingly, both by prior foreordination and by the priesthood authority he possessed, John's was the assignment to reveal the great apocalyptic message his beloved Lord entrusted to the care of his writing (1 Ne. 14:19–28; Ether 4:16).

In this context it must be remembered that the person of Jesus Christ is as central to the message of the Book of Revelation as He is to any of John's writings. The revelation begins with a vision of the glorified Lord, the Son of Man, with head and hair of the purest white, eyes as the flame of fire, a voice with the sound of many waters, and a countenance as glorious as the sun when it shines in its strength (Rev. 1:12–16). John had seen the resurrected Savior, and witnessed His Ascension, but the Lord had then not yet entered into His glory. Even John, who knew Jesus so well, was astounded to behold his Master in His eternal glory. John's reaction was to fall as if dead, at the feet of this glorified eternal being. But John recounts that his beloved Master "laid his right hand upon me, saying unto me, Fear not; I am the first and the last: I am he that liveth, and was dead; and behold, I am alive for evermore, Amen; and have the keys of hell and of death" (Rev. 1:17–18). With these words quoted by John as they were spoken by the Lord Jesus Christ, is pronounced the message of the Book of Revelation. Fear not. He that liveth and was dead is now alive forevermore. The Savior holds the keys of hell and death. He lives, and lives eternally. As did John, so did the Prophet Joseph Smith understand "all other things which pertain to our religion are only appendages to this testimony."[12] As we obey His commandments and become filled with His love, He will exercise the keys that only He holds to bring to pass our individual salvation, safe from hell and death, to live with Him forevermore. Such a message, transmitted through John, is absolutely in keeping with the other messages left by John. The Beloved Disciple continues to declare the divinity and saving mission of his Master.

The Savior instructed John to communicate the apocalyptic vision, along with an individual charge, to each of seven churches in Asia. Each struggled to remain strong in the faith as different challenges confronted John's beloved little children in their respective cities. Individual messages to the cities accord well with what is known of them as centers of the Christian community. Nevertheless, the message is for all followers of Christ.

John identifies those who were to receive his letter. They are seven of the churches in the Roman province of Asia. Elder James E. Talmage has suggested that these seven were the last bastions of faith, the great apostasy having eaten up all other areas. John was writing a letter of comfort and warning to the surviving remnant of the true Church. However, implications from John's symbolic use of numbers should not be overlooked. John possibly uses seven to denote that the message is universal for all branches of the church, even those outside of Asia, and those beyond John's day.[13]

By the end of the first century, Christians had become very confused about the doctrine of the Second Coming, which they referred to by the Greek term, *parousia,* signifying "being present with." Faithful members of the Church longed for the Savior to be present with them again. The expectation that He would return soon after His Ascension spread as a false hope. That the Apostasy would first take place and many centuries pass was clearly known, but not fully comprehended by many followers of Christ. This was a question which had vexed the branch of the Church at Thessalonica. Paul counseled the Thessalonian Christians to be more concerned about living in a righteous manner in order to be prepared to meet the Savior either at His return, or upon their own passing to the other side (1 Thess. 5:1–11). It was necessary for Paul to write a second time to the Thessalonians about the subject in more explicit fashion, instructing them not to let anyone deceive them about the Second Coming, "for there shall come a falling away first" (JST, 2 Thess. 2:3).

The increase of concern that Christ had not yet returned was a contributing factor to the spreading Apostasy of John's day. No doubt one function of the Book of Revelation was to provide legitimate signs of the Second Coming. In a new revelation to a modern prophet, the Lord declared that themes in the Book of Revelation pertain to "the revealed will, mysteries, and the works of God; the hidden things of his economy concerning this earth during the seven thousand years of its continuance, or its temporal existence" (D&C 77:6). Nevertheless, in connection with the great-awaited event that will occur in the final stage of the earth's temporality, other important information is revealed. Profound truths are declared regarding the relationship between the earth and the eternal heavens organized by Jesus as Creator, the premortal plan of salvation put into effect by the atoning mission of the Savior, and the ultimate eternal destiny of those who are faithful to the example of the Son of God. Christ is central to each instance. Such are the basic fundamental doctrines of the glad tidings brought by Jesus and conveyed by His true disciples. They are found in the Book of Revelation, as elsewhere. Thus the vision revealed to John does not merely contain prophecy given to recognize the "fullness of times" which precedes Jesus' *parousia,* but profound, yet simple to understand, gospel truths about the person and eternal mission of Jesus Christ. Symbolism may put off a generation unfamiliar with that traditional mode of information, yet the Prophet Joseph Smith declared John's Book of Revelation to be "one of the plainest books God ever caused to be written."[14]

John's Apocalypse provides important prophetic and doctrinal information. Both kinds of information proclaim the glad tidings of Jesus Christ. After directing specific counsel to the seven selected churches in Asia Minor, the Lord issues an invitation to anyone who might receive the message revealed to John.

> Behold, I stand at the door, and knock: if any man hear my voice, and open the door, I will come in to him, and will sup with him, and he with me. To him that overcometh will I grant to sit with me in my throne, even as I also overcame, and am set down with my Father in his throne (Rev. 3:20–21).

To the faithful of John's time, a clear invitation was offered. Despite external opposition and growing apostasy within, those who continued to follow Jesus, overcoming the world with its adverse conditions, could be confident in communing with their Savior and one day sharing His glory in the eternities. The message is, of course, timeless and of universal application. The invitation is repeated at the end of the Book of Revelation. The Lord declares in the final words of the great vision, "I Jesus . . . am the root and the offspring of David, and the bright and morning star. And the Spirit and the bride say, Come. And let him that heareth say, Come. And let him that is athirst come. And whosoever will, let him take the water of life freely" (Rev. 22:16–17).

The Composition of the Gospel of John

The authorship of the Gospel of John has been debated by contemporary scholars seeking to determine whether the Apostle

John or Eusebius's hypothesized Elder John composed this witness of the Christ.[15] As with other of John's writings, the common view of Christian historians and commentators before Eusebius was firm in accepting the Apostle John as the writer of the Gospel which bears his name. Irenaeus was clear in his assertion that the Apostle John published his gospel at Ephesus, and Clement of Alexandria explained that John wrote the Gospel in response to continual urging by students and disciples to record his personal experiences with Jesus.[16] A Latin translation of a prologue to an edition of the scriptures, part of the famed *Muratorian Canon,* encapsulates the opinion of second-century Christians by describing "the fourth of the gospels, that of John, one of the disciples."[17]

A prologue introducing the Gospel of John survives that is of even earlier date, the so-called anti-Marcionite prologue to John. These writings are accepted as predating even Irenaeus and are generally dated to A.D. 160–180.[18] The introduction to John reads:

> The Gospel of John was revealed and given to the church by John while he was yet in the body as one Papias of Hierapolis, a dear disciple of John has reported . . . Indeed, he took down the gospel word for word while John was dictating. But the heretic Marcion was cast out by John after having been disapproved by him because of his opposite opinions. Marcion had, however, carried to John writings or letters from the brethren who dwelt in Pontus.[19]

The passage is important in that several allusions make it clear the John referred to is the Apostle and Evangelist. The phrase "while he was yet in the body" may mean much more than to simply describe him as not yet dead, and, instead, refer to John's later translation. The carrying of reports from Pontus along the Black Sea shore to Ephesus would be appropriate only if the John mentioned were the presiding officer of the entire Church. Finally, the connection of Marcion with the author of the Fourth Gospel makes John's identity clear, for Tertullian is explicit in his account of the condemnation of the apostate Marcion at the hands of the Apostle John.[20]

Yet another text found in Corderius's *Catena,* but attributed to anonymous early Christian leaders, confirms the authorship of John, son of Zebedee. "Last of all the evangelists, John, called the son of thunder, being far advanced in years, dictated his gospel against the frightful here-sies springing up at that time, to his disciple Papias, bishop of Hierapolis."[21] This text not only confirms the Apostle John as the author of the Gospel, but provides important contextual information about the time the Gospel of John was composed—time of emerging apostasy.

Although modern scholarship remains divided on the question of the Gospel of John's authorship, many leading scholars adhere to the same tradition as the earliest Christians. The Apostle John wrote the Fourth Gospel. One of the soundest lines of examination presented in support of that tradition is the analysis of the text itself, a process which led one commentator to conclude that "The internal evidence of the Gospel indicates it was written a) by a Palestinian Jew, b) by an eyewit-ness, c) by the disciple whom Jesus loved, d) by John the son of Zebedee."[22] This important observation recognizes that the author of the Gospel of John was an eyewitness of the events he described, a close follower of Jesus. Indeed, "in the epilogue to the Gospel the 'disciple whom Jesus loved' is said to be the one who 'bears witness to these things and wrote these things.'"[23] Central to the intent and organization of this gospel is the notion of an eyewitness who can say what he had seen and heard, and describe with absolute accuracy the person of the Lord Jesus Christ. As a leading contemporary New Testament scholar, F. F. Bruce, asserts in his important commentary on the Gospel of John, the final word on the question of authorship is, "As early as the ascription of this Gospel to John can be traced back, it is regularly assumed that the John in question was John the son of Zebedee, one of the Twelve.[24]

The date for John's composition of his Gospel is a more compli-cated matter because of the dearth of pertinent evidence. The earliest surviving manuscript of any part of the Gospel of John is the John Rylands Papyrus. It preserves a portion of chapter 18 and is dated to about A.D. 125. On the basis of this papyrological evidence, the Gospel would have to have been written before that time and is some-times dated to about A.D. 100.[25] Because the Book of Revelation is the last in the arrangement of the books of the modern Bible, the public generally assumes that it was the last composed, and that consequently John must have written his Gospel before producing Revelation.[26] Of course, the books of the New Testament are arranged not by chronology, but by topic; for example, Gospels, Acts, Pauline Epistles, general Epistles, and Revelation. Indeed, even within *these* categories, chronology is no factor for arrangement. For example, the Pauline Epistles are not arranged chronologically, but rather by length of text.

It is quite plausible that the Gospel of John was written after the Book of Revelation. Both are obviously composed late in John's ministry, at a time when apostasy is transpiring. If Revelation was received on Patmos during the reign of Domitian, that ended in 96, it would have been written and disseminated from Ephesus no more than a few years later. John's own residence at Ephesus, as noted in the previous chapter, is known to have extended into the reign of Trajan, encompassing the years 98–117. There is no reason to suppose that John could not have written the Gospel during that period of time. Incorrect teachings about the person and mission of Christ would have proliferated by that time. The Gospel of John seems very much intended to counteract such false teachings by providing John's own eyewitness account and testimony of what he saw and heard, and whom he knew Jesus to be. Indeed, more than forty times throughout his narrative, John employs a form of the Greek word *martureo* (to testify or give witness). As the last living apostolic witness, John's task is clearly indicated: to testify of the person and divinity of Jesus Christ.

The Message of John the Evangelist

Whether to help the faithful of his own time resist the messages of Docetism, Gnosticism, or the Nicolaitans, or to provide a gift of knowledge and testimony to men of all times, the Beloved Disciple articulated his purpose as evangelist toward the end of his own text.[27] "But these are written that ye might believe that Jesus is the Christ, the Son of God; and that believing ye might have life through his name" (John 20:31). The Gospel of John was designed to correct misunderstanding of the person and nature of Christ on the one hand, but was chiefly concerned on the other hand with assisting those who read its text to come to believe in Christ and, through faith in Him and love for Him, attain the eternal life the Lord proffers to His true followers. The former purpose entails the endowment of knowledge, the latter provides the spiritual witness of one who loved and would instill that same love of Christ in all who come to know the Master through his words and testimony.

Unlike the three synoptic Gospels, which provide a narrative of Jesus' life and teachings, John's purpose is not to chronicle Jesus' deeds, but rather to provide a selective account of the Savior's teachings, through which men may come to know the Lord. John's own testimony of Christ's ministry provides assurance to his reader of the truthfulness of his account. The final words of John—in his distinctive third-person style—make this clear.

> This is the disciple which testifieth of these things, and wrote these things: and we know that his testimony is true. And there are also many other things which Jesus did, the which, if they should be written every one, I suppose that even the world itself could not contain the books that should be written (John 21:24–25).

In the Gospel of John, narratives are secondary to discourses. John provides firsthand information about what Jesus taught, so that through the Savior's own teachings the faithful might become better acquainted with Christ. John's use of narrative passages normally establishes the context of an address or discussion which follows. His discourses are carefully crafted monologues or conversations leading to the exposition of an important principle relating to the person or mission of Christ. Through these discourses, Jesus is revealed as Lord and Savior. One commentator explains that unlike the modern critic or revisionist scholar,

> John is not attempting to give a historical picture of the man Jesus, but what he sees to be a true picture of the historical Jesus—the historical Jesus as John now sees him to be, the historical Jesus with the glory that was to be his by virtue of his death, resurrection, and ascension already visible in his earthly life.[28]

John's understanding of Jesus was as Creator, Son of God, Savior, and Lord; his purpose was to facilitate his reader in coming to know Christ in all these aspects of His person. The depiction of this being of eternal majesty, who was John's own friend, begins with Christ's pre-earthly role, not merely as the "word" of the King James Translation, nor the Platonic *logos* of later Christian philosopher theologians, but the *logos,* or spokesman, of that great premortal Heavenly Council (John 1:1), the agent of His Father from the beginning (John 1:2), creator of all things (John 1:3), source of life (John 1:4), and light or truth (John 1:5). To reveal this personage to the "little children" of John's time, whose vision of the true cosmic Christ was dimmed, and to communicate the same to the generations to follow is the design of John's glad tidings.

These roles of Christ's person and mission are reflected in the discourses of the Fourth Gospel. Of many possible examples, a few will suffice to demonstrate. The Bread of Life sermon of John 6 follows the narrative circumstance of the miracle of the loaves and fishes, by representing Christ as the Bread of Life sent from the Father. In concluding the passage, John recounts the departure of many who were disappointed that Christ did not claim the role of militant messiah, for which the misinformed Jewish people vainly sought. The climax of the entire section comes when Jesus asks Peter if the disciples will also go away. Peter replies with those great words of testimony, "Lord, to whom shall we go? thou hast the words of eternal life. And we believe and are sure that thou art that Christ, the Son of the living God" (John 6:68–69). Jesus is the Son of God. He has the words of eternal life. Only through this true Messiah may the glory of eternal life be attained.

The sermon of the Way, the Truth, and the Life in John 14 reemphasizes this doctrine that the keys of eternal life belong to the Son of God. It establishes the principle that by following Christ as the Way, Truth can be learned and Life received. The message is simple but profound: "He that believeth on me, the works that I do shall he do also" (John 14:12). Jesus' exhortation to those who would be like Him is to keep the commandments. "He that hath my commandments, and keepeth them, he it is that loveth me" (John 14:21). Jesus' discourse with the Twelve at the Last Supper is connected with this injunction to love, wherein He links the great atoning sacrifice He will soon make with the new commandment He gives, "That ye love one another; as I have loved you, that ye also love one another. By this shall all men know that ye are my disciples, if ye have love one to another" (John 13:34–35).

In these passages John not only speaks about Jesus as Son of God, but demonstrates that a chief characteristic of both the Son and the Father is love. They act out of love toward men, and so should men, if they wish to have life eternal, act out of love. In such a manner John reveals the way Christ has given to men to join Him and His Father.

"And this is life eternal, that they might know thee the only true God, and Jesus Christ, whom thou hast sent" (John 17:3). Jesus' sermon on the True Vine and the Branches in John 15 develops the concept of a unified band of disciples, motivated by love, whom Jesus has given the distinction of being not servants, but friends. It is His friends for whom Jesus prays in the great Intercessory Prayer of John 17. His final petition to His Father is "that the love wherewith thou hast loved me may be in them, and I in them" (John 17:26).

The great Evangelist has in his inspired exposition of the glad tidings not only testified of the divine person and mission of the Christ, but by relating Jesus' own teachings revealed the loving Good Shepherd whose concern for the care of His flock is paramount. As John's beloved Master is revealed through words and deeds, John's own devotion to his Friend is manifest. The sincere reader of the Gospel of John cannot help but desire similar devotion to so loving and courageous a being.

The Gospel of John, lovingly composed by the aged Beloved Disciple, Apostle for more than eighty years and last of his dispensation to hold the keys of priesthood authority, represents his final witness, that Jesus is the Christ, the Son of God, the Savior of the World.

Endnotes

1.   Hugh W. Nibley, *When the Lights Went Out,* 6.

2.   Vicotinus, *Commentary on the Apocalypse,* On Revelation 10:11 and 11:1.

3.   Roland H. Worth, *The Seven Cities of the Apocalypse* (1999).

4.   J. P. V. D. Balsdon, *Romans and Aliens* (1979), 113–15.

5.   Worth, *Seven Cities,* 98.

6.   See the above discussion on pages 53–54.

7.   Roman historian Cassius Dio provides a detailed account (67.14) about Domitian's execution of his cousins on charges of atheism, but makes no mention of Christian persecutions, as would have been expected.

8.   Suetonius, *Domitian,* 12.2, provides near contemporary detailed information in this regard. Also see James C. Walters, "Romans, Jews, and Christians," in Karl Donfried and Peter Richardson, *Judaism and Christianity in First Century Rome* (1998), 175–95.

9. Wolfgang Kunke, *An Introduction to Roman Legal and Constitutional History*, 2nd ed., trans J.M. Kelly (1979), 73. Peter Garnsey, *Social Status and Legal Privilege in the Roman Empire* (1970), 116–17.

10. Tertullian, *On the Prescription against Heretics*, 36.

11. Worth, *Seven Cities*, 130.

12. Joseph Smith, *TPJS*, 121.

13. Richard Draper, *Opening the Seven Seals* (1991), 27–28.

14. Joseph Smith, *History of the Church*, 5: 342.

15. A summary of pertinent issues and scholarly opinion is provided by Raymond Brown, *The Gospel According to John*, 1:lxxxvii–civ.

16. Irenaeus, *Against Heresies*, 3.1.1; Eusebius, *Ecclesiastical History*, 6.14.7.

17. Hennecke and Schneemelcher, *New Testament Apocrypha*, 1:43–45.

18. Culpepper, *John*, 129-30.

19. Robert M. Grant, "The Oldest Gospel Prologues," *Anglican Theological Review*, 23 (1941), 241–42.

20. Tertullian, *On the Flesh of Christ*, 3; *On the Prescription against Heretics*, 33.

21. Culpepper, *John*, 112 and note 19.

22. B. F. Westcott, *The Gospel according to St. John*, (1880), xxiv.

23. F. F. Bruce, *Gospel of John*, 3.

24. Ibid., 1.

25. Culpepper, *John*, 108.

26. Revelation was regularly, but not in every instance, last in the lists of New Testament books known from ancient times. See Lee M. McDonald, *The Formation of the Christian Biblical Canon* (1995), 274–76.

27. The problems of Docetism are discussed earlier on pages 148–49, in conjunction with the Johannine Epistles. Gnosticism similarly portrays Christ in a manner that calls into question his corporeality. The Nicolaitans propounded a dualism that asserted "what was done in the body had no bearing on the soul," so leading to sexual licentiousness and permissiveness regarding consumption of pagan sacrificial meats. See D.F. Watson, "Nicolaitans," *Anchor Bible Dictionary*, 4:1106–07.

28. Dunn, *Unity*, 27.

CHAPTER FOUR

The Last of Those Who Had Seen

"When my ashes scatter," says John, "there is left on earth
No one alive who knew
Saw with his eyes and handled with his hands
That which was from the first, the Word of Life
How will it be when none more saith 'I saw'?"

The poet's insight reveals much of truth. Robert Browning's poem, "A Death in the Desert," lamented John's departure, an event which brought about the world's loss of the priesthood keys he held and the acceleration of apostasy that it occasioned. Yet John himself, as a translated being, continued to labor in the cause of his Master. The Beloved Disciple's continuing mission, known and understood by those familiar with the revelation given on the matter to the Prophet Joseph Smith (D&C 7), is dimly recollected by Christendom, where the significance of the Savior's allusion to John's tarrying until He came again (John 21:22), has become the stuff of legend. In Longfellow's poem, "St. John's, Cambridge," the elder Apostle is characterized as living still, waiting for the Savior's return.

Then I remember one of whom was said
In the world's darkest hour, "Behold thy son!"
And see him living still, and wandering
And waiting for the advent long delayed.

The Last Apostle

John was the last Apostle of Jesus to function in the Dispensation of the Meridian of Time. He was last to possess the keys of the priesthood and so serve as the authoritative link between heaven and earth. Only he could activate legitimate transmission of priesthood authority from one man to another. When John departed, such authority could no longer be conferred, for the keys of power ceased to function in the absence of one commissioned to employ them. By the fourth century, Eusebius may have "sought with dedicated zeal to prove the survival of the Church by blazing a trail back to the Apostles," altering the definition of the Church in structural, practical, and theological terms to make everything seem to fit.[1] But nearly a hundred years before, Origen perceived the truth in writing *iam finem venisse,* "the end has already come."[2] Origen was aware that without legitimate authority the powers of heaven could not be called upon by those claiming to possess priesthood.

As presiding officer of the Church, possessing the keys of priesthood authority, John had the right and power to call new Apostles and fill up the Quorum of the Twelve again. Why he did not do so is readily apparent. The Lord did not so instruct him. The Apostasy was prophesied about and expected. Christians of the first generations understood that "collectively and individually the Church was here only on a brief pilgrimage. They were *das wanderunde Gottesvolk,* strangers and pilgrims all, destined for but a short time upon the earth."[3] B. H. Roberts offers this explanation for why the Church ceased to function as an authorized arm of the heavenly Church.

> There is no account in any of the writings of the Apostles or fathers of the first century of any attempt to perpetuate the quorum of the twelve by filling up the vacancies occasioned by the death of the original Apostles. . . . The reason for this will doubtless be found in the fact that in the very days of the Apostles the great "falling away" which was to end eventually in the subversion of the Christian religion, had begun . . . and men were rapidly proving themselves unworthy of the church of Christ, the Lord did not permit his servants to perpetuate these quorums of the higher Priesthood.[4]

John had done what he was able to do to provide for his "little children." He had taught and preached salvation through faith in Jesus and the practice of Christ's doctrine of love. The same message was left for the faithful—for those who had eyes to see—in the writings of the Beloved Disciple. The apocalyptic vision the Savior had bestowed on

John was also committed to writing, serving as a guide to the faithful of his day and later times. John had left his warning along with his love. He may have lingered long to inspire with his presence, but the time finally arrived for John to "do more, or a greater work yet among men than what he has before done" (D&C 7:5).

The *Acts of John* (103–05) records a concluding address attributed to the Elder Apostle. It encourages his brethren at Ephesus by reminding them that the Lord will be with them even after John is gone.

> Now, my brothers, since we have seen the grace of the Lord and his affection towards us, let us worship him, since we have obtained mercy from him; not with our fingers, nor with our mouths, nor with our tongue, nor with any other member of our body at all, but with the disposition of our soul. And let us watch, since he is at hand even now in prisons for our sakes, and in tombs, and in bonds, in reproaches and insults, by sea and dry land. . . . in a word he is with all of us and with the sufferers he suffers himself, my brethren. If he is called upon by any of us he does not hold out against hearing us, but, being everywhere, he hears us all. . . . You therefore, beloved also be persuaded, that it is not a man that I exhort you to worship, but a God unchangeable, God invincible, God who is higher than all authority and all power . . . so if you hold fast to him and are built upon by him, you shall possess your soul indestructible.[5]

After John left his last message with his "little children," he seems to have simply walked away. In this account there is no word of death. A different ending apparently attached later to the original text, probably of fifth-century composition, depicts John as laying down to enter the sleep of death after a disquisition of the virtues of celibacy. Such a context, and significant textual differences serve to identify the passage as a significantly later addendum of spurious authorship. Accordingly, verse 105 of the section in question seems to be the last segment of the original *Acts of John*. It reads, very simply, "And when John had delivered these things to the brethren, he went out with Andronicus to walk."[6]

There did exist in Ephesus traditions of multiple burial places for John. The great Basilica of John, built by Justinian in the fifth century over an earlier church, perhaps constructed two hundred years before by Constantine, supposedly rests upon the most likely site of John's remains. However, there also exists the counter tradition that John's body was not really there at all. This old Ephesian legend is indicated in a single manuscript version of the *Acts of John by Prochorus,* which claims John did not die.[7] Similarly, even Augustine preserves the tradition that not all was right with the idea of John's death, indicating that it was said that where John was buried the ground rose and fell as with the rhythm of the Apostle's breathing, a sign that he only slept and had not died.[8]

Such local traditions, when combined with Christ's statement to Peter about John that "if I will that he tarry till I come, what is that to thee?" (John 21:22), produced a general tradition that John still walked the earth, from which arose legends of the Beloved Disciple's activities. A purported fifth-century appearance links John to Ravenna and its most ancient church of Gallia Placidia. Several traditions place the Apostle John in England, including one of his personal interaction with English king Edward the Confessor, whose 1066 death was foretold by John. The king's chapel preserved at Westminster is decorated with artistic depiction of Edward's experience with John and an account of the same is recorded in Johannis Brompton's *Cronicon.* Other traditions of John occur in England and not only in Anglo-Saxon, but also in Celtic Christian tradition.[9]

The Translated John

From the ancient world comes a notice in an obscure work of Alexandrian Christian scholars, the *Synaxarium Alexandrinum,* of the date of a Christian feast day in honor of the "Translation of John."[10] The term may be used just as we use it, for the notion of translated beings was certainly familiar to early Christians as it had been to the Jews. Best known, of course, were the translated prophets of the Transfiguration, Moses and Elijah.

In 1829, as a result of discussion with Oliver Cowdery over the meaning of John 21:22 about whether John had died or continued to live, the Prophet Joseph Smith received the revelation that gave understanding to seventeen hundred years of Christian enigma regarding John. John was, in fact, a translated being with a special continuing mission that he could perform only in that state. The revelation is a translated version of a record made on parchment by John and hidden up by himself.

And the Lord said unto me: John, my beloved, what desirest thou? For if you ask what you will, it shall be granted unto you. And I said unto him: Lord, give unto me power over death, that I may live and bring souls unto thee. And the Lord said unto me: Verily, verily, I say unto thee, because thou desirest this thou shalt tarry until I come in my glory, and shalt prophesy before nations, kindreds, tongues and people. . . . My beloved has desired that he might do more, or a greater work yet among men than what he has before done. Yea, he has undertaken a greater work; therefore I will make him as flaming fire and a ministering angel; he shall minister for those who shall be heirs of salvation who dwell on the earth (D&C 7:1–3, 5–6).

David Marsh provides a thorough study of John as a translated being. In it he points out that,

Accounts of translated beings are found in all five books that compose the standard works. The existence of such beings and the doctrine they are founded upon can be an inspiring testimony to the mercy of our Heavenly Father in his plan to help us know him and return to his presence. Once we understand the reason for their miraculous condition and power, we begin to realize just how vital they are to the fulfillment of the plan of salvation and the everlasting covenant. . . . At least five principles taught in the scriptures and by the prophets of this last dispensation reveal to us the doctrine of translated beings. Translated beings exist by virtue of the Melchizedek Priesthood, have been given future missions, have power over death, have the convincing power of God, and can conceal their identity.[11]

The special mission that John was to fulfil until the Savior's return is made clear in the text the Lord revealed to Joseph Smith. John was to "minister for those who shall be heirs of salvation who dwell on the earth" (D&C 7:6). The Beloved Disciple was granted this privilege due to his desire to possess "power over death, that I may live and bring souls unto thee." The Savior acknowledged the sincerity of His friend's devotion by allowing John to "tarry until I come in my glory," with the charge to "prophesy before nations, kindreds, tongues and people" (D&C 7:3).

The revelation given to the Prophet Joseph regarding John's translation is corroborated by the additional witness of the Book of Mormon. To three of the Nephite Twelve, the resurrected Lord declared:

Behold, I know your thoughts, and ye have desired the thing which John, my beloved, who was with me in my ministry, before that I was lifted up by the Jews, desired of me. Therefore, more blessed are ye for ye shall never taste of death; but ye shall live to behold all . . . until all things shall be fulfilled according to the will of the Father, when I shall come in my glory with the powers of heaven (3 Ne. 28:6–7).

The promise of translation provides for an ultimate passage from this life that "shall never endure the pains of death"; but entails the promise of being "changed in the twinkling of an eye from mortality to immortality" (3 Ne. 28:8). Similarly, the promise was given to the Three Nephites that "ye shall not have pain while ye shall dwell in the flesh, neither sorrow save it be for the sins of the world" (3 Ne. 28:9). The purpose of the special mission bestowed by the Savior upon His Nephite disciples was the same as that of John, to "bring the souls of men unto me, while the world shall stand" (3 Ne. 28:9). One commentator has noted that John was particularly well suited to such a mission.

As a trusted friend of Christ and as one of the special witnesses of the Savior, John occupies a singular position to testify to the world of both the reality and the divinity of the Son of God. The design and focus of John's testimony, as contained in the Bible, is to convince us that Jesus of Nazareth is indeed the Christ. Every story, event, and discourse recorded by John seems geared toward persuading us to believe in the Only Begotten and to come unto him for salvation.[12]

The particulars of John's postmortal ministry are not known to us at this time. No doubt countless numbers of individuals, both before and after the latter-day restoration of the gospel, have been brought to a greater testimony and understanding of his Master by the direct effort of the translated Beloved Disciple.

Who can calculate the influence and effect John the Beloved has had during the centuries of the Apostasy as well as throughout the history and development of the Restoration in these last days? Indeed, as a translated being, he has done a greater work among men than that he did during his mortal life in Jerusalem (see D&C 7:5). It is possible that many of our ancestors who belonged to the scattered tribes of Israel have been brought to the Savior through John's divinely conferred convincing power. Furthermore, we can only imagine the service he will render in our day and through the Millennium. Unfettered and unaffected by death or disease and aided by an increased ability to preach and persuade, John the Beloved will no doubt accomplish great things in building up the kingdom of God in this last dispensation. Though his identity may be concealed as he works among us, we can suppose that in a future day he will be known for what he is—a "flaming fire and a ministering angel" (D&C 7:6).[13]

While specific actions of John in respect to the above cannot be determined, one special aspect of the translated Apostle's ministry was revealed in these latter days. In response to a query concerning the meaning of Revelation 10, wherein it is said that John ate a little book, the Lord explained that this represented "a mission, and an ordinance, for him to gather the tribes of Israel" (D&C 77:14). In addition, the record of a June 1831 Church conference records that,

> The Spirit of the Lord fell upon Joseph in an unusual manner, and he proph-esied that John the Revelator was then among the Ten Tribes of Israel who had been led away by Shalmaneser, king of Assyria, to prepare them for their return from their long dispersion, to again possess the land of their fathers.[14]

Both pieces of information about John's activities with the lost ten tribes illuminate the scope of the Beloved Disciple's continuing mission. On the one hand it seems to entail working with individuals, or coming to their aid in time of need, to assist as well as to teach using the special gift of the convincing power of God. On the other hand, a highly organized aspect of John's calling appears to relate to the gathering of the full house of Israel.

It may happen that a record of the ten tribes, and John's work with them, will come forth at some future time. (See 2 Ne. 29:12–13.) An important aspect of John's service to the people of this earth has been to provide written testimony of the person and mission of the Savior. Indeed, as related above, John's role in revealing his Master's plan is so significant that, by name, John was prophesied of centuries before his own time (1 Ne. 14:19–27). The five books of John that appear in the

New Testament deliver an undying witness of the Christ. But some four hundred years after their publication and dissemination, the prophet Moroni wrote in his abridgment of Ether that at a future date "shall my revelations which I have caused to be written by my servant John be unfolded in the eyes of all the people" (Ether 4:16).

> Moroni was writing after the New Testament ministry of John had ended, but the promise the Lord gave through Moroni is similar to the promise spoken by the angel to Nephi more than a thousand years earlier, before the days of John. The angel revealed that the writings of John and others "are sealed to come forth in their purity . . . in the own due time of the Lord, unto the house of Israel" (1 Ne. 14:26). As great as our appreciation is of John's biblical writings, the Book of Mormon gives us an elevated vision of his work and writings, with an open invitation from the Lord to qualify ourselves to receive John's writings that have been sealed up.[15]

Whether such writings are limited to purer versions of John's biblical writings, or whether, as seems to be suggested, they provide an expanded version of John's apocalyptic vision, or whether they contain writings regarding the ten tribes, or simply other writings of John unknown to us, cannot be presumed. We can but wait for "the own due time of the Lord."

The discovery fifty years ago of the buried Coptic Christian library at Nag Hammadi produced the *Apocryphon of John,* attributed to the Apostle John. Because the text, at least in part, provides an account of a ritual portrayal of the Creation, Adam and Eve in the garden, and other information designed to endow the celebrant with special blessings from heaven, some have become enthusiastic about the work as an ancient temple ritual text. Although it may have begun in a purer form as such a composition, perhaps even written by John, as it claims, the text as we have it has been altered and had much appended to it by way of later writing, Gnostic and Hermetic, which is not related at all to the teachings of the gospel as John knew them.[16] Great care must be exercised in the use of such a text. Possibly an accurate original *Apocryphon of John,* if it is a legitimate writing of the Elder Apostle, will also come forth one day along with John's other writings preserved by the Lord.

Perhaps other as yet unsupported writings of the Beloved Disciple will also appear at that time, the work of either his mortal or translated ministries. Indeed, the existence of such writings may be suggested in Doctrine and Covenants 93:18, where the Lord makes the promise that "it shall come to pass, that if you are faithful you shall receive the fulness of the record of John." When those writings are received, they will doubtless declare with the boldness of the Son of Thunder the divinity of the Son of God, and with the sincerest concern of the Beloved Disciple reveal the loving nature of his own Master, the example the Father has provided for all His children. In a modern-day scripture, the Lord Himself quotes a witness about Him written by this friend, who labors still in His service spanning dispensations of time.

> And he bore record, saying: I saw his glory, that he was in the beginning, before the world was; Therefore, in the beginning the Word was, for he was the Word, even the messenger of salvation—The light and the Redeemer of the world; the Spirit of truth, who came into the world, because the world was made by him, and in him was the life of men and the light of men. The worlds were made by him; men were made by him; all things were made by him, and through him, and of him. And I, John, bear record that I beheld his glory, as the glory of the Only Begotten of the Father, full of grace and truth, even the Spirit of truth, which came and dwelt in the flesh, and dwelt among us. And I, John, saw that he received not of the fulness at the first, but received grace for grace; And he received not of the fulness at first, but continued from grace to grace, until he received a fulness; And thus he was called the Son of God, because he received not of the fulness at the first. And I, John, bear record, and lo, the heavens were opened, and the Holy Ghost descended upon him in the form of a dove, and sat upon him, and there came a voice out of heaven saying: This is my beloved Son. And I, John, bear record that he received a fulness of the glory of the Father; And he received all power, both in heaven and on earth, and the glory of the Father was with him, for he dwelt in him (D&C 93:7–17).

Endnotes

1. Nibley, *When the Lights Went Out,* 1.
2. For a lengthy discussion of the whole matter, see Nibley, *When the Lights Went Out,* 1–32. For his Latin paraphrase of Origen, see particularly p. 5, and n. 22.
3. Ibid., 14.
4. B. H. Roberts, *The Outlines of Ecclesiastical History* (repr. 1979), 151.

5. Hennecke and Schneemelcher, *New Testament Apocrypha,* 1:235.

6. Ibid.

7. Culpepper, *John,* 148 and note 38.

8. Ibid., 149 and note 41.

9. Ibid., 255–60.

10. Weidmann, *Polycarp and John,* 73–74.

11. David B. Marsh, "Give unto Me Power over Death," *The Testimony of John the Beloved,* (1998), 141–42.

12. Ibid., 146.

13. Ibid., 153.

14. Joseph Smith, *History of the Church,* 1: 176.

15. Jonn D. Claybaugh, "What Latter-day Scriptures Teach about John the Beloved," *The Testimony of John the Beloved,* 23–24.

16. Hennecke and Schneemelcher, *New Testament Apocrypha,* 1:314-38.

SECTION FOUR

James

CHAPTER ONE

Brother of the Lord

The New Testament occasionally mentions James, the brother of the Lord, who became one of the stalwarts of the early Christian movement. After the resurrected Lord appeared to him, James labored for the remainder of his life to teach and care for the members of the Church. He maintained special ties to the Christian community that remained in Jerusalem, of which he had been appointed the first bishop. James, this third pillar of Christianity, concerned himself with the day-to-day practice of religion, and emphasized such focus in his general Epistle to the Church. He himself lived a life of such purity and faithfulness that, even among Jewish enemies of the followers of Jesus, the brother of the Lord was revered as James the Just.

The Family of James

In connection with the activities of Jesus' ministry in the vicinity of Nazareth, Mark's synoptic account (Mark 6:3) briefly mentions Jesus' mother and his siblings, James, Joses, Judas, Simon, and sisters. Matthew's chronicle (Matt. 13:55) similarly names Jesus' four brothers as James, Joseph, Simon, and Judas. The names are the same except that a transliteration of the Hebrew is given as Joseph, rather than the more Greek Joses. Of course, James is but an English variation of the Hebrew Jacob, given throughout the New Testament in its transliterated Greek form *Iakobos*. Matthew's order reverses the last brothers on the list, leading some scholars to suppose that the lists are given in order of seniority, or age, and that Matthew appears to be correcting Mark on the order of the youngest two brothers. Since James is mentioned first in both accounts, scholars hold that they may be fairly sure James was the eldest of the four. Of the sisters mentioned in Mark, the New Testament itself supplies neither number nor name, though one early Christian writer, Epiphanius, reports Jesus' sisters to have been named for their mother and her sister, Mary and Salome.[1]

Other references in the New Testament refer simply to "Jesus' brothers" or make use of the expression "his mother and his brethren" (Matt. 12:46; Mark 3:31; Luke 8:19; John 2:12; 7:3–10; Acts 1:14). Paul makes mention of the Lord's brothers, noting that they and the Apostles took their wives with them as they traveled preaching the gospel (1 Cor. 9:5). The latter reference implies that, like the Apostles, the brothers of the Lord were dedicated to proclaiming the gospel. Indeed, one critic asserts that "the preservation of all four names of the brothers of Jesus in Matthew and Mark indicates that all four brothers were well-known figures in the early church."[2]

That the early Christian community knew and clearly accepted James, Joses, Jude, and Simon as brothers of Christ, referring to them, almost as if by title, as "brothers of the Lord," should have prevented the controversy that later arose on purely theological grounds: whether the four brethren were actually brothers, step-brothers, or cousins of Jesus. Before examining such contentions, it may be beneficial to note that the term invariably used in the New Testament to designate their relationship to Christ is the Greek *adelphos,* signifying "brother."[3] Greek has other words that mean step-brother and cousin, which could have been used, but were not.

Views on the relationship of Jesus and His brothers, from the fourth century to the modern era, take form depending on one's opinion of the question of Mary's perpetual virginity, a doctrine emerging in the fourth century and still adhered to by Catholic and Orthodox churches. Indeed, in Catholicism a similar doctrine still later arose in connection with celibacy which portrayed Joseph as also perpetually virginal.[4] Bauckham provides an excellent summary of the historical reinterpretations that derived from such theologies.

> The relationship to Jesus of the four men known in the early church as the "brothers of the Lord" has been extensively discussed mainly because of its bearing on the traditional doctrine of the perpetual virginity of Mary. In the Greek patristic and eastern Orthodox tradition this doctrine has been accompanied by the view that the "brothers of the Lord" were the sons of

Joseph by a marriage prior to his marriage to Mary. Since Jerome the Latin western and Roman Catholic tradition has preferred that they were not brothers in any modern sense, but first cousins of Jesus. Only in modern Protestant scholarship, with no commitment to and often deeply suspicious of the idea of the perpetual virginity of Mary, has the view become at all common that the "brothers of the Lord" were the sons of Joseph and Mary, though probably the majority of exegetes, including a few Roman Catholic scholars, now take this view. The three views have come to be known by the names of fourth-century proponents of each, as the Helvidian view (son of Joseph and Mary), the Epiphanian view (sons of Joseph by his first marriage), and the Hieronymian view (cousins).[5]

Catholic scholarship has offered various scenarios under which the form "brothers of the Lord" could have been cousins by hypothesizing that Clopas, whose wife Mary is mentioned in the New Testament, could have been a brother of Joseph and that Joseph may also have had a sister Mary whose husband may have been Alphaeus and whose son, the Apostle known as James the Less, could have been the James we know as "brother of the Lord."[6] It is important to realize that for such supposition no evidence exists at all. Efforts to explain away the words of the New Testament presume that New Testament writers either did not understand the relationship or were insufficiently versed in Greek language to know the Greek words for step-brother or cousin, and simply employed *adelphos* instead. However, no comment is or can be made to dismiss two important facts. First, throughout the Gospel accounts, Mary herself is often mentioned as in company with the brothers of the Lord, an expected situation if she is their mother, but unlikely if she were not. Second, there exists a strong tradition both in the New Testament and in other early Christian writings, for calling these four men collectively or individually, brothers of the Lord. Moreover, two passages from the New Testament indicate that Mary did eventually come to know Joseph as her husband (Matt. 1:18–25), and that by referring to Jesus as Mary's "first" born son, she did have other children (Luke 2:7). These things cannot be explained away in order for the exigencies of later formulated theology to fit. In commenting on these passages of scripture, one critic writes,

Paul, Mark, and John give the reader no reason to think that those called brothers and sisters of Jesus were anything but full brothers and sisters. There is no suggestion anywhere in the New Testament that there were children born to Joseph by an earlier marriage. . . . The reader naturally assumes that they were children born to Mary and Joseph subsequent to the birth of Jesus.[7]

The restored gospel has ever recognized the virgin birth of the Lord Jesus Christ and accepted the truthfulness of both Old Testament and Book of Mormon prophecy concerning that circumstance of Mary's conception of the Savior (Isa. 7:14; 9:6; 1 Ne. 11:18; 2 Ne. 17:14; 19:6; Alma 7:10). The issue of Mary's bearing other children has not been a topic of modern revelation, nor remarked upon by the Prophet Joseph Smith. In *Jesus the Christ,* Elder James Talmage quoted Matthew 1:24–25, indicating that Joseph "knew her not till she had brought forth her first born son."[8] Perhaps the fullest discussion of the matter by any Church leader of this dispensation appears in a chapter entitled "Mariology and Mariolatry" in *On the Way to Immortality and Eternal Life,* by President J. Reuben Clark, Jr., Apostle and counselor in the First Presidency for more than thirty years. President Clark considered the teaching of Mary's perpetual virginity to be the basis of the Roman Catholic veneration of the Virgin Mother of God. To explain his own view, President Clark provided an English translation of the eminent scholar Otto Zoeckler's *Kritische Geschichte der Askese.*[9] President Clark prefaced his reproduction of Zoeckler's comments as follows:

> Since the idea of the perpetual virginity of Mary is perhaps basic to the whole dogma and cult involved in Mariolatry, we may make one quotation dealing with this matter from the opposite point of view, which, on the scriptural texts, seems to us the true view. Dr. Zoeckler treats the subject as follows:[10]

President Clark is very clear in stating that Zoeckler's quoted commentary "seems to us the true view." He then includes a long quotation of Zoeckler's statement in his own text:

> The question of her maternal relationship to Jesus on the one hand and to the "brethren of the Lord" on the other is a less difficult one. The designation

of Jesus as her "first-born son" (Luke ii.7) and the statement as to her relations with Joseph (Matt i.25, cf. i.13) seems to point to the conclusion that
the persons called in the Gospels and in Acts i.14 the brethren of the Lord
were the younger sons of Joseph and Mary. For various reasons the theory of
Jerome that they were cousins, and that of Epiphanius that they were children of Joseph by a former marriage are untenable. The unprejudiced reader
of the New Testament can not avoid the view represented in antiquity by
Helvidius and stamped as heresy after Jerome and Ambrose, that they were
the children of Joseph and Mary, while Jesus was the son of Mary in a miraculous manner by the Holy Ghost. The latter assertion rests upon distinct
passages of scripture (Matt i.18–25; Luke i.26–38, ii.7–14).[11]

Jesus' Relatives and the Church

Separate scriptural reference to James in his later guise as one of the
leaders of the Church is, of course, also found in the New Testament.
Paul makes James's standing very clear when he places him with Peter
and John in naming them the pillars of early Christianity (Gal. 2:9).

Similarly, the other relatives of Jesus were much involved in
supporting the work of the Church. This is especially true in the case
of Christ's four brothers.

> The "brethren of the Lord" are recognized as an influential group in the
> primitive church. Paul and Luke alike mention them alongside the
> Apostles. According to Luke, they were closely associated with the
> Apostles and other followers of Jesus in the days immediately following his
> resurrection (Acts 1:14); according to Paul, one of them, James, had actu-
> ally seen the risen Christ (1 Cor. 15:7).[12]

The question has arisen, however, whether the family of Jesus
were always believers in their Elder Brother's divine person and
mission. A not altogether justifiable assumption has prevailed among
scholars that "James and the brothers and sisters of Jesus were not
believers during the ministry of Jesus," and that "James became a
believer through a resurrection appearance of Jesus to him."[13]

The assumption that the brothers did not become true believers until
after Christ's Resurrection derives from the Gospel written by John,
whose status as a cousin of Jesus perhaps lends greater weight to his

knowledge of the inner workings and dynamics of Jesus' family. John provides information that Jesus' brothers, along with their sisters and their mother, Mary, journeyed with Jesus and his disciples. They were with the Lord at Capernaum and Cana (John 2:12), and also during later stages of Christ's Galilean ministry (John 7:1–13). That they were a part of Jesus' retinue seems fairly certain and, therefore, they should most likely be included among His followers. John records that the brothers urged Jesus to go up to the Feast of Tabernacles at Jerusalem so that all the Jews might witness the Savior's miraculous deeds and acts. They counseled their Brother to "Depart hence, and go into Judæa, that thy disciples also may see the works that thou doest. For there is no man that doeth any thing in secret, and he himself seeketh to be known openly. If thou do these things, shew thyself to the world" (John 7:3–4). At this point in his narrative, John offers the assessment that "neither did his brethren believe in him" (John 7:5). As the text proceeds, Jesus explains that He will not go up to Jerusalem "for my time is not yet full come" (John 7:8).

The incident is intriguing. Certainly it shows that Jesus' brothers are an integral component of His followers. It also demonstrates that they support Him and are concerned that He make the decisions that will bring His disciples to Him. But what about John's declaration that they did not believe in Him? Could the Beloved Disciple, who, with his brother James and with Peter, had alone been privy to certain events and special actions of Jesus and thereby possessed greater knowledge and understanding of the Lord's person and the true purpose of His mission, have intended to communicate that the brothers of Jesus did not yet believe in their brother as Son of God and Savior? Were they, as were many of Jesus' followers, confused about His actual purpose, instead viewing Him as a Messiah who, as heir to the throne of David, was expected to use miraculous powers to restore the Davidic kingdom? Did the brothers understand what Jesus meant when He explained His time had not yet come? Perhaps not; and, if not, Jesus' brothers could not yet have believed in the Christ in the way that Peter, James, and John believed in Him.

It seems unlikely that John's intent is to indict the brothers of Jesus, but rather to explain that they were not yet partakers of the greater knowledge of the true mission their brother had been ordained to perform. That the brothers were loyal to Jesus seems clear. That they supported His work, at least as they understood it, should not be questioned. They, and indeed most of the Apostles, did not yet fully grasp the eternal significance of the Master's purposes.

There seems to be no evidence that at any time the brothers of Jesus were not included among Christ's followers. James's contributions to the work of his brother would be of the same magnitude as those of the other pillars of the Church. The other brothers contributed as well, though, except perhaps for Jude, little is known of their individual efforts. Of the second son, Joseph, or, in Greek, Joses, nothing is known at all. Of Simon or Symeon, Eusebius reports that he succeeded his brother James as bishop of Jerusalem. Symeon's name occurs second on a preserved list of Jerusalem's bishops. The time of this transition is not known. Clearly Eusebius presumes it to be at the time of James's execution by the high priest and Sanhedrin, but if James had ceased to function as Jerusalem's bishop to become an Apostle, it may have occurred decades before Jerusalem's fall.[14]

Ancient lore identifies the Lord's brother, Jude, with the Apostle Thomas, known in the tradition of Syrian Christianity as Judas Thomas. "Some recent scholars have appeared to favour the historicity of this tradition," but it is important to maintain the perspective that "only in works from this particular geographic area of the early church is the name Judas given to the Apostle Thomas."[15] Yet, that is the very region where Thomas labored. Thomas is the Aramaic word for twin, which in Greek is rendered by the name Didymus. Reference to Judas Thomas or Jude Didymus seems to signify the Apostle who was thought to resemble his brother Jesus so greatly that he almost seemed His twin. One critic cautions against wholesale acceptance of the Syrian tradition asserting,

> What has not been sufficiently noticed is that in several of the sources which attest the name Judas Thomas there is no hint of his identification with the Lord's brother. In particular, Ephraem distinguishes Judas Thomas from both the Apostle Judas of James and Jude the Lord's brother, but regards the last two as the same person. The explicit identification of Judas Thomas as Jesus' twin brother is confined to the *Acts of Thomas* and the *Book of Thomas,* though it may well be presupposed in the *Gospel of Thomas.*[16]

The three works alluded to appear to have been compositions of great importance for eastern Christians. If actually based on writings by the Lord's brother, they may be considered major contributions. *The Acts of Thomas* survives in a tenth-century Syriac text which may derive from a Greek original of probably fifth-century date. The text is a narrative of traditions regarding Thomas's missionary activities on the way to India and back.[17] More reliable in terms of authorship and of very early date is the *Gospel of Thomas,* a collection of the sayings of Jesus, preserved in several fragmentary Greek manuscripts, but in full in a Coptic Nag Hammadi manuscript.[18] Also of special interest is the *Book of Thomas* or the *Book of Thomas the Contender,* surviving as one of the Nag Hammadi Coptic manuscripts. The work claims to be a revelation from Jesus to His brother Judas Thomas, recorded by the Apostle Mathaias.[19]

Whether Jude was or was not the same person as the Apostle Thomas, it is clear that he spent his life in the service of the Lord. The Epistle that bears his name reveals Jude's faith and loving concern for the Church members who remained steadfast in the adverse circumstances of the late first century. If the three works of Judas Thomas remain spurious, the canonical Epistle of Jude can be said with confidence to have been composed by Jude, the brother of the Lord. The text of Jude's letter identifies its author as "brother of James" (Jude 1:1). Of late first century composition, with topics of coming apostasy and the hope of vindication at the Second Coming for those who endure, the Epistle corresponds in theme and period with the Epistles of John. It also serves to provide evidence for Jude, Christ's youngest brother, having lived into the late first century.

Not just the four brothers of Christ, but the extended family of the Savior, were not only held in honor by early Christians and seem to have continued in their dedication to the Christian movement. A special Greek epithet was applied to the relatives of Jesus—*deposynoi,* "those who belong to the Master." As late as the mid-third century Julius Africanus, in his *Letter to Aristides,* wrote of the *deposynoi,* "From the Jewish village of Nazareth and Kokhaba they traveled around the rest of the land and interpreted the genealogy they had from family tradition and from the Book of Days as far as they could trace it."[20]

Modern commentators suggest that the emphasis on genealogy not only relates to the family's connection to the Lord, but also to their claims to be Davidic heirs and the legitimate rulers of the Jews.[21] Indeed, the third century writer Hegessipus links the succession of Symeon as bishop of Jerusalem and his legendary pursuit after the fall of Jerusalem to Vespasian's order to search out members of the royal family of David.[22] Moreover, Eusebius preserves an intriguing account that as late as the reign of Domitian, members of the family were sought by the authorities, whether as relatives of Christ, descendants of David, or both.

> The same Domitian ordered the execution of all who were of the family of David, and there is an old and firm tradition that a group of heretics accused descendants of Jude, the brother, according to the flesh, of the Savior—alleging that they were of the family of David and related to Christ himself. Hegesippus relates this as follows. "Now there still survived of the family of the Lord the grandsons of Jude—who was said to his brother according to the flesh—and they were informed against as being of the family of David. These the summoner brought before Domitian Caesar. For he was afraid of the coming of Christ as Herod had been also."[23]

After learning that they owned a small plot of land that they worked themselves, as Domitian ascertained by examining their hands, the emperor

> Did not condemn them but looked down upon them as simple folk, released them, and decreed an end to persecution. When they were released they were the leaders of churches both because of their testimony and because they were of the family of the Lord and remained alive in the peace which lasted until Trajan. This we learn from Hegesippus.[24]

The passage is important for two reasons. First, it demonstrates the continued importance of Jesus' relatives in the first-century Church. Secondly, it provides indication that as late as the third or fourth centuries there were still Christians who believed the brothers of the Lord to be brothers of the Lord and had not yet come to adhere to Jerome's belief that they were but cousins of some sort.

As one of the Lord's actual brothers, James was not only devoted to Jesus during His earthly sojourn, but after His departure James seems to have provided leadership both to his brothers and the Church. James, the brother of the Lord, gave service to the entire Church through offering counsel and doctrinal teaching in the epistle that bears his name. James also offered lifetime devotion to the welfare of Jerusalem's Church members, in a manner befitting the brother of the Lord.

Endnotes

1. Richard Bauckham, *Jude and the Relatives of Jesus in the Early Church* (1990), 7 and 37.

2. Ibid., 7.

3. Kittel, *Dictionary,* 144–45.

4. Ibid.

5. Bauckham, *Jude and the Relatives of Jesus,* 19.

6. Ibid., 20–23.

7. John Painter, *Just James: The Brother of Jesus in History and Tradition* (1999), 12, 35.

8. James Talmage, *Jesus the Christ,* 85.

9. The translation of Zoeckler's text appears in *The New Schaff-Herzog Encyclopedia of Religious Knowledge,* s.v. "Mary," 223. See J. Reuben Clark, Jr., *On the Way to Immortality and Eternal Life* (1949), 330.

10. J. Reuben Clark, Jr., *Immortality and Eternal Life,* 29.

11. Ibid., 30 and note 49.

12. Bruce, *Peter, Stephen, James, & John,* 86.

13. John Painter, *Just James,* 13.

14. Eusebius, *Ecclesiastical History,* 4.22.4. Also see Painter, *Just James,* 147–48.

15. Bauckham, *Jude and the Relatives of Jesus,* 32.

16. Ibid., 33.

17. H.W. Attridge, "Acts of Thomas," *Anchor Bible Dictionary,* 6:531–34.

18. Ron Cameron, "Gospel of Thomas," in *Anchor Bible Dictionary,* 6:535–40.

19. John D. Turner, "Book of Thomas the Contender," *Anchor Bible Dictionary,* 6:529–30.

20. Eusebius, *Ecclesiastical History,* 1.7.14.

21. Painter, *Just James,* 144–56; Bauckham, *Jude and the Relations of Jesus,* 60–70.

22. Bauckham, *Jude and the Relation of Jesus*, 79–106.
23. Eusebius, *Ecclesiastical History*, 3.19–3.20.
24. Ibid., 3.20.

CHAPTER TWO

James of Jerusalem

James is perhaps more closely associated with Jerusalem than any of the other early Christian leaders. His connection to the city endured for nearly forty years after the death of his brother, Jesus, at the hands of the rulers of Judea's capitol. From Jerusalem, James exerted great influence over early Christians, particularly those who lived in Judea and nearby areas. As the first bishop at Jerusalem and later as an Apostle who lived the duration of his life at Jerusalem, one of James's most important concerns was the welfare of the local members of the Church. The Jerusalem Church seems to have faced continuing problems of indigence as well as periodic persecution from the leaders of the Jews. It fell to James to provide for the safety and care of Church members in these adverse circumstances.

James's Position in the Church

After the Ascension of the Savior, the remaining eleven Apostles retired to an upper room to pray. "These all continued with one accord in prayer and supplication, with the women, and Mary the mother of Jesus, and with his brethren" (Acts 1:14). According to Acts, the brothers of Jesus seemed to occupy an important place in the nascent Church, a place perhaps second only to the Twelve who functioned under the direction and leadership of Peter, John, and James, son of Zebedee. Most scholars find this passage astounding, since they assume that the brothers of the Lord had not been among the followers of Jesus before this time. In this instance even F. F. Bruce joins this common opinion of modern scholarship in raising the question, "how then did it come about that his relatives who do not figure at all among his followers before his death, should so soon afterward be found taking a leading place among them?"[1] In Paul's statement that James, the brother of the Lord, had been accorded the special privilege of a post-resurrection appearance of the Savior (1 Cor. 15:7), Bruce finds the answer to his own question. "Paul's statement that in resurrection Jesus 'appeared to James' provides an answer to our question. This experience produced in James a revolutionary effect comparable to that which a similar experience later produced in Paul himself."[2] Most scholars offer much the same explanation to account for the prominent role that James came to exercise. Critics variously posit that James refused to follow Jesus because of sibling rivalry, or natural rebelliousness, or lack of interest. Most agree that in the account of James's visionary experience with the resurrected Christ is to be found the conversion that produced a stalwart Church leader.[3]

All such theories are, of course, based on little more than empty speculation. As noted in the previous chapter, the account of the Gospels can readily be construed as indicating that the brothers of the Lord were in fact included among Jesus' followers from the earliest days of the Savior's ministry. Indeed, in respect to their long-term association with the followers of Christ and their role in Acts 1:14, one commentator notes that,

> After the ascension of Jesus Luke portrays the return of the disciples from the Mount of Olives to an upper room in Jerusalem where they are depicted gathered for prayer with women, indirectly Mary the mother of Jesus, and his brothers. Luke portrays the mother and brothers of Jesus as "believers" and faithful followers of Jesus, and there is no indication of any recent radical "conversion" subsequent to his death, through, for example, some resurrection appearance.[4]

Clearly James did see the resurrected Lord as Paul informs us. If James were already a faithful follower of Jesus, it would not have constituted a conversion experience, but would certainly have served to strengthen his testimony to the point that he would be prepared to exercise high callings of priesthood leadership within the Church. Very intriguing, however, is a passage from the *Gospel of the Hebrews*, an apocryphal work popular in the second century throughout Judea and other eastern reaches of the Christian movement. It offers an account of the appearance of Christ to His brother James.

> And when the Lord had given the linen cloth to the servant of the priest, he went to James and appeared to him. For James had sworn that he would not eat bread from the hour in which he had drunk the cup of the Lord until he should see him risen from among them that sleep. And shortly thereafter the Lord said: Bring a table and bread! And immediately it is added: He took the bread, blessed it, broke it, and gave it to James the Just and said to him: My brother, eat thy bread, for the son of Man is risen from among them that sleep.[5]

If any truth is to be found in the quotation from the apocryphal account, it would appear that James fasted from the "hour in which he had drunk the cup of the Lord" until the Savior had risen from the dead. Whether James began his fast at the death of his brother when Jesus drank the bitter cup, or after a sacramental rite, reminiscent of the Last Supper, when James drank of a cup given to him by Jesus, is unclear in the above account. What is clear, however, is that James was indisputably already a faithful believer to have fasted through the time of the Savior's Crucifixion until after His resurrection. The appearance of the risen Lord to His brother seems, then, not to have transpired for purposes of conversion, but to reward James's deep faith and loyalty.

It is by no means surprising that James, the brother of the Lord, was called to the position of bishop when Church organization took form at Jerusalem. Indeed, James was not only the first bishop at Jerusalem, but seemingly the first bishop in the entire Church. In the jargon of his own fourth century, Eusebius speaks about James being "elected" bishop at Jerusalem. "Then there was James, who was called the Lord's brother, for he too was named Joseph's son. . . . This James whom the people of old called the Just because of his outstanding virtue was the first, as the record tells us, to be elected to the episcopal throne of the Jerusalem church."[6] Despite Eusebius's use of anachronistic terminology, earlier sources provide surer information about James's calling. Clement of Alexandria unambiguously attributes James's assignment as bishop at

Jerusalem to appointment by the presiding Apostles, Peter, James, and John.[7] Apocryphal sources contemporary with Clement declare that James was appointed bishop by the risen Lord.[8] If the apocryphal sources present accurate information, it does not conflict with the notion of Peter, James, and John's role in the appointment of the Lord's brother, for the three Apostles would have issued a call based on the Lord's instruction to them. Men are called of God through priesthood lines of authority, in ancient times just as in the era of the Restoration.

Hugh Nibley offers an intriguing supposition that James may not have been bishop of Jerusalem, but rather have held the office of Presiding Bishop in the ancient Church. Nibley acknowledges that the office is mentioned neither in the New Testament nor in other early Christian sources, but concludes that James's high standing among the Brethren and his composition of a general epistle to the Church membership, which treats several themes that may be expected to belong to the concerns of a Presiding Bishop, all serve to suggest that James's activities were more representative of a General Church Authority than a local bishop, even a bishop of Jerusalem.[9]

Paul attributed to James General Authority status as an Apostle. He reported that on the occasion of a visit to Jerusalem when he abode with Peter for fifteen days, "other of the Apostles saw I none, save James the Lord's brother" (Gal. 1:19). Many scholars refuse to accept Paul's recognition of James as an Apostle at its word. Rather, they believe that Paul used the term in reference not only to James, but also to himself, merely to indicate one who is "sent forth" in the Lord's service, the literal meaning of the Greek *apostolos*.[10] Protestant scholars, in particular, view Paul's apostolate as self-proclaimed, the consequence of his receiving in his heart a call to serve, much in the way that today's ministers speak of being called to serve. Nevertheless, Paul seems to refer to the Apostles as a specifically constituted and special group, rather than the composite of all who went forth as missionaries to proclaim the gospel. Indeed, Paul's use of the phrase "others of the Apostles" (Gal. 1:19) suggests as much. To address the question, Richard Anderson brings to bear the evidence not just of Paul's writings, but also of Luke, who without doubt used the term Apostle in its most restrictive sense in both his Gospel and in Acts, and who referred to Paul by the very same title.

On the mission immediately following the Jerusalem return, Paul and Barnabas are twice called "Apostles" (Acts 14:4,14). The term occasionally preserves its general sense of "one sent" in nonformal New Testament references, so some have thought that Paul and Barnabas were only messengers and not members of the Twelve. But Luke uses *Apostle* thirty-four other times in his Gospel and Acts, and every time this word designates the Twelve or its members. Indeed, his first mention seems to define what he means, since out of all Christ's "disciples," only twelve were called, and these were named "Apostles" (Luke 6:13). And Paul certainly puts his office on a parity with the Twelve, speaking of those who were "Apostles before me" (Gal 1:17) and humbly calling himself "least of the Apostles" after mentioning the Twelve (1Cor 15:9). His confident authority as "an Apostle of Jesus Christ" in the openings of ten of fourteen letters matches the similar assertion of Peter beginning both of his personal letters.[11]

Clearly, Paul is considered one of the Twelve Apostles by Luke as well as those leaders of the Twelve who gave to Paul "the right hands of fellowship" (Gal. 2:9). Accordingly, if Paul, an Apostle, identified James as an Apostle, no doubt he meant it as a title of Church authority, that is, as one of the Quorum of the Twelve. Just as Matthias replaced Judas among the Twelve, as other Apostles, such as James, son of Zebedee, passed from this world, it appears that (at least up until the A.D. 49 Jerusalem Council), vacancies in the Quorum were filled. James, the brother of the Lord, whether he served as bishop of Jerusalem or Presiding Bishop of the Church, obviously came to receive a calling to join the Twelve, as did Paul and Barnabas.

James in Acts

James is introduced when Peter, released by angelic intervention from imprisonment at the hands of Herod Agrippa, who had "killed James the brother of John with the sword" (Acts 12:2), instructed Church members gathered at the house of Mary, mother of John Mark, to take the information of his miraculous release and his departure from the city "unto James, and to the brethren" (Acts 12:17). This James is certainly the brother of the Lord, since James, son of Zebedee, had already been executed by Herod Agrippa. The brethren referred to may have been the brothers of the Lord or, in a generic sense, simply

Church brethren. Whether James had as yet attained the apostolate is unknown, though he was certainly an Apostle a few years later at the time of Paul's first visit to Jerusalem. Indeed, James, the brother of the Lord, may quite possibly have replaced James, son of Zebedee, in the Quorum of the Twelve. If this were so, and if enough time elapsed between that James's beheading and the imprisonment of Peter, it is not impossible that James was already ordained an Apostle.

When Peter sent word to James of his escape and his planned departure from Jerusalem, it could have been because James was the senior officer of the Church remaining in Jerusalem. Other Apostles may have already fled or have been conducting their labors of teaching and testifying elsewhere. None of this can be known as more than speculation, however, since the chronicle of Acts and other sources do not treat these matters.

By contrast, a very different interpretation is connected to this event by a number of scholars who hold that James, by virtue of his episcopal authority, had already superseded Peter as leader of Jerusalem's Christians, and that Peter's reporting of his release and imminent departure from the city is to his superior in the Church. Still others see in Peter's departure the occasion for the reduction of Peter's influence with the Jerusalem Church and the increase of James's. Both groups assert that by the time of the Jerusalem Council James was the leader of Christianity at Jerusalem and, by extension, of all Christians.[12]

The Jerusalem Council is treated in detail in the first chapter of the present work. It is important because it is the only documented occasion where all four great pillars of the Christian movement interacted together. They were able to resolve the crisis that threatened the Church through the attempted imposition of Jewish law and practice upon early Christianity. It is the author's expressed belief that the specific evidence of Acts, and certainly the more general testimony of modern revelation, leaves no doubt whatsoever that Peter acted as presiding officer not only of the conference but of the whole Church, as he had been appointed by the Savior. James's role in the events of the meetings is crucial, and James was clearly one of the most important leaders in the Church, but his place was not above that of Peter. When James rose last to give his opinion on the matter, his purpose was twofold: to support the decision Peter had already pronounced, and to outline in detail the plan for implementing this new Church policy as it had been worked out in the presiding councils previous to the commencement of the conference. The Brethren collaborated and came to agreement in their support of Peter as presiding officer. Theirs was a unity of purpose and a unity of faith. In a similarly formulated opinion, Elder Bruce R. McConkie provides what we must take as the final word on the circumstances of the Council of Jerusalem and James's role in it:

> Commentators and others who are unaware of the true system of apostolic succession falsely assume that James was making a decision in the case and therefore was head of the Church in Jerusalem, having some pre-eminence over Peter. . . . The fact is that Peter was the presiding officer in the Church and had in fact rendered and announced judgement on the issue of circumcision. James is simply proposing the detailed instructions to put in force the decision already announced by Peter.[13]

For the presiding Brethren the matter was closed, sorted out, and finalized through inspiration. But some members of the Church, particularly some at Jerusalem who still adhered to Pharasaic dogma regarding circumcision and Mosaic law, refused to align their views with doctrine taught by Peter, John, Paul, and also by James.

> Gentile disciples had already been baptized and taught strictly to "continue in the faith" as a condition of salvation (Acts 14:22). But this did not satisfy Jewish Christians strictly observing the Law of Moses. Circumcision symbolized this issue, but Judaizers were talking about hundreds of obligations beyond circumcision. The orthodox Jews count 613 commandments in the five books of Moses, and the rabbinical rules of the Mishnah multiply the commandments to thousands.[14]

Despite the decision of the presiding Brethren that Gentile converts should not have to undergo circumcision or practice the law of Moses, problems still arose as at Antioch from "certain [who] came from James" (Gal. 2:12), who demanded greater observance of Jewish practices. According to Elder McConkie, "the Jewish members of the Church, however, had not been able to accept this decision without reservation.

They themselves continued to conform to Mosaic performances, and they expected Gentile converts to do likewise."[15] Quite naturally, James became associated in popular belief with those brethren from Jerusalem, where James appears to have been the leading Church official upon the departure of Peter, John, and others after the Council of Jerusalem. James's support of a more stringent position is not necessarily the case, nor is it fair to assume that James revised his views in any way contrary to the support he gave the new policy formulated at the Jerusalem Council.

Nevertheless, modern scholarship links James to the most uncompromising component of Jewish followers of Jesus. One critic goes so far as to claim that "James was not a 'Jewish Christian,'" but "he was a Christian Jew."[16] Modern scholarly treatments of the subject generally adhere to Raymond Brown's schematic of early Christian doctrinal stances on this divisive question. Brown believes there were four distinct divisions of members of the Church. The first group demanded "full observance of the Mosaic law, including circumcision," insisting "that Gentiles had to become Jews to receive the messianic blessings brought by Jesus." The second group consisted of "Jewish Christians and their Gentile converts, who did not insist on circumcision but did require converted Gentiles to keep some Jewish observances." The third group were those "who did not insist on circumcision and did not require observance of the Jewish ('Kosher') food laws." Finally, remaining as a fourth group were those who "saw no abiding significance in Jewish cult" and practiced it in nowise whatever. Brown places both Peter and James in the second group with Peter leaning toward the third and James leaning toward the first. Paul is categorized in the third group.[17]

The transition from Judaism to Christianity was no doubt difficult for many who believed Jesus was the Messiah. When even a number of Pharisees associated themselves with the followers of Jesus or, as they were known at Jerusalem, the Nazarenes, they formed a group devoted to purification through observance of the law of Moses within the Christian community. That the opposition of such Judaizers, as Paul refers to them, occasioned great difficulty within the Church is clear from Paul's own writings. Moreover, these may be those to whom the Lord refers in Doctrine and Covenants 64:8, saying, "My disciples, in days of old, sought occasion against one another and forgave not one another in their hearts; and for this evil they were afflicted and sorely chastened."

To what degree James was connected to Church members from Jerusalem who, with or without authorization, used his name cannot be surmised. That James must have been scrupulous in his own observance of the law is suggested by a variety of ancient writers who recount the legends of James the Just.[18] Nevertheless, no tradition nor any scriptural reference is explicit or even implicit in the insinuation that James demanded such observance from any other Christian.

The task that confronted James at Jerusalem must have been overwhelming in its complexity and seemingly unending. James not only had to facilitate cooperation within the Church community of congregants of all manner of views concerning the observance of Judaic religious practice, but he also must have exercised tremendous effort to protect followers of Christ from Jewish authorities who looked upon them as heretical apostates from Jerusalem. Indeed, such coexistence with the majority Jewish community may have provided considerable impetus for Jewish Christians who looked upon Jesus as the Messiah of the Jews to continue observing Mosaic law, Jewish festivals, and other aspects of the rabbinical Judaism that had evolved from the faith of Abraham, Isaac, and Jacob.

Eusebius and Hegesippus recount much about James's reputation not only among the followers of Jesus, but even among the Jews and James's enemies and detractors, the leaders of the Jews.[19] All are portrayed as agreed that James was a man of great personal holiness. He is referred to as "the Just" or "the Righteous" and called by the Hebrew honorific, "Oblias." James's reputation for righteousness is based not only on his personal morality and high ethical behavior, but also on his daily temple ministrations and his exacting observance of the law, even Nazarite elements, though no evidence exists that James himself took Nazarite vows.[20] It is not impossible that James's own scrupulousness as pertaining to Mosaic law was undertaken, at least in part, to deprive the leaders of the Jews of reason to find any fault with himself as leader of the Christian community, and, by extension, with the Jewish Christians of Jerusalem and Judea. Whether for these reasons or purely on personal grounds, James's observance of Jewish law does not imply that he was opposed to the Gentile policy formulated at the Jerusalem Council, to which the Acts account portrays James as thoroughly committed. Nor should we surmise that James in any manner supported the efforts of the Judaizers, even if they may have used his name to afford their claims greater credence and authority. More significantly, James should not be characterized as being in disharmony with Peter, the presiding Apostle, or with Paul, the Apostle designated by Peter and recognized by James as directing the Gentile mission. Indeed, one modern commentator has endeavored to closely follow the testimony of the New Testament scriptures and on those grounds aptly describes James as appearing to remain

> Thoroughly Jewish after his conversion and apparently a faithful adherent of the Torah–but certainly neither an ally of the Judaizers nor a zealot of the ceremonial Torah. Nevertheless, by his breadth of vision James was able to sympathize with the problems of the Gentiles, does not insist on their circumcision, and appears in every way anxious to cooperate with Paul in his efforts to evangelize them.[21]

The once-accepted efforts of a group of German scholars to portray Paul and James at odds, one Apostle of the Gentiles, the other Apostle of the Jewish Christians, has today been largely rejected in favor of a view of cooperation and warm acceptance between the two. Indeed, Paul's comments about James are without attack or negative reference, and from the record of Acts, James seems a supporter of Paul.[22] Indeed, when Paul returned to Jerusalem to convey in person the collection he had gathered from the churches he visited, James cordially received Paul and appears to have made sure that the elders of the Jerusalem congregations agreed to accept Paul and the monies he brought (Acts 21). Indeed, after gladly receiving Paul, James glorified God to learn of Paul's great successes (Acts 21:17–20). In this connection and overall, one commentator characterizes James as having "excellent relations with Paul and the Gentiles."[23]

As an Apostle, as a brother of Jesus, James's first priority was to accomplish the work of the Church in the way that its head, the Lord Jesus Christ, directed. This objective was shared with Peter and with Paul. During the years Peter was at Antioch and Paul traveled throughout Asia, Greece, Italy, and other places, James remained at Jerusalem, seeing to the needs of the churches and their members throughout Judea. Each had a different assignment, but were of one purpose. Moreover, that one purpose must not be disregarded to emphasize instead conditions and circumstances originating in the respective locales and with the local followers of Jesus with whom the four pillars labored. This is particularly true in the case of James the Just of Jerusalem. Scholarly theorists and revisionist historians have done the Lord's brother a disservice by neglecting the most important role he filled, that of an Apostle of the Lord Jesus Christ. Paul not only mentions James as an Apostle, but implies the devotion with which James exercised that calling by placing the brother of the Lord in the company of Peter and John as one of the three greatest witnesses of the Savior and His work (Gal. 2:9).

Endnotes

1. F. F. Bruce, *Peter, Stephen, James & John*, 87.

2. Ibid.

3. Painter, *Just James*, 11–41 summarizes a variety of opinions on how the brothers of Jesus were not followers of Christ.

4. Painter, *Just James*, 42.

5. The account is preserved in a quotation found in Jerome, *Concerning Illustrious Men* 2. See Hennecke and Schneemelcher, *New Testament Apocrypha*, 1:165. Also see Painter, *Just James*, 182–85.

6. Eusebius, *Ecclesiastical History*, 2.1.2.

7. Ibid., 2.1.4–5.

8. The *Gospel of Thomas, Ascents of James*, and *Kerygmata Petrou*, accord in their presentation of this information. See Painter, *Just James*, 5 and note 7.

9. Hugh Nibley, *Apostles and Bishops in Early Christianity*, 21, a manuscript in process of publication under the above title, originally written in 1954. F.A.R.M.S. expects the book to be issued in 2003.

10. See Bruce, *Peter, Stephen, James & John*, 88–90, for this matter as relates to Paul and James.

11. Anderson, *Understanding Paul*, 35.

12. For various discussions of these views see, for example, Bruce *Peter, Stephen, James & John*, 28–34, 90–101; Painter, *Just James*, 42–52; James B. Adamson, *James the Man and His Message* (1989), 12–20; Walter Schmithals, *Paul and James* (1963), 38–64; F. F. Bruce, *Commentary on Galatians* (1982), 105–34.

13. Bruce R. McConkie, *Doctrinal New Testament Commentary*, 2:143.

14. Anderson, *Understanding Paul*, 51.

15. McConkie, *Doctrinal Commentary*, 2:464.

16. Adamson, *James,* 19.

17. Brown, *Antioch and Rome,* 2–8.

18. Painter, *Just James,* 115–18.

19. Hegesippus, quoted by Eusebius, *Ecclesiastical History,* 2.23, 3.11, 4.22.

20. Epiphanius, 29.3–4, indicates that James not only attended the temple but entered the holy of holies, the function not merely of a temple priest, but of the high priest. Eusebius, *Ecclesiastical History,* 2.23.6 also suggests as much. The question of whether James was at some time presented as a rival Christian high priest or more likely, rival high priest of the Pharisees has elicited scholarly debate. See S. G. F. Brandon, *The Fall of Jerusalem and the Christian Church* (1951), 51–53, 120–27. However, for the view that James was a Nazarite, see Adamson, *James,* 20.

21. Adamson, *James,* 21.

22. Schmithals, *Paul and James,* 13.

23. Adamson, *James,* 21.

CHAPTER THREE

James's Writing and the Message of Christian Life

The doctrinal thought of James, brother of the Lord, survives of a surety only in the Epistle that bears his name. Other books attributed to James range from those that may possibly be based on original writings of the Apostle to those that are clearly of later composition. The latter appropriate James as author in order to legitimize their claims. What James himself may have written seems centered on the practical aspects of assisting the righteous follower of the Way of the Lord through the travails of this earthly existence. James's teachings treat the importance of righteous works of one person to another in the community of Jesus' followers. It is the religion of practicality that one might well expect from a Presiding Bishop or an Apostle who had once labored diligently in the office of bishop. For James, "pure religion and undefiled before God and the Father is this, To visit the fatherless and widows in their affliction, and to keep himself unspotted from the world" (James 1:27).

Apocryphal Works Attributed to James

Four apocryphal works bear the name of James. Three are part of the Coptic Christian writings discovered at Nag Hammadi, and one, the *Protoevangelium of James,* is as its title indicates, an "early gospel" or infancy gospel, largely describing Mary's life, but providing some material that relates to the early years of Christ's life. James the brother of Christ is named as its author, but despite such a claim, James's authorship is clearly pseudonymous. The composition was originally written in Greek and can be dated no later than the early third century, since it is mentioned in the writings of both Origen and Clement of Alexandria. Because the apparent purpose of the text is the glorification of Mary, by historical context it should be dated as late as possible so that it falls within the era when Mary had begun to receive various kinds of veneration, probably very late in the second century. James himself, of course, had no real connection to this text.[1]

No doubt the same may be said for two of the Nag Hammadi documents that claim James as their composer. The *First Apocalypse of James* is presented as a revelation dialogue between James and his Brother, the risen Lord, in which Christ reveals the "way of redemption" to James. Present scholarly assessment is that some aspects of the setting of the text, chiefly the "choice of James himself as the bearer of the revelation and particularly reference to him as James the Just . . . suggest that it had its roots in Jewish Christianity . . . but there is little in the doctrine of the apocalypse that is reminiscent of Jewish Christianity."[2] Rather, as is typical of the Nag Hammadi corpus, Gnostic doctrines prevail. It is not impossible, however, that some version of an Apocalypse of James may have originated among Jewish Christians, and there been tampered with, being revised or added upon by the Coptic-speaking Christians of Egypt. Lending authenticity to the text is an intriguing passage that treats a preexistence and provides James with the formulaic ritual that will enable him to return to the "Pre-existent One."[3]

The *Second Apocalypse of James* has been characterized as only superficially Gnostic. On the whole it may be more representative of the kind of writing prevalent among what Jewish Christian communities remained throughout the Near East by the time of the second century. The original text was certainly in Greek and has been dated as early as the first half of the second century.[4] The place of James in this apocalyptic account reflects the important and preeminent role among Church leaders that James seems to have filled for the Christians of Judea and neighboring districts.

> The text draws extensively on Jewish-Christian traditions. James the Just, who held a position of special prominence in early Jewish-Christian circles is presented as the possessor of a special revelation from Jesus and assigned a role that rivals, and perhaps exceeds that of Peter in canonical tradition. James is the revealer who escorts the "illuminated" ones through the door of the heavenly kingdom and rewards them.[5]

The name *Apocryphon of James* is assigned by scholars to an untitled Nag Hammadi document which refers to itself as a secret book (apocryphon) revealed by Christ to His brother James. The text is composed in the form of a dialogue of the risen Lord with Peter and James. It "has no narrative structure; instead, it is composed largely of sayings: parables, prophecies, wisdom sayings, rules for the community, and creedal formulas."[6] This non-structural preservation of sayings is associated with the earliest period of Christian writing. Indeed, the *Apocryphon of James* often employs the phrase "remembering" in connection with its effort to preserve the *logia* (sayings) of Jesus. One commentator notes that,

> This scene portrays a situation in which the literary production of sayings of Jesus was still being vigorously pursued; it reflects a time in which written texts with scriptural authority were not yet normative. The reference to "remembering" provides the critical clue to the date and character of this activity, since this term was employed technically in the early Church to describe the process of creating, collecting and transmitting sayings of Jesus.[7]

For these reasons the text today called the *Apocryphon of James* seems to be of mid-first century composition, sufficiently early that it is not inconceivable for the work to have been legitimately associated with James. Moreover, it does not possess the strong Gnostic character and themes of other writings collected and translated into Coptic by the Christians of Egypt. Only its apocalyptic setting is at all reminiscent of that pervasive Gnostic genre.

Of the apocryphal works attributed to James, only the so-called *Apocryphon of James* possesses even the smallest possibility of any connection to James. These works do serve, however, to demonstrate the importance James held for centuries in the tradition of the Christianity practiced in Judea and its neighboring regions. That James's name is attached to texts of later composition provides evidence of the authority James possessed. Moreover, such appeals to James's name to legitimize a composition suggests the widespread dissemination, at least throughout this quarter of the Christian world, of the Epistle that authentically bears James's name.

The Authorship and Background of the Epistle of James

Martin Luther threatened to throw the Epistle of James out of the Bible and burn it up. Luther interpreted James as setting faith at odds with works, the subject of many long years of debate between Luther, for whom faith alone defined the foundation of his theology, and the great classical scholar, Erasmus, for whom works, ordinances, sacraments, and observance of commandments stood along with faith as legitimate modes of religious observance requisite for practicing Christians. Since the time of the Reformation, scholarly opinion has varied greatly on the question of James's authorship of this Epistle and not until recent decades has James begun to be seriously considered among critics as the author of the Epistle. However, such modern interpretation views the Epistle of James in the context of a Christianity divided between Jew and Gentile, with James at odds with Peter or Paul. The latter point of view goes back to Luther's erroneous portrayal of works versus faith, James versus Paul, in as polemical a stance as Luther versus Erasmus.[8]

One important commentator recently expressed his opinion that the Epistle of James was, indeed, the work of the Lord's brother and explains the evidentiary grounds for his position.

> We believe that the author of the Epistle is James the Lord's brother and that the Epistle is correspondingly important in its exposition of the Christian life and faith. This deduction rests on several considerations of thought, style, structure and other evidence. . . . Whether the Epistle of James is by James the Lord's brother or someone else can be decided only on the basis of a study of the Epistle itself—the final court of appeal.[9]

Historical context must be added to considerations of the text itself as evidence for authorship. Is the Epistle of James a work whose content accords with James's circumstances and concerns, based on information about James in other scriptures or other writings that mention the Lord's brother?

The first verse of the Epistle of James identifies the author and his audience, "James, a servant of God and of the Lord Jesus Christ, to the twelve tribes which are scattered abroad, greeting" (James 1:1). Perhaps because of the existence of other works that spuriously claimed James as their author, the Council of Nicea did not include the Epistle of James in its list of canonical scripture, and so did not recognize James as its author. Nevertheless, earlier ecclesiastical authorities, such as Irenaeus, Origen, and Eusebius, seem to recognize the Epistle and connect it to James, the brother of the Lord. Acceptance of the work as James's did not falter in the African and Near Eastern provinces of the empire; and because of the influence of Origen and especially Athanasius, who greatly advocated the work, the Epistle of James was accepted in Asia Minor and finally at Rome by Jerome, who included it in the Vulgate and cited it in his teachings as well.[10]

One of the reasons ancient and modern scholars have been reluctant to accept James as author of the Epistle is the high quality of the Greek style and syntax employed in its composition. Nevertheless, the context of the Epistle, its concern for the poor, and its very Jewish tone accords with what might be expected to have come from James. In short, its historical setting is very accurate for the era that James guided the Church in Jerusalem.

> The social injustice of those years, with the oppression of the poor by the wealthy landed aristocracy, including the chief-priestly families, could provide an appropriate life-setting for . . . the letter of James. There is much in its content that reads very well as if it could be the work of James the Just, with its emphasis on self-control, righteousness, mercy, impartiality, poverty and patience, and its excoriation of hypocrisy, partiality and exploitation of the weak. One feature that has given pause to readers who might otherwise be ready to ascribe it to our James is its Greek style.[11]

The same argument that was raised against the legitimacy of the writings of Peter or John is resorted to in the case of James. How could an ignorant Galilean produce such fine Greek? Why would the supposed leader of Jewish Christians and presumed antagonist of Greek-speaking Gentiles deign to write in any tongue but Aramaic? As suggested above with reference to both Peter and John, the Lord's chief disciples were not men of rabbinical training, but were men of accomplishment and education, men raised in areas where they would have been exposed to Greek from childhood. The same applies to James. That not only Paul, but other early leaders of the Christian movement possessed linguistic expertise in the Greek that was the prime language of communication throughout the eastern Mediterranean hinterland is increasingly recognized.

> Many scholars hold that while the possible range of James's education should not be underrated, it is hardly likely that he would possess the wide culture, the acquaintance with classical literature, or the vernacular and literary Greek. "Perhaps our accepted picture of James and of other members of his family," observes F. F. Bruce, "is not as accurate as we imagine; it is based on very inadequate information."[12]

Accordingly, James may well have been a person of exquisite Greek language skills which he used to proclaim the gospel with equal eloquence and devotion.[13]

The Message of James's Epistle

The addressing of the Epistle of James to the twelve tribes of the diaspora is normally interpreted in one of two ways: to show that James restricted his teachings to Jewish Christians whenever the Epistle may have been composed, or to assign the letter an early date before the Council of Jerusalem when issues of Gentile Christians living the law confronted the Church. Its broad direction beyond the local areas of Judæa indicates that James was probably already an Apostle. Thus the most likely date of the composition of the Epistle is between the years 44 and 49, making it the earliest composed of New Testament writings.[14]

The Epistle of James is often viewed as a special document of Jewish Christians, the most Jewish of New Testament writings, reflecting "a pre-Christological, almost pre-crucifixion stage containing the 'simplest expression of Christian consciousness, still untouched by complex dogmatic reflections.'"[15] Even though the Lord and His teachings are referred to throughout the work, because the Epistle makes direct and explicit mention of Jesus or Christ only twice (James 1:1, 2:1), critics view it as less a testimonial of Christ than direction for righteous living, which could apply as readily to Jews as to Christians. It is variously interpreted as didactic instruction in moral conduct or as a guide for the righteous sufferer in a world of sin, of whom James the Just, or James the Righteous, may be the prototype.[16]

Such interpretations completely miss the pervasive theme that continues throughout the letter of the Lord's brother to his fellow followers of Christ. James proclaims that it is Jesus the Messiah who is the exemplar for righteousness. The teachings that James articulates are those found in the later composed Gospels as the teachings of Jesus. James attributes many of the principles he reminds his readers of to the Lord. All would understand such a reference to signify the Christ. Most interestingly, the simple, point-by-point expression of the precepts of righteous living are reminiscent of the *logia* found in the *Apocryphon of James*.

The first chapter of the Epistle constitutes an eloquent expression of the most important qualities of religious life that a follower of Jesus can attain. The cardinal virtue is patience, occasioned by the trying of faith, and when brought to a completed state it is patience that makes one "perfect and entire, wanting nothing" (James 1:4). The trying of faith, then, leads to patience, which, when complete, ultimately produces perfection. To assist in maintaining patience is given God's great promise: "If any of you lack wisdom, let him ask of God, that giveth to all men liberally, and upbraideth not; and it shall be given him. But let him ask in faith, nothing wavering" (James 1:5–6). Through the practice of prayer with faith the Lord's inspiration can be received by all men. This makes patience possible even at the most difficult time. The latter scripture, of course, possesses very special significance for the Restoration of the gospel. Joseph Smith, the boy prophet, accepted the Lord's promise with sincerity, exercised the prayer of real faith, and received the response that broke eighteen centuries of silence from the heavens to God's children in this world. How thrilling to speculate that as James penned these words he could have had intimations of the effect they would have in ushering in a new and final dispensation of prophetic authority and devoted worship of Jesus Christ as the true and living Son of God!

James went on to command the faithful followers of the Lord to make no distinction among rich or poor, for the former may not be as greatly blessed as the latter (James 1:9–11). He encouraged endurance of temptation, which does not originate with God (James 1:12–18). Also of importance is slowness to wrath and slowness to speak evil (James 1:19–21). This practice of righteous living, each and every day, will make actual "doers of the word, and not hearers only" (James 1:22); only doers can avoid self-deception, thinking that they know themselves when it is, in fact, only a reflection in a looking glass they see, rather than their real selves (James 1:23–24). To act in righteousness is to observe properly what James calls the perfect law of liberty (James 1:25). We know it better as the law of agency. Its true purpose is to allow God's children to do righteousness. James summarizes the Christian life in a few eloquent and inspired words. "Pure religion and undefiled before God and the Father is this, To visit the fatherless and widows in their affliction, and to keep himself unspotted from the world" (James 1:27).

Because we have fewer writings from James than from Peter, John, and Paul, and because less information about James survives from the writings of others than survives about Peter, John, and Paul, it is challenging to portray James's person and character in an extended fashion. James is the most difficult to come to know of the four great New Testament witnesses of Christ. Perhaps more than any other source, the first chapter of his Epistle reveals the brother of the Lord as he must have been. James was surely a patient man, who exercised faith to build that patience and to receive continual strengthening support from the Lord through prayer. He must have worked hard to resist temptation, to be slow to wrath even against the leaders of the Jews who caused such distress for his flock. Perhaps, more than any other quality, James exemplified the precept to be a doer of the word and not a hearer only. His motto, like that of a latter-day leader, may well have been "Do it!" James makes clear what needed to be done—maintain personal purity, keeping oneself unspotted from this world, and serve the Savior by serving others, especially those in greatest need. In all these matters, James had the unparalleled example of his own much-loved Brother to follow, and he followed it with both love and devotion.

The second chapter of James may be one of the most misunderstood passages of scripture. The first half of the chapter presents little problem as James discourses about the great wrong done in despising the poor (James 2:1–7), and reiterates what he terms "the royal law" of loving "thy neighbour as thyself" (James 2:8). After reminding his readers of several of the Ten Commandments, James turns his attention again to the law of liberty and the importance of judging with mercy so that mercy will be applied to one's own judgment. These teachings, of course, are familiar as restatements of Christ's own teachings, the most fundamental aspects of religious practice in the community of the Savior's followers.

The second part of the chapter contains James's exposition of the inadequacy of faith without works, and is the part that many people misunderstand. James in nowise denigrates the importance of faith. Quite the contrary! Faith is of paramount importance, but the proof of faith are the works that develop from it. For James, faith is wrought with works and by works faith is made perfect (James 2:22). The two, faith and works, are inextricably linked, companions leading to perfection after the example of Christ.

The remaining chapters of the Epistle address a variety of practices that should be observed by the follower of Christ. Governing the tongue so as not to give offense to another (James 3:1–10) is a practical application of the golden rule and a contributor to the peaceful conduct of interpersonal relations (James 3:13–18). Humility is of tremendous importance, for the humble man will refrain from evil speaking against another (James 4:10). Pray for one another, anoint the sick in the prayer of faith that they may be healed, for the true believer is involved with the community of the faithful, providing loving service as an observer of pure religion (James 5:10–20).

Two important doctrines are alluded to in the fourth chapter that are central to early Christianity and frequently addressed by subsequent writers of the late first and second centuries. Their presence in the Epistle of James disqualifies it as a Jewish work and places it directly in the mainstream of early Christian thought. The teachings are related. One is the famed "Doctrine of the Two Ways," seldom better defined than by James's statement "that the friendship of the world is enmity with God," and "whosoever therefore will be a friend of the world is the enemy of God" (James 4:4).[17] The other relates to early Christian eschatological views that the time of both the Church and also the individual in the world was brief and would quickly end.[18] James puts it this way:

> Go to now, ye that say, To day or to morrow we will go into such a city, and continue there a year, and buy and sell, and get gain: Whereas ye know not what shall be on the morrow. For what is your life? It is even a vapour, that appeareth for a little time, and then vanisheth away (James 4:13–14).

Accordingly, the righteous man will observe the practices that James indicates must comprise the way of life of a follower of Jesus.

Very possibly the earliest writing of those books that comprise the New Testament, the Epistle of James reveals the concerns that the brother of the Lord held for his fellow worshipers. They provide great insight into the day-to-day practice of the followers of the Way, a name by which the earliest followers of Jesus identified themselves at Jerusalem in the years just after the Savior's earthly mission was completed.

James is himself revealed as a righteous follower of the Way through his own teachings of which he was not a hearer only, but also a doer. Through his observance of the teachings of Jesus, James, of course, came to be known among friend and foe as James the Just. That appellation is the greatest witness of James's faithfulness in practicing the righteous way of life.

Endnotes

1. William S. Vorster, "Protoevangelium of James," *Anchor Bible Dictionary,* 3:629–32.

2. William R. Schoedel, "First Apocalypse of James," *Anchor Bible Dictionary,* 3:628–29.

3. Ibid.

4. Charles W. Heduch, "Second Apocalypse of James," *Anchor Bible Dictionary,* 3:632–33.

5. Ibid.

6. Ron Cameron, "The Apocryphon of James," *Anchor Bible Dictionary,* 3:619–20.

7. Ibid.

8. On Luther's view of James's Epistle and scholarly opinion on the legitimacy of its authorship, see the excellent summary in Adamson, *James,* IX–52.

9. Ibid., XIV.

10. Painter, *Just James,* 235.

11. Bruce, *Peter, Stephen, James & John,* 113.

12. Adamson, *James,* 5 with a citation to Bruce, *Peter, Stephen, James, & John,* 96.

13. For arguments establishing the multilingualism of James, and his brother Jesus, see Painter, *Just James,* 238–46.

14. For issues of dating, see Joseph B. Mayor, *The Epistle of St. James* (1910), vii, xci–xcii, cxliv, clxxxiii–clxxxviii; C. Powell, "'Faith' in James and its Bearing on

the Problem of the Date of the Epistle," *Expository Times* 62 (1950–51), 311–14.

15. Adamson, *James,* 31.

16. Ibid., 27-33; Painter, *Just James,* 227–76.

17. Nibley, *When the Lights Went Out,* 7, 23–25.

18. Ibid., 2–5.

CHAPTER FOUR

The Killing of James the Just

In the year A.D. 62, the brother of the Lord, James the Just, was executed on trumped-up charges by the leaders of the Jews, high priest and Sanhedrin. His death was said to have occasioned an outcry not only among Christians but even among the Jews of Jerusalem, angry that so righteous a man would so wrongly be put to death. The killing of James has been linked to great changes at Jerusalem: for Christians, abandonment of Jerusalem and departure to new homes at Pella; for Jews, destruction of the Holy City as retribution for the murder of Christians and for crucifying the Messiah.

Josephus's Account of James's Execution

It is a testament to James's fame and reputation for goodness that a non-Christian source would include in his history of the Jews so lengthy and detailed an account of James's killing. Moreover, Josephus's chronicling of this event stands as evidence of the hue and outcry with which it had been met.[1]

Josephus sets James's execution in the period between the death of the Roman procurator Festus and the arrival of his successor Albinus. In the interim the province of Judea seems to have been administered by the newly appointed Sadducee high priest, Ananus. This ambitious man was characterized by Josephus as "rash in his temper and unusually daring."[2] Josephus describes Ananus's plot against James as follows:

> Possessed with such a character, Ananus thought that he had a favorable
> opportunity because Festus was dead and Albinus was on the way. And

so he convened the judges of the Sanhedrin and brought before them a
man named James, the brother of Jesus who was called the Christ, and
certain others. He accused them of having transgressed the law and
delivered them up to be stoned. Those of the inhabitants of the city who
were considered the most fair minded and were strict in the observance
of the law were offended at this. They therefore secretly sent to King
Agrippa urging him, for Ananus had not even been correct in his first
step, to order him to desist from any further such actions. Certain of
them even went to meet Albinus, who was on his way from Alexandria,
and informed him that Ananus had no authority to convene the
Sanhedrin without his consent. Convinced by these words, Albinus
angrily wrote to Ananus threatening to take vengeance upon him. King
Agrippa, because of Ananus' action, deposed him from the high priesthood which he had held for three months and replaced him with Jesus
son of Damnaeus.[3]

Josephus lays at the feet of Ananus's flawed character his wrongful
execution of James and others of the Christians. The outrage at these
events of a group of upright Jews apparently resulted in the undertaking
of embassies to both Agrippa (son of Herod Agrippa who had killed
James, son of Zebedee) and the new Roman procurator, Albinus. These
actions of just Jews may well have prevented the continued execution of
other Christians that Ananus had decided upon.

Josephus's account of the actual mode of death of James is brief. It
is implied that he died by stoning. Most important, perhaps, is the
identification by a non-Christian of James as brother of Jesus, who was
called the Christ. The historicity of the relationship so debated by
modern scholars of religion is clearly established in Josephus's account.

Eusebius's Chronicle of the Martyrdom of James

More than two hundred years after Josephus wrote his account,
using both Josephus and the Christian author Hegesippus as sources,
Eusebius provided a lengthy narrative of James's martyrdom at the
hands of Jewish leaders.

Eusebius claims to give in his Ecclesiastical History an account of the death
of James the Just which is taken from the writings of Hegesippus. This

account, which is very much longer than that of Josephus, presents a quite different version of the antecedent circumstances and the death of James.[4]

Eusebius begins his paraphrase of Hegesippus with the Sanhedrin's inquisition of James, questioning him about the cryptic phrase "the door of Jesus." Apparently James had been successful in converting many leading Jews to belief in the doctrines of resurrection and rewards for righteousness in the next life. These converts would have come from the upper classes, from those who did not accept life after death, namely the very Sadducees who comprised much of the Sanhedrin. Eusebius describes the Sanhedrin's questioning and attempted manipulation of James as follows:

Since therefore many even of the ruling class believed, there was an uproar among the Jews and scribes and Pharisees, who said there was a danger that the entire people would expect Jesus as the Christ. So they collected and said to James: "Be good enough to restrain the people, for they have gone astray after Jesus on the belief that he is the Christ. Be good enough to make the facts about Jesus clear to all who come for the Passover Day. We all accept what you say: we can vouch for it, and so can all the people, that you are a righteous man and take no one at his face value. So make it clear to the crowd that they must not go astray as regards Jesus. . . . So take your stand in the Temple parapet, so that from that height you may be easily seen, and your words audible to the whole people. For because of the Passover all the tribes have come together and the Gentiles too."[5]

The plan of the Sanhedrin and the leaders of the Jews was, of course, flawed, as they supposed James could be intimidated into denying his brother, the Savior. Quite the contrary, to testify that Jesus was the Messiah was all important for James. He had long taught Jesus' followers at Jerusalem that to follow Jesus' teachings of righteous living was the "Way" and that the atoning sacrifice of the Savior opened the door to eternal life. James used the occasion and opportunity given him by these leaders of the Jews, who did not understand that unlike they themselves, threats of death could not deter for even a moment James the Just from his paramount responsibility as an apostolic witness of the Lord Jesus Christ. And so, high upon the temple walls, James offered up his final testimony, knowing it would be sealed with his blood.

> So the scribes and Pharisees made James stand on the Sanctuary parapet and shouted to him: "Just one whose word we are all obliged to accept, the people are going astray after Jesus who was crucified; so tell us what is meant by 'the door of Jesus'." He replied as loudly as he could: "Why do you question me about the Son of Man? I tell you he is sitting in heaven at the right hand of the great power, and he will come on the clouds of heaven." Many were convinced and gloried in James's testimony, crying: "Hosanna to the Son of David!"[6]

Realizing their strategic error, the Jewish leaders decided to simply murder James. In Eusebius's account, there is no mention of trial or legal proceeding. The Sanhedrin, in moblike fashion and giving full vent to their fury, simply hurled the righteous man down from the temple walls to his death.

> Then again the Scribes and Pharisees said to each other: "We made a bad mistake in affording such testimony of Jesus. We had better go up and throw him down, so that they will be frightened and not believe him." . . . So they went up and threw down the Just one. Then they said to each other "Let us stone James the Just" and began to stone him, as in spite of his fall he was still alive. But he turned and knelt uttering the words: "I beseech Thee, Lord God and Father, forgive them; they do not know what they are doing." While they pelted him with stones, one of the descendants of Rechab the son of Rechabim, the priestly family to which Jeremiah the prophet bore witness, called out, "Stop! What are you doing? the Just one is praying for you. Then one of them, a fuller, took the club he used to beat clothes and brought it down on the head of the Just one. Such was his martyrdom.[7]

So ended the life of a just and faithful servant of the Master, who devoted his life to righteousness and to the service of the Lord through acting as loving servant to the Master's flock at Jerusalem. James's witness of the Savior served to inspire those who heard and to bring many into the fold.

After James

Eusebius's account of James's martyrdom concludes strangely with a single sentence, "and at once Vespasian began to besiege them."[8] The siege and destruction of Jerusalem is depicted as a direct result of the killing of James the Just and a long awaited retribution for the Crucifixion of the Savior many years before. Indeed, James is also described by Eusebius—quoting Hegesippus—as "Oblias, that is in Greek, rampart of the people in righteousness."[9] Elsewhere Eusebius explains the significance of the phrase as making reference to the Apostles as bulwarks of protection for the Jews that,

> There is no necessity to add to the narratives of what happened to the whole nation after the passion of the Savior and those words in which the multitude of the Jews begged off from death the robber and murderer and besought that the author of Life should be taken from them; but it would be right to add a possible confirmation of the kindliness of beneficent Providence. For forty whole years it suspended their destruction, after their crime against the Christ, and during all of them many of the apostles and disciples, and James himself who is called the Lord's brother, the first bishop of the city, still survived in this world. By their dwelling in Jerusalem they afforded, as it were, a strong protection to the place; for the government of God had still patience, if haply they might at last by repenting of their deeds, be able to obtain pardon and salvation; and in addition to such great long-suffering it sent wonderful tokens from God of what would happen to them if they did not repent.[10]

Eusebius even attributes to Josephus a similar viewpoint that the destruction of Jerusalem occurred as God's retribution for the killing of James. Eusebius quotes Josephus as saying "These things happened to the Jews to avenge James the Just, who was a brother of Jesus who is called the Christ, for the Jews put him to death in spite of his great righteousness." But the passage does not appear in any extant text of Josephus, so definite conclusions about Josephus's opinions regarding the causes of Jerusalem's destruction ought not be ventured.[11]

In any case, Eusebius's chronology is somewhat flawed. Josephus establishes the death of James at the time of the procuratorial interregnum between Festus and Albinus in the year 62. Despite Eusebius's claim that Vespasian's siege began immediately, four more years intervened before the beginning of the revolt of Jewish zealots.[12] It appears that during this period of time the followers of Jesus vacated Jerusalem. Eusebius himself relates the flight of Christians and the reestablishment of the Christian community of Jerusalem at Pella, across the Jordan. Eusebius attributes this exodus to "an oracle given by revelation before the war to those in the city who were worthy of it, to depart and dwell in one of the cities of Perea which they called Pella."[13]

With this departure ended the early Christian community of Jewish Christians at Jerusalem. Christians would, of course, one day return to Jerusalem, refounded some years later after the Bar Kochba rebellion as the Hadrianic city of Aelia Capitolina. But the Jerusalem Christian community begun by those who had known the Savior Himself had departed. James, the brother of the Lord, had devoted his lifelong labor to teaching and caring for the followers of Jesus at Jerusalem. After his death, his flock scattered, but his example of righteousness, his testimony that Jesus was the Christ, and his exhortation to the practicalities of righteous living remained.

Endnotes

1.   Josephus, *Jewish Antiquities,* 20.197–203.

2.   Ibid., 20.199.

3.   Ibid., 20.200—203.

4.   Brandon, *Fall of Jerusalem,* 97.

5.   Eusebius, *Ecclesiastical History,* 2.23.10–11.

6.   Ibid., 2.23.12–14.

7.   Ibid., 2.23.14–18.

8.   Ibid., 2.23.18.

9.   Ibid., 2.23.7.

10. Ibid., 3.7.7–9.

11. See Painter, *Just James,* 131–33 and Eusebius, *Ecclesiastical History,* 2.23.20.

12. Hall and Welch, *Masada,* 129–40, 319–36.

13. Eusebius, *Ecclesiastical History,* 3.5.3.

SECTION FIVE
Paul

CHAPTER ONE

Citizen of Three Worlds

At the organization of an instructional facility on January 5, 1841, the Prophet Joseph Smith gave the following description of the Apostle Paul:

> He is about five feet high; very dark hair; dark complexion; dark skin; large Roman nose; sharp face; small black eyes, penetrating as eternity; round shoulders; a whining voice, except when elevated, and then it almost resembled the roaring of a lion. He was a good orator, active and diligent, always employing himself in doing good to his fellow men.[1]

How appropriate a description, for it both describes Paul physically and also provides an indication of his goodness, his energy, the power of his oratory, and the strength of that mighty voice so often lifted in testimony of the Lord Jesus Christ. The reference to his Roman nose brings to mind Paul's high place as one of the very few who not only possessed Roman citizenship, but was born a Roman citizen. The notice of his oratorical skill betokens Paul's superb Greek education. Finally, Paul's emphasis on doing good to his fellowmen is perhaps reflective of his training in the ways of Jewish law and tradition. Paul possessed Jewish, Greek, and Roman backgrounds. He was, indeed, a citizen of all three of these worlds that coexisted during the first century in the eastern Mediterranean region.

Paul would have been one of a handful who shared so thoroughly in all three of these cultures. From each of them he drew different knowledge and skills that prepared him uniquely for the special task the Lord would assign him. The Apostle to the Gentiles may well have been the only man of his age qualified to assume the burden that was his. Certainly he was the best prepared to undertake a mission that would bring his teaching and testimony to Jew, Greek, and Roman alike. Paul was in very fact the mighty Lion of God, whose voice roared across the greatest of man's empires, to proclaim a heavenly King in sonorous tones to which ears could not be closed. The Apostle's bold message of faith and salvation, carried by the Spirit into the hearts of men, brought those who had never even heard mention of the God of heaven into the fold of the righteous who would dwell with Him forever.

The Man from Tarsus

Luke records Paul's declaration that "I am a man which am a Jew of Tarsus, a city in Cilicia, a citizen of no mean city" (Acts 21:39), and an additional but similar statement, "I am verily a man which am a Jew, born in Tarsus, a city in Cilicia" (Acts 22:3). The second reference confirms Tarsus not only as Paul's place of residence, but also as his place of birth. The same information is also implied in the first passage's use of the term citizen. In the ancient world, to be a citizen of a particular city required not merely residency, but birth. Only Rome was sufficiently innovative to develop citizenship that could be extended to those not born as citizens. By the first century, this had definitely become a national citizen status, but available outside of Italy only to the most elite residents of the provinces. As for citizenship of local towns and cities throughout the empire, that lesser distinction was held only by those born in those individual locales.[2] Moreover, Tarsus possessed a peculiar local requirement for admission to its citizen rolls, a property qualification to ensure that only men of achievement could participate in the administration of the city's civic corporation. Of course, a family among the very privileged few to hold Roman citizenship would certainly have met any qualification of wealth or property to be included in the far less exclusive group of Tarsian citizens.[3] Accordingly, Paul's birth and residence, as well as his local citizen status, are clearly established as belonging to Tarsus.

Paul was correct to declare that he was "a citizen of no mean city" (Acts 21:39). The description has greater significance in the original Greek text.

In Greek that is "no insignificant city," a label used in ancient literature for a place with distinguishing marks. Tarsus could boast of its size, commercial importance, and educational tradition. The largest city in its province, its fame compared well with the two dozen provincial centers of the empire.[4]

Tarsus ranked as the metropolis of southeastern Anatolia, the chief city of the region known as Cilicia, and a major economic and educational center. Four hundred years before the time of Paul, the Greek general and historian Xenophon, passing through Cilicia, called Tarsus a "great and prosperous city."[5] The city was located on an expansive fertile plain, and as an important textile center, it was famous for its fine linen produced from locally grown flax of high quality. The primary overland trade route from Syria and the East into the interior of Asia Minor passed through Tarsus, making it an important economic center. Similarly, the River Cyndus, which flowed through the city was still a navigable stream at Tarsus, allowing ships to bring trade from the Mediterranean ten miles downstream. So Tarsus qualified as a center of maritime trade as well.

Hittite records make note of Tarsus as early as the second millenium B.C. The city seems to have been devastated by invasion of sea peoples by around 1200 B.C., and was later resettled by Greeks, though it was ruled by Assyrians in the eighth and seventh centuries B.C. Afterward Tarsus became part of the Persian Empire and was not to return to self-rule by its Greek population until the advent of Alexander the Great in 333 B.C. By the first century B.C., Tarsus had come under Roman control. Rome at various periods utilized Tarsus as a major center for staging military operations in the East and it served as capital of the Roman province of Cilicia, though during Paul's lifetime Cilicia was attached to the larger Roman province of Syria.[6]

Tarsus had achieved a certain renown as an educational center. As a Greek *polis,* the city's culture was Hellenized, although its location near non-Greek peoples of the East (Syrians, Persians, Phoenicians, etc.) made it something of a melting pot of peoples and cultures. Nevertheless, the educational system of Tarsus was thoroughly Greek. Many of its residents, certainly any from its citizen families, would have obtained basic and advanced education in Greek language and rhetoric, history, and thought. Strabo reports that "the city of Tarsus has all kinds of schools of rhetoric," suggesting the ancient equivalent of broad secondary education, not only for the privileged, but no doubt for its prosperous merchant class as well.[7] People from Tarsus knew their Greek well and could use it skillfully in times of rhetorical need: for debate, to make speeches, or to write and compose. Tarsus had also acquired a reputation for higher education, particularly as a center for the study of philosophy.

> According to the geographer Strabo, writing probably in the early years of the first century A.D., the people were avid in the pursuit of culture. They applied themselves to the study of philosophy, the liberal arts and "the whole round of learning in general"—the whole "encyclopedia"—so much so that Tarsus in this respect surpassed even Athens and Alexandria, whose schools were frequented more by visitors than by their own citizens. Tarsus, in short, was what we might call a university city. Yet people did not come from other places to study in its schools: the students of Tarsus were natives of the city.[8]

Paul's experience would have been greatly affected in many ways by growing up in "no mean city" as Tarsus was. His hometown's prosperity, educational opportunities, civic pride, Greek culture, and exposure to customs and new ways brought by traders from throughout the world gave Paul a background he never could have acquired had he been born at Jerusalem. As one commentator has remarked, "the city, therefore, into which Paul was born was well governed and prosperous. Its Greek orientation had to struggle with a strong Eastern spirit. It stood on the frontier of East and West, and its citizens were prepared to function in both."[9] The "Man from Tarsus" possessed just such a preparation that in part qualified him to become the Apostle to the nations, able to function in East or West, comfortable in the world of Jews, or Greeks, or Romans.

A Hebrew of the Hebrews

Paul declared his Hebraic credentials to the Philippians, saying he was "circumcised the eighth day, of the stock of Israel, of the tribe of Benjamin, an Hebrew of the Hebrews; as touching the law, a Pharisee" (Phil 3:5). He leaves no doubt of his descent from Abraham, Isaac, and Jacob, but it is perhaps also significant that while Paul was of the house of Israel, he was not technically a Jew. Rather, he disclosed his lineage to be of the tribe of Benjamin, a claim he reiterated elsewhere (Rom 11:1). Indeed, he bore as the name by which he was known in Jewish circles that of the most illustrious Benjaminite in Old Testament history, Saul, first king of Israel. Although many from the tribe of Benjamin "tended to lose their tribal identity" during the years the tribes of Judah and Benjamin comprised the southern kingdom of Judea, "some at least did not allow it to be obliterated."[10] For Paul's family to have so carefully maintained such distinction sets them apart from most, and may indicate that they descended from Benjaminites of some prominence.

Scholars suggest that Paul's use of the expression "Hebrew of the Hebrews" was less a genealogical matter than a linguistic. Through this phrase, Paul became further set apart in that he was not merely a Greek-speaking Jew of the diaspora, but a Benjamite who could employ Aramaic, or in the case of the highly educated young Pharisee, Saul, even the Hebrew that so few of the Jews of that era still understood.[11] Certainly, the writings of Paul confirm that in his citation of the Old Testament, he demonstrated a facility with Hebrew/Aramaic versions of scripture, as well as the *Septuagint*. This Hellenistic Greek translation of the Hebrew scriptures was used throughout the Jewish communities of the diaspora, where only Greek was understood and employed even in the worship at the synagogue.[12]

From Paul's words and what we know of the history of Tarsus and the Jewish people, certain conclusions and inferences may be drawn about the family of Saul. It is entirely possible that they came to Tarsus during the period when it was under Persian control, at the time that Jews were released from their Babylonian captivity and given the freedom to migrate throughout the Persian Empire. The large Jewish populations of the cities of Asia Minor uniformly seem to begin development during that era.[13] Accordingly, by Paul's time his family may have been in Tarsus for four or five centuries, quite long enough a period to have acquired the wealth and status they appear to have possessed. Moreover, their preservation of their own Benjaminite genealogy and their apparent continued use of Aramaic in an environment that for at least three centuries had been overwhelmingly Greek, betoken a long-standing prominence that suggests their wealth was by no means of recent acquisition. The high position of the family is indicated by their rare Roman citizen status, and their inclusion among the restricted citizen body of Tarsus. Their ability to maintain contact with leading Jews at Jerusalem such as Saul's mentor, Gamaliel, marks them as a chief family of the Jewish community at Tarsus.

It is not known how Paul's family rose through the years to become one of the wealthy and prominent families of Tarsus. Luke describes Paul as having knowledge of the trade of the *skenopoios*. King James's translators rendered the Greek word into English as "tentmaker." The second part of the Greek term, *poios*, does signify one who makes, but what Paul is described as knowing how to make is a *skenos,* which can mean tent, but in reality refers to anything made from a large quantity of cloth. For example, the curtains of a stage, or the painted cloth backdrops of a dramatic production can be a *skenos*, from which our English word "scene" is a derivative. A *skenopoios* could also manufacture great cloth sails for the ships of the period or awnings to cover courtyards, marketplaces, or amphitheaters. In that era, cloth was used more widely than it is in our own time. When it is remembered that Tarsus was the location of one of the Roman world's most important textile industries, it is perhaps not amiss to suggest that Paul's family wealth and status came from their involvement in the manufacture and further utilization of cloth in the ways suggested above, and in a very large-scale operation.

Paul was unquestionably multilingual. No doubt Aramaic was spoken at home, perhaps, but not necessarily, as the first language of the family. Certainly all would have been just as fluent in Greek, the primary language of their native city. For a well-to-do family of Israel concerned with matters of heritage, Hebrew was undoubtedly part of the children's instruction. Certainly Saul must have received excellent training in Hebrew language and religion to qualify to study under so eminent a teacher as Gamaliel. A family that could afford to pay for its son later to study at Jerusalem with the most famous rabbi of the day could easily afford tutorial instruction in Hebrew and the original Hebrew scriptures of the *Torah* and the *Nevi'im*. Finally, as one of a very few families of Tarsus to possess the distinction of Roman citizenship, it is possible that Paul was also conversant with Latin. No direct evidence from Paul's writings indicates this, but knowledge of the language may perhaps be inferred not only from his teaching at

Rome, but also from the Apostle's work at both Philippi and Corinth, Roman provincial capitals, but, more importantly, Roman citizen colonies, where Latin was used as much as Greek.[14]

Young Paul's education in Jewish religion included, of course, the Old Testament tradition of the law of Moses and the teachings of the prophets, and also the materials of the new rabbinical Judaism that had developed since the return of a portion of the Jews to Judea. While it is likely that as a family of the diaspora, Paul's family would not have been exposed to as rigid a Judaism as had they lived at Jerusalem, nevertheless, Paul identifies his Jewish training as belonging to the party of the Pharisees. Certainly some contact between the Jews at Jerusalem and Jewish congregations of the diaspora was to be expected, even if by the first century those congregations represented heavily Hellenized strains of Judaism. Although towns deep in the interior of Asia Minor may have had minimal contact with Pharisees, the Jewish community of an important city like Tarsus, located on trade routes and thereby readily accessible, surely would have become a target of Pharisees intent on purifying Hellenistic influence from the religious practice of the Jews at Tarsus.[15] Not only Paul, but his fathers before him, adhered to the doctrine of the Pharisees and may, in all likelihood, have been the most important supporters at Tarsus of the teachings of the Pharisees (Acts 23:6). Paul's early religious training was no doubt received from many sources: his family, tutors, local rabbis, or even visiting Pharisees from Jerusalem. But whatever the source of this education in the revised religion of the new Judaism, Paul became well versed. Gamaliel would not have accepted an unqualified student, no matter how much money his family could pay.

Paul's professional training took him to Jerusalem and was intended to make him a scribe and a Pharisee, a protegé of the most renowned rabbi of the day. It was training for which much prerequisite knowledge was needed, and training that was expensive. Paul was, of course, among the most successful of Gamaliel's disciples. Many years later, as Paul explained the credentials he possessed to certify his ability to comment on Jewish practices, he recounted that he "profited in the Jews' religion above many my equals in mine own nation, being more exceedingly zealous of the traditions of my fathers" (Gal 1:14). To be among the best of Gamaliel's students placed Paul in a position to one day become himself a leader of the Pharisees.

Gamaliel is said to have been the grandson of Hillel himself, the originator of the movement of Pharasaic rabbinism and founder of the "school of Pharasaic rabbinic leaders that ultimately shaped the Jewish tradition."[16] In many ways Hillel can be described as holding a place second only to the scribe Ezra as a founder of modern Judaism. Either as head of Hillel's school or founder of a school of his own, Gamaliel exercised tremendous influence on the Pharisee movement.[17] Gamaliel had achieved his authoritative standing not merely as director of the most important school for rabbis, but as an expert in the *Torah* and the *Mishnah*. Indeed, to him is attributed the elevation of the rabbinical oral commentary on the *Torah* to a level with the *Torah* itself. In response to the question of "how many Torah's were given to Israel? Rabban Gamaliel said, 'Two, one in writing and one orally.' Not only was the written Law binding on the Pharisees, but also its traditional understanding and expansion," according to Gamaliel.[18] So important was Gamaliel to the Pharisees that upon his death it was written in their Mishnah, "When Rabban Gamaliel the elder died, the glory of the Torah ceased, and purity and 'separateness' died."[19] One modern commentator emphasizes the significance of the statement by interpreting the phrase "separateness" as equivalent to Pharasaism, "which is almost to say that he was the last of the true Pharisees, since 'separateness' (Heb. p'risut) is a formation of the same root as 'Pharisee.'"[20]

Gamaliel is depicted as a man of wisdom even in Christian sources. Indeed, his role in the Sanhedrin afforded followers of Jesus protection from the Sadducees who, after the death of the Savior, sought to kill the Apostles Peter and John because of their miraculous acts and success in bringing many to a knowledge of the Son of Man. In Acts, he is described as "one in the council, a Pharisee, named Gamaliel, a doctor of the law, had in reputation among all the people" (Acts 5:34). Gamaliel's message reflects the Pharisee's doctrine that the will of heaven shall prevail regardless of the actions of men, "And now I say unto you, Refrain from these men, and let them alone: for if this counsel or this work be of men, it will come to naught: But if it be of God, ye cannot overthrow it; lest haply ye be found even to fight against God" (Acts 5:38–39). Gamaliel's counsel prevailed in the Sanhedrin, much to the benefit of the Christians.

After completing his training under Gamaliel, Paul appears to have left Jerusalem for a time. None of Paul's many Epistles, nor the record of Luke about Paul, give any indication that Paul ever knew or even heard Jesus the Messiah. If he had any experience at all with the Savior while he was alive, indication of such a meeting would unquestionably be found somewhere in Paul's prolific writings. The only sensible explanation is that Paul had left Jerusalem during the years of Christ's ministry and was not present to meet Jesus or to witness His acts and to hear His teachings. Perhaps Paul had returned to Tarsus during that time to act as rabbi in his native city and to bring home the latest teachings of the Pharisees. Although his precise whereabouts remain unknown, it is virtually impossible that Paul stayed in Judea.

A number of years must have passed between the death of Jesus and Saul's appearance in the New Testament. Gradually, not only Sadducees, but Pharisees like Saul who no longer heeded Gamaliel's advice, began to engage in persecution of Jesus' followers. From the point of view of Pharisees, such persecution must have been intended to purge Israel of the "followers of the Way" whom Pharisees would have considered apostates from the law and their new oral traditions, soon to be compiled into the *Mishnah*. Indeed, Luke records Paul as explaining his own persecution of Christians in such terms. "And I persecuted this way unto the death, binding and delivering into prisons both men and women" (Acts 22:4). Paul's purpose was to imprison and beat believers in Christ until, in his current perspective, they renounced their apostasy and returned to the proper observance of the law, or were removed from the body of Israel by their deaths. Paul was so effective in this work commissioned by the chief priests (Acts 26:10) that Luke recounts that "he made havock of the church, entering into every house, and haling men and women committed them to prison" (Acts 8:3).

As Paul described himself, "beyond measure I persecuted the church of God, and wasted it . . . being more exceedingly zealous of the traditions of my fathers" (Gal. 1:13–14). Paul's zealousness in the matter of persecuting Christians derived from his deep devotion and dedication to his religion. He perceived himself to be defending his religion from those who were trying to lead the righteous away from Judaism. "The cherished object of his zeal was the ancestral traditions—the ancient law of Israel and its interpretation as taught in the school of Gamaliel."[21] Paul's devotion was a positive quality ill-applied, since it was used to defend a religion that was no longer true, a religion that had itself passed through an apostasy, as discussed earlier, to become the new Judaism of the rabbis.[22] Indeed, it was the same zealous devotion that later would be redirected and better applied as a converted Paul dedicated himself to the propagation of belief in Christ. Paul's almost blind devotion was a consequence of his training in the precepts of Mosaic law and the Pharisaic interpretation of the same. His views and beliefs were acquired as a result of the instruction in Judaism that he received as a youth in Tarsus, and when a young man, as a student of Gamaliel in Jerusalem.

> [In this] one respect Paul did deviate from his master's example: he repudiated the idea that a temporizing policy was the proper one to adopt towards the disciples of Jesus. To his mind, this new movement posed a more deadly threat to all that he had learned to hold dear than Gamaliel seemed able to appreciate. Moreover, Paul's temperament appears to have been quite different from Gamaliel's: as against Gamaliel's statesmanlike patience and tolerance, Paul was characterized on his own confession, by a superabundance of zeal, which indeed he never entirely lost, but redirected so that what once had been Saul's weakness became for Paul a great strength.[23]

Educated in the Greek Way

Paul was as at home in the Greek world as he was among the Jews. Indeed, most of his life was spent in the lands and cities where Greek was spoken and where either Hellenic or Hellenistic culture predominated. He was uniquely qualified by linguistic, cultural, and educational background to carry the gospel through the great Hellenistic *oecumene* of which he was very much a member.

As a youth growing up in one of the most important Greek educational centers, and coming from a family not only of high standing in the Tarsian community but even possessing Roman citizenship, Paul can be expected to have received a superb education in the Greek schools of Tarsus. The educational opportunities were close at hand and Paul's family could pay for them without any difficulty at all.

Greek *paedeia*, the educational system in which a student was trained in Greek language and grammar, Greek literature, Greek composition and rhetoric, and finally in Greek philosophic thought and argument, would have been pursued in full by Paul in a variety of schools at Tarsus, before he reached the necessary age to go to Jerusalem and complete his Jewish rabbinical preparation under the tutelage of Gamaliel. No details of Paul's particular education are known, but the generalities of the system are well established. Paul would have received the very training noted above. Language with emphasis on grammar, composition, and rhetoric would have been extensively pursued for the advanced curriculum of philosophic thought and argument, with even more training in rhetorical technique. That Paul did, in fact, undergo this sort of Greek education is very clear when the Apostle's own writings are examined, revealing an excellent command of Greek language, skilled expertise for Greek composition, and the talent of an accomplished student in respect to argumentation, rhetorical style, and grounding in philosophic topics and methods. Paul possessed skills and abilities that could have been acquired only by one who had experienced Greek *paideia*. These comprise the ultimate proof of an excellent training in Greek education, and with it a thorough familiarity with all things Greek on the part of Paul of Tarsus.[24]

Paul's writings are composed in Greek of superb quality and style. From his use of language alone Paul is revealed as a highly educated man. Beyond his skill in the use of Greek language, Paul also employs in his Epistles the Greek literary technique of rhetorical devices. Stylistic figures such as simile and oxymoron, climax and synecdoche, chiasmus and antithesis, as well as many other syntactical or rhetorical figures abound in Paul's writing. His extended use of figurative language enlivens his message by incorporating familiar aspects of the Greek or Roman world into colorful metaphors to teach gospel principles.[25] Clearly sound, grammatical Greek can be written without the incorporation of such literary language, but rhetorical style is the mark of a Greek educated man. In addition to the use of stylistic devices, a more substantial component of the Greek art of persuasion, rhetoric, is found in compositional technique and the proper organization of argument or evidence. A Greek speaking audience would expect to read in epistles or to hear in speeches Greek of the sort that employed stylistic devices and was composed in accordance with the methods of rhetoric. Paul and other early Christians engaged in writing or public speaking would:

Have been hard put to escape an awareness of rhetoric as practiced in the culture around them, for the rhetorical theory of the schools found its immediate application in almost every form of oral and written communication: in official documents and public letters, in private correspondence, in the lawcourts and assemblies, in speeches at festivals and commemorations, and in literary compositions in both prose and verse. In addressing a Greek audience, even when he pointedly rejected the "wisdom of this world," Paul could not expect to be persuasive unless there was some overlap between the content and form of what he said and the expectations of his audience. What we need to do is to try to hear his words as a Greek-speaking audience would have heard them, and that involves some understanding of classical rhetoric. . . . The Greeks gave names to rhetorical techniques, many of which are found all over the world. They organized these techniques into a system which could be taught and learned. What we mean by classical rhetorical theory is this structured system.[26]

Paul's education had made him very skilled in the application of classical rhetoric in his speaking and writing in Greek. Many of Paul's speeches as recorded in Acts and his Epistles demonstrate various kinds of rhetorical composition, leaving no doubt about the extended training he must have received to be able to apply rhetorical technique with such facility. Paul's Epistles include many rhetorically structured passages. As an example, the Epistle to the Galatians is a perfect paradigm of the *encomium*. This is a particularly arranged kind of argument designed to justify one's self, one's beliefs, or one's ideals and values. It is organized into five sections, each with a different function: the *exordium* (Gal. 1:6–11) or introduction, the *narratio* (Gal. 1:12–2:14) or summary exposition of the facts, the *propositio* (Gal. 2:15–21) or statement of the logical premise upon which the proof of the argument is based, the *probatio* (Gal. 3:1–4:31) or laying out of evidence, and the *exhortatio* (Gal. 5:1–6:10) or final encouragement. The structure of Galatians as a classic example of encomiastic argumentation is developed by a number of scholars.[27]

In Galatians Paul uses the *exordium* (1:6–11) to establish background information about how some of the Galatians had abandoned the teachings to which they had been converted by Paul to return to Jewish doctrines. But Paul certifies that he did not teach them such doctrines of men, but rather the truths of Jesus Christ. In the *narratio*

(1:12–2:14) Paul recounts how his own training in Jerusalem surpassed that of the itinerant Judaizers and how he left Judaism behind when he received the vision of the resurrected Lord. He goes on to establish other facts: his service in teaching the gospel in Arabia and Syria, the disputes and divisiveness that Judaizers occasioned among the Christians of Antioch, how these were resolved and doctrine established by the presiding Apostles of the Church to delineate bounds and limit Gentile observance of Mosaic law and Jewish practice. The *propositio* (2:15–21) demonstrates how Mosaic teachings were fulfilled in the sacrifice of Christ and how not detailed observance of Mosaic law but rather the application of faith and love, following the example of Christ, would lead men to individual salvation through Christ's Atonement. In the *probatio* (3:1–4:31) Paul lays out evidence to show that Abraham, as father of the Hebrews, practiced a spiritual rather than a temporal religion. For Abraham as for the followers of Jesus, faith was the key to gospel progress. Finally, the *exhortatio* (5:1–6:10) offers the Apostle's encouragement to find in Jesus Christ "neither circumcision . . . nor uncircumcision; but faith which worketh by love" (Gal. 5:6).

An example of a different kind of argument, the forensic defense speech, is found in Luke's account of Paul's defense before Herod Agrippa (Acts 26). It, too, consists of five component parts, three of which repeat elements of the *encomium*. The speech begins, of course, with the *exordium* and, as usual, follows with the *narratio*. However, a *probatio* comes directly afterward, omitting the *propositio* of the *encomium*. The final two stages of the defense are a *refutatio,* or argument against charges brought, and finally a summation of arguments delivered with energy and power, known as the *peroratio.* Many of Paul's other speeches in Acts and his Epistles readily lend themselves to structural analysis in terms of the argumentation types and methods of classical rhetoric.[28]

Paul's intellectual abilities were themselves organized and arranged according to the paradigms of Greek education. This made it possible for Paul to think, act, and teach in a manner consistent with the world in which he moved. Of course, the object of Paul's teaching was to proclaim the glad tidings to the nations, or Gentile peoples. The training Paul received as a youth at Tarsus transformed him into a bona fide citizen of a world ordered around principles of Greek education and Roman law.

Roman Citizen

If his Greek education facilitated Paul's ability to carry out his mission, his Roman citizenship (a very rare commodity anywhere in the empire, outside of Italy) guaranteed his personal safety as he traveled through new towns and cities where he was unfamiliar to local authorities. It has been said that the three most powerful words in the world of the New Testament era were *civis Romanus sum*, "I am a Roman citizen." The words proclaimed an individual's right to certain treatment and privileges under the law, available from far away Britain in the west to the deserts dividing Syria and Palestine from Mesopotamia, and from the barbarian-infested forests of upper and lower Germany to the sands of the Sahara. The many lands that comprised the vast Roman domain all recognized and gave special status to the person who had obtained Roman citizenship, and accorded even higher prestige to one who had been born a Roman citizen. Luke provides information throughout Acts of Paul's use of his Roman citizen status to secure protection. Most significantly, on his last visit to Jerusalem, when the Jews of that city sought to destroy Paul, the prized Roman citizenship saved him.

> And as they bound him with thongs, Paul said unto the centurion that stood by, Is it lawful for you to scourge a man that is a Roman, and uncondemned? When the centurion heard that, he went and told the chief captain saying, Take heed what thou doest: for this man is a Roman. Then the chief captain came, and said unto him, Tell me, art thou a Roman? He said, Yea. And the chief captain answered, With a great sum obtained I this freedom. And Paul said, But I was free born. (Acts 22:25–28).

The word King James translators rendered in this passage as "freedom" is found in the original Greek as *politeia*. The word means "citizenship," not "freedom." It is puzzling why the King James translation erroneously uses the English word freedom when the term "citizenship" was available to them, despite their status as subjects to a monarch. Indeed, when Jerome translated the Latin Vulgate from the Greek text of Acts, the Latin word he chose to render *politeia* was *civitas,* the Roman word for citizenship and the word found in all Roman citizenship laws to indicate citizen status.

Citizenship was most commonly obtained by being the child of a citizen. It was an inheritable legal right under Roman law. So Paul, born a citizen, would have received his citizen status from his father. Rome was innovative in coming to view citizenship not merely as a right passed from parent to child, but as obtainable by non-citizens. In early Rome, persons from Latin towns of central Italy, by then under Roman rule, could, upon moving to Roman territory, apply for citizenship. The magistrates, or leading citizens of Italian territories ruled by Rome, could also receive Roman citizen status in recognition of their standing and without the necessity of relocating. Similar opportunities, known as Latin rights, were granted in the imperial era to a number of important cities in the provinces of Gaul and Spain. In 89 B.C. in Italy, decades before the transition from Roman Republic to Roman Empire, all persons of local citizen status in any Italian municipality were awarded full Roman citizen rights. By the time of the empire, non-citizens who completed a full term of twenty years' service in the Roman military could also receive citizenship. Finally, throughout the Empire, in eastern provinces as well as western, individuals who had performed particularly meritorious service for Rome were rewarded with citizenship. Occasionally those, as in the case of the captain of the Jerusalem detachment of units of the local Roman cohort, who paid large sums to local Roman officials also acquired citizenship. In both instances, individuals received citizenship by virtue of what was known as a viritane grant of citizenship. Viritane signifies "man by man" or citizenship given on an individual basis.[29] It could only have been on the basis of such a viritane grant that Paul's father, grandfather, or some more distant progenitor had acquired Roman citizen status.

The circumstances under which Paul's family received Roman citizenship are unknown and cannot be known with the present state of evidence. Roman legal scholar, Sherwin-White, draws attention to this problem in writing "to speculate how and when the family of Paul acquired the citizenship is a fruitless task, though lack of evidence has not deterred the ingenious."[30] Despite lack of specific information, the most likely times that proper conditions and opportunities existed for the family to receive citizenship can be surmised.

Tarsus and its residents delivered assistance on three occasions to Roman commanders who used the city as a military staging area, Cn.

Pompeius Magnus in 63 B.C., C. Julius Caesar in 47 B.C., and M. Antonius during the 30s B.C. It is possible that as these commanders resupplied and outfitted troops, Tarsians who did them significant service were rewarded with citizenship. Paul's family, if they were in fact well-to-do cloth manufacturers, certainly had the ability to supply tents, or clothing, or sails for fleets to Roman armies. At any of these times citizenship could have been bestowed as a reward through a viritane grant facilitated by these princely commanders, or any of their subordinates of senatorial rank.

Most Roman citizens followed the practice of using official Roman *tripartite nomenclature,* that is, bearing three names. This was a right limited to Roman citizens. Others using the triple name could be charged with masquerading as a citizen, a crime of dire consequence. The first name, or *praenomen,* was one of less than thirty Latin personal names, and was generally simply abbreviated in official nomenclature. For example, in the names above, Cn. signified Cnaeus, C. indicated Caius, and M. stood for Marcus. The second name, the *nomen,* was the *gentilicium,* or name of the clan or extended family to which one belonged. Julius was not Caesar's first name, but it was his family name. He belonged to the Julian clan or family. The third name, or *cognomen,* indicated a branch of the clan or family. In some ways it was a more specific family name. It was by this third name that Romans were normally identified, for example, Caesar.

As Roman citizens, Paul's family would have possessed and used a Roman name, from the time of the first family member who received citizenship. For Paul's family, however, only their *cognomen* is known. It is the common Latin *cognomen,* Paulus or Paullus. In keeping with Roman practice, Paul was called by his *cognomen*—Paulus. Many have the impression that when he converted to Christianity, he changed his name to Paul. That is simply not accurate. The name Paul was already his Roman *cognomen* and had been employed by his father, and perhaps as well by his grandfather going back to whatever progenitor first held the citizenship of Rome. Paul was a family name, not a first name. It is interesting, of course, that Paul never refers to himself as Saul. It is Luke's convention in the book of Acts to use Saul before the conversion, and Paul afterward. Nevertheless, this does not alter the fact that Paulus was a family *cognomen* long in use.

A common convention entailed the adoption by new citizens of a Roman *nomen* or *cognomen*, or sometimes both, from a Roman who may have been instrumental in their reception of citizenship. For example, C. Julius Caesar arranged for the citizenship of many. Accordingly, in Roman records and inscriptions can be found many bearing the *nomen* Julius. There were three aristocratic Roman families that used the *cognomen* Paullus. They were the Aemilii Pauli, the Sergii Pauli, and the Vettenii Pauli.[31] The first two clans were prominent during the era that Paul's father, grandfather, or more distant grandfather might be expected to have acquired citizen status. It is by no means impossible that a Roman Paulus was in Tarsus either on one of the occasions noted above, or at another time, and was instrumental in procuring citizenship for a progenitor of Paul. Regrettably, records are insufficiently detailed to place such a Paulus at Tarsus. Unless new evidence turns up, we cannot know the exact facts about how Paul's family came to be Roman citizens.

With that citizenship, however, came to the ancestors of Paul of Tarsus not merely prestige and high standing in their local community, but rights and privileges that could be exercised throughout the empire. In addition to his use of Roman tripartite nomenclature, Paul could also exercise the right to wear the toga, a privilege reserved to those of citizen status. Financial privileges included exemption from taxation, and business rights accorded to citizens allowing for the making of contracts under Roman law with concomittant standing within the Roman legal system. Citizens possessed certain political rights, some of which could be exercised in the provinces as well as at Rome. For example, a Roman citizen could be appointed to government office by provincial governors and could expect to be granted audience before provincial officials, including even the governor. If at Rome, voting rights could be exercised.[32] Perhaps the greatest advantage accorded to the Roman citizen was a higher protection of personal privilege within the legal system. All inhabitants of the empire were protected by Roman law, but the Roman citizen was guaranteed certain procedural rights under the law. Exemption from death or punishment of any kind without due process of the trial and appeal process provided a protection that Paul, for example, is known to have called into play on a number of occasions. Citizens possessed the right of judgment by peers, that is, juries of other Roman citizens, or by Roman officials, even the emperor himself.

Under the Empire all holders of Roman citizenship possessed among their citizen rights the *ius appellationis ad Caesarem*, or right of appeal to Caesar. According to the great third century jurist, Ulpian, the right of appeal was guaranteed to all Roman citizens whether residents of Italy or the provinces under the provisions of a *lex Iulia de vi publica*, enacted at the beginning of the Empire by Augustus, who thereby instructed Roman magistrates and officials that citizens should not only have the right of appeal from local judicial authority to Rome, but should also not be inflicted with death, scourging, prolonged imprisonment, or torture without full due process of law including the right of *appellatio* (Dig. 48.6.7).[33]

In addition to such rights guaranteed for citizens when under investigation or indictment by Roman officials, there were protections from the authority of non-Roman local officials, or from accusations by non-citizens. Moreover, the death of any Roman citizen was required to be investigated by Roman officials and could not be relegated to local officials.[34]

Paul had access to the rights of a Roman citizen and used them when necessary to provide protection in order that he might accomplish his work of proclaiming the gospel. He not only received protection from the local Jewish officials of Jerusalem, but exercised appeal to Roman magistrates and even the emperor. His citizen status preserved Paul on his journeys through the provinces, though occasionally overzealous non-Roman local officials beat Paul, thinking him to be only an itinerant Jew. On such occasions the subsequent revelation of Paul's citizen status brought distress to officials, fearful of retribution at the hands of Roman justice.[35] The neglect of citizen rights did happen from time to time even though "a Roman citizen in the provinces was a privileged person," and while "his citizenship could, at times, save him from non-Roman provincial justice, yet only those" known locally as "citizens" and "who also possessed wealth and prestige as well as citizenship were in the position to procure any certain legal advantages."[36] Despite such occasional failure in the observance of the protected rights of Roman citizens, that privileged status made it possible for Paul to function in places and in ways that other early witnesses of Christ could not, for they were not, as Paul was, comfortable in the worlds of the Roman, Greek, and Jew.

Endnotes

1. Joseph Fielding Smith, *Teachings,* 180.

2. For a book-length treatment of Roman citizenship issues see Sherwin-White, *The Roman Citizenship.*

3. F. F. Bruce, *Paul, Apostle of the Heart Set Free* (1977), 35.

4. Anderson, *Understanding Paul,* 21.

5. Xenophon, *Anabasis,* 1.2.23.

6. For background on Tarsus, see Bruce, *Paul,* 32–36; Jerome Murphy-O'Connor, *Paul, A Critical Life* (1996), 32–35.

7. Strabo, *Geography,* 14.5.13.

8. Bruce, *Paul,* 34–35. Also see Strabo, *Geography,* 14.5.12–13.

9. Murphy-O'Connor, *Paul,* 35.

10. Bruce, *Paul,* 41.

11. Murphy-O'Connor, *Paul,* 36–37; Bruce, *Paul,* 42–43.

12. A comparison of Paul's quotation from the *Septuagint* and other Hebrew or Aramaic Old Testament texts is elucidated in full in Welch and Hall, *Charting the New Testament,* chart 2-5.

13. See previous pages 32–33 (typescript) and Section I, Chapter 3, note 23.

14. Inscriptions at both Corinth and Philippi are primarily in Latin. Combined with the fact that both cities were resettled by Roman citizens primarily from Italy guarantees the use of Latin in both locations. However, given the widespread bilingualism of the Roman educated classes, and the residence at both sites of local people, communication in Greek would have been easily accomplished. Paul's Epistles to the Church members of both Corinth and Philippi were undeniably in Greek. Also see Jeffers, *Greco-Roman World,* 260–65, 281–84.

15. Feldman, *Jew and Gentile,* 45–83.

16. Robert Goldenberg, "Hillel," *Anchor Bible Dictionary,* 3:201.

17. Bruce Chilton, "Gamaliel," *Anchor Bible Dictionary,* 2:903–06.

18. Murphy-O'Connor, *Paul,* 56. Also see Mishnah, Sifre Deut. 351.

19. Mishnah, *Sotah,* 9:15.

20. Bruce, *Paul,* 50.

21. Ibid., 51.

22. See earlier pages 27–29 (typescript).

23. Bruce, *Paul,* 51.

24. Jaeger, *Paideia,* 3 vols., is the best modern treatment of Greek educational method and curriculum.

25. A book-length study of Paul's fascinating development of imagery is to be found in David J. Williams, *Paul's Metaphors* (1999).

26. George A. Kennedy, *New Testament Interpretation through Rhetorical Criticism* (1984), 10–11.

27. Hans-Dieter Betz, *Galatians: A Commentary on Paul's Letter to the Churches in Galatia* (1979), 14–25; Bruce J. Malina and Jerome H. Neyrey, *Portraits of Paul* (1996), 34–51, offer excellent summary analyses of rhetoric in Galatians.

28. Kennedy, *New Testament Interpretation,* 129–56.

29. An excellent summary of the history of Roman Citizenship is Sherwin-White, *The Roman Citizenship.*

30. A. N. Sherwin-White, *Roman Society and Roman Law in the New Testament* (1963), 151.

31. Murphy-O'Connor, *Paul,* 42.

32. Welch and Hall, *Charting the New Testament,* chart 15–4.

33. John F. Hall, "Appeal to Caesar," *Anchor Bible Dictionary,* 1:317.

34. Welch and Hall, *Charting the New Testament,* chart 15–4.

35. A summary and analysis of the times of Paul was brought before judges and officials is provided by Welch and Hall, *Charting the New Testament,* chart 15–6.

36. J. C. Lentz, *Luke's Portrayal of Paul* (1993), 127.

CHAPTER TWO

Missionary to the Gentiles

Paul of Tarsus was a man devoted to the faith of his fathers. He had prepared himself professionally to be an expert in Mosaic law and the doctrines of Judaism, old and new. His life was intertwined in every way with the interests of the Jewish and Pharisaic establishment. With the clear conscience of the zealot defending a system of belief with which he could not allow himself to find fault, Paul directed his energies to the persecution of Jesus' followers even unto death (see John 16:2–3). Like the prosecutors of the great Inquisition many centuries after Paul, the young Pharisee no doubt perceived himself as trying to return apostates to the faith and to protect the faithful from apostasy. Even as a young man, Paul had been given the trust of the Sanhedrin to act in its behalf against Christians. As he grew older, membership in that ruling body of the Jews increasingly beckoned and was ever more likely for so favored an agent. On a single afternoon, in the briefest of moments, Paul's world was transformed, and from the Damascus road emerged the great missionary of early Christianity. The Lord in His infinite knowledge realized that to divert one so faithful from his dedication to a now-false religion would require His own intervention. Perhaps Paul indicates as much when he alludes to having been apprehended of Jesus Christ, "not as though I had already attained, either were already perfect: but I follow after, if that I may apprehend that for which also I am apprehended of Christ Jesus" (Philip. 3:12). That brief vision of the resurrected and glorified Lord of Israel took Paul and transformed his entire being in such a way that his devotion to Jesus Christ could be measured with that of the other pillars of Christianity, the New Testament witnesses of Christ.

The Road to Damascus

Paul journeyed from Jerusalem to Damascus intending to seize and bring back to Judea Jews who had converted to Christianity and later emigrated to Damascus. Since they had departed from Judea, they did not suffer official persecution because they were no longer under the jurisdiction of the high priest or Sanhedrin. Paul's authority to undertake this task in Luke's account of the event is attributed to the high priest (Acts 9:1–2). Later, Luke seems to contradict himself by assigning Paul's commission to the Sanhedrin (Acts 22:5), though in reality it is likely that Paul acted with the sanction of both Sanhedrin and high priest. However, neither had any authority that extended outside the boundaries of Judea. Accordingly, Jews living in Damascus should have been beyond apprehension by Jewish leaders. In his 47 B.C. edict of privileges for Jews, Julius Caesar had allowed an ethnocentered authority of the high priest and Sanhedrin over the Jewish people and in that connection had accorded them the right to exercise extradition from other provinces. Extradition requests, however, should have been made through proper channels and via provincial officials, in any case—not through Paul. It is likely that Paul's job was simply to grab the offending Christians and return them to Jerusalem, without concerns for jurisdiction or the authority of Roman laws of extradition.[1]

It was with this design to seize and return Christians of Jewish background that Paul experienced the great epiphany. Luke's account in Acts provides the most complete narrative of the event, for in his own writings Paul never describes in detail what was surely the great occurrence of his life. Perhaps it was for him too sacred a matter to treat at length in the context of the Epistles. Nevertheless, Paul makes brief allusion to the appearance of the Savior in four passages declaring: that he had seen Jesus the Lord (1 Cor. 9:1), that to Paul, the least of all, the Lord appeared (1 Cor. 15:8), that he was privileged to receive the revelation of Jesus Christ Himself (Gal. 1:12), and that Christ was revealed by God to Paul (Gal. 1:16). Luke's version of the event is dramatic. A bright heavenly light shone around Paul. Paul, of course, fell to the ground, physically overcome and left blinded for a time. Those with him heard the voice, but did not behold the vision of the resurrected Lord. When he heard "Saul, Saul, why persecutest thou me?" Paul could barely answer with the faint inquiry "Who art thou, Lord?" What astonishment and perhaps immediate grief for the prior course of his actions must have seized Paul when he realized the identity of this speaker from the heavens! "I am Jesus whom thou persecutest: it is hard for thee to kick against the pricks" (Acts 9:3–5). Paul followed the Lord's direction to go to Damascus and was not only healed of his blindness at the hand of Ananias but received baptism as well (Acts 9:6–18).

The Lord's purpose was fulfilled. As He declared to Ananias, Paul was "a chosen vessel unto me, to bear my name before the Gentiles, and kings, and the children of Israel: For I will shew him how great things he must suffer for my name's sake" (Acts 9:15–16). The Lord must also have revealed such a declaration to Paul, who was aware that his conversion was accomplished in order to extend the gospel throughout the Gentile lands, and that he had been divinely called to such labor since before birth, "when . . . God, who separated me from my mother's womb, and called me his grace, To reveal his Son in me, that I might preach him among the heathen" (Gal. 1:15–16). The Apostle to the Gentiles was ready to begin his great missionary labor.

Paul's Missionary Methods and Results

Paul commenced his labor immediately after his healing and his baptism. He burned to proclaim the knowledge of the special witness which he had been granted—that Jesus is the Christ. One modern commentator characterizes the Apostle's zealous enthusiasm, saying,

> Paul found himself instantaneously compelled by what he saw and heard to acknowledge that Jesus of Nazareth, the crucified one, was alive after his passion, vindicated and exalted by God, and was now conscripting him into his service."[2] Paul's eagerness to declare the glad tidings of which he had become a partaker, through a literal divine intervention, resulted in his immediate instruction to those he had been sent to apprehend and to the Jews of Damascus, all being amazed that a chief persecutor of Christians was now a chief preacher of Christ resurrected. As Luke describes Paul's action, "straightway he preached Christ in the synagogues, that he is the Son of God" (Acts 9:20).

In his first act of teaching and testifying, Paul established a pattern of proselyting that would serve him throughout his lifetime of missionary service. Whether in Damascus, where he first began to stand as a witness of Christ, or during his journeys through Asia Minor and Greece, Paul's first stop for teaching was the synagogue. Therein could be found both Jews and what Gentile proselytes may have converted to Judaism, an audience containing some individuals who would be receptive to Paul's testimony. The subject of Paul's discourse in synagogic settings was how the law of Moses had been fulfilled with the coming of the Messiah, who introduced a higher law, a rule of faith, hope, and charity, of repentance and forgiveness through the Atonement of the Son of God. Typical of Paul's approach is the sermon he delivered in the synagogue at Antioch of Pisidia (Acts 13:16–41). Also not uncommon was the result of his teaching:

> And when the Jews were gone out of the synagogue, the Gentiles besought that these words might be preached to them the next sabbath. Now when the congregation was broken up, many of the Jews and religious proselytes followed Paul and Barnabas: who, speaking to them, persuaded them to continue in the grace of God. And the next sabbath day came almost the whole city together to hear the word of God. But when the Jews saw the multitudes, they were filled with envy, and spake against those things which were spoken by Paul, contradicting and blaspheming. Then Paul and Barnabas waxed bold, and said, It was necessary that the word of God should first have been spoken to you: but seeing ye put it from you, and judge yourselves unworthy of everlasting life, lo, we turn to the Gentiles. . . . But the Jews stirred up the devout and honourable women, and the chief men of the city, and raised persecution against Paul and Barnabas, and expelled them out of their coasts (Acts 13:42–46, 50).

The Jews of Antioch in Pisidia reacted out of envy and anger that some of their own number, their Gentile proselytes and other Gentiles, had been persuaded by Paul's teaching, a doctrine that proclaimed Christ and accused the rabbinical Judaism of having fallen away from the truths of the gospel taught by the patriarchs and Moses. City officials were involved and, after the local Jewish leaders exercised their political influence, Paul and his companions were compelled to depart. But many of the city had already been brought to a knowledge of the truthfulness of the glad tidings and had become followers of Jesus.

In Lyaconia, where Paul traveled to from Pisidia, he and Barnabas performed miraculous healings at Lystra that clearly attracted the attention of the local populace, who resorted to their knowledge of Greek mythology to explain the astounding occurrences they had witnessed. They thought Paul and Barnabas to be Zeus and Hermes, Greek gods famed in mythological lore for visiting cities in the guise of travelers and rewarding the hospitable, but taking retribution on the inhospitable.[3] Jews from Antioch in Pisidia had followed Paul's company to stir up against them the residents of whatever city they journeyed to. Despite the healings they had performed, the local inhabitants, enraged by the Jews, stoned Paul and carried him out of the city, "supposing he had been dead" (Acts 14:19).

The pattern repeated itself again and again. Paul entered a city and taught in the synagogue, attracting converts and followers (many from the local Jewish congregation), thereby enraging local Jewish leaders, who used all their influence with city officials or the local townspeople to try to kill, harm, or convict Paul of whatever crime, real or imagined, they could allege against him. No fewer than eighteen times of which we actually possess scriptural record, Paul was brought before judges or other town officials and accused of a variety of wrongdoing, invariably by the rabbis and elders of the Jewish synagogue.[4]

Not only was Paul's missionary effort subjected to regular harassment by Jews, but the Christian congregations of Paul's converts, both Jew and Gentile, were also badgered by certain Jewish Christians, many of whom traveled from Jerusalem to the predominantly Gentile branches of the Church in Asia Minor, without authorization, to initiate their own private doctrinal campaigns. The efforts of this vociferous minority, who apparently refused to follow the decisions and directives of the presiding Apostles, occasioned great harm in the early Christian community.[5]

Paul's missionary efforts were directed to all segments of the population: not merely Jew and Gentile, but rich and poor, free and slave. Paul also carried the gospel message to the most prominent members of society, including local officials—even provincial governors who typically belonged to the Roman aristocracy, such as Sergius Paulus (Acts 13:6–12) in Cyprus, or Gallio in Corinth (Acts 18:1–18).[6]

Paul's techniques and methods were employed repeatedly. His Jewish rabbinical background facilitated his teaching of members of synagogues. Paul's superb training in Greek rhetoric made possible persuasive arguments to the Hellenistic Gentile populations he encountered. Paul used different aspects of the doctrine of Christ, depending upon his audience. To convert Jews, Paul presented Jesus as the Christ, the Anointed One, the long-awaited Messiah. To convert Gentiles, Jesus Christ was proclaimed as Son of God and Savior. Both concepts resonated with Greek populations accustomed to *soter* (savior) cults of Hellenistic kings and rulers once common in the empires of Alexander and his successors. They could readily understand the need to put one's trust in the true Savior and develop continually increasing faith in Christ. Of all the aspects of Paul's teaching, including the roaring of his lionlike voice in testimony of Jesus' divinity and Atonement, perhaps most important to the success of the work the Lord had commissioned to Paul was the Spirit of God that accompanied the Apostle to the Gentiles. Paul understood the workings of the Spirit and the gifts of the Spirit. His explanation of such spiritual aspects of the gospel leaves no doubt that Paul himself lived close to the Spirit. The presence of the Spirit is indispensable for bringing people to a knowledge of Jesus Christ. "No man can say that Jesus is the Lord, but by the Holy Ghost" (1 Cor. 12:3).

Paul realized that the Church he was helping to establish was the Church of Jesus Christ, in reality as well as name. Paul, whose conversion had come directly at the Savior's intervention, understood that the Lord Jesus Christ personally directed the Church and its work. Paul followed what directions he was given through the Spirit. For example, it was the Holy Ghost that forbade Paul in his second missionary journey to continue to preach in Asia. Soon Paul was directed by a vision to carry the gospel to Europe, journeying to the Roman province of Macedonia in northern Greece and later to the province of Achaea in central and southern Greece. In following the directions of the Spirit, Paul was able to accomplish the Lord's work when and how the Savior wished.

Early Missionary Efforts

Paul informs us that immediately after his conversion and brief stay at Damascus, he departed into Arabia (Gal. 1:17). The Roman province of Arabia Petrea lay to the east of southern Syria and Judea and to the south of the latter, in Nabataean territory "from the Hauran down through Moab and Edom and expanded on both sides of the Gulf of Aqaba."[7] Many speculate that Paul's sojourn in this desert region was to allow him time for contemplation to adjust to his changed faith. The fact that the Nabataean authorities sought to arrest Paul (2 Cor. 11:32–33) suggests otherwise. As one modern biographer of Paul concludes, "the only explanation is that Paul was trying to make converts. This first act subsequent to his conversion confirms his understanding of his conversion as a commission to preach the gospel among pagans."[8] Such an explanation seems much in keeping with the Paul who had begun to preach at Damascus as soon as his sight was restored to him. With the unshakable faith of one privileged to have beheld the glorified Christ, Paul needed no contemplative retreat. He was already about the Master's work.

Fleeing from Arabia, Paul returned to Damascus, where he dwelt for three years (Gal. 1:17–18), teaching and testifying of the Christ. At length, Paul departed Damascus to go to Peter in Jerusalem on which occasion he met with one other Apostle, James the brother of the Lord (Gal. 1:18–19). As a result of his meetings with Peter, Paul journeyed through "the regions of Syria and Cilicia" (Gal. 1:21) during the years from A.D. 37–42.[9] No information is available to identify specific places Paul may have visited. It is likely that he went to Antioch, where there was a burgeoning Christian community, and to his own native city of Tarsus. Whether Paul taught the gospel to his own family is entirely unknown. Sometimes commentators construe the remark Paul made to the Philippians that "I count all things but loss for the excellency of the knowledge of Christ Jesus my Lord: for whom I have suffered the loss of all things" (Philip. 3:8), as indication of Paul's disinheritance by a father who is known to have followed the Pharisees, to whom he sent Paul for training. That Paul had to support himself as a tentmaker (1 Thess. 2:9; 2 Thess, 3:7–9; 1 Cor. 4:12), manual labor which he looked down upon (2 Cor. 6:5; 11:7, 23, 27), is also interpreted as evidence that Paul no longer had access to his family's wealth.[10] Other explanations, such as a temporary cash-flow problem or a delay in receiving funds from Tarsus, could just as readily explain Paul's need to practice the trade of those who worked for his family. For these reasons, not even valid speculation can be made regarding the later religious attitudes of Paul's family.

By the year 44, Paul was laboring among the Christians of Antioch, where many Greek converts had fled from persecution at Jerusalem and had initiated extremely successful proselyting among the Greek and Hellenistic peoples of Antioch. Barnabas, sent as representative of the Apostles at Jerusalem to supervise the Church activity at Antioch, perhaps had

> Begun to feel the need of a colleague to share the responsibility of super-vising the life and activity of "the Antiochene church," and his mind turned to Paul. He knew of Paul's vocation to the evangelizing of Gentiles, and perhaps heard reports from time to time of what Paul had been doing in this regard in Cilicia, all that he knew of Paul convinced him that there was no man more suitable to join him in his work at Antioch, so he journeyed to Tarsus to find him, and persuaded him to return to Antioch with him."[11]

Barnabas and Paul worked well together at Antioch and undertook missionary efforts, journeying for several years both through Cyprus, where Barnabas was from, and also through southwestern and south central Asia Minor, traversing regions of Cilicia, Pamphylia, Pisidia, and Lyaconia (Acts 13–14). By the end of A.D. 47, they had resumed their work at Antioch, but were confronted by problems that had arisen in their absence.[12] Judaizers from Jerusalem had demanded the circumci-sion and full observance of Mosaic law on the part of Gentile converts to Christianity, which caused a serious division between Jewish Christians in Antioch and Greek and Hellenistic converts. The resolution of these problems ultimately required an apostolic council and conference of the Church at Jerusalem in 49. The events and actions of the Jerusalem Council are examined in detail in the first chapter of the present work.

Paul's Apostolic Calling

Apart from their resolution of the issue of Gentile observance of Jewish law and custom, another event of great consequence seems to have occurred during the meeting of the Apostles preliminary to the convening of the conference of Church members. Paul alluded to it in extremely self-effacing language, writing that when Peter, John, and James "perceived the grace that was given unto me, they gave to me and Barnabas the right hands of fellowship" (Gal. 2:9). In other words, when Peter, the presiding Apostle, along with his counselor John and with James, the brother of the Lord, also by that time an Apostle, was given to understand the grace or favor of the Lord that rested upon Paul, and realized the high calling the Lord wished Paul to fill, these three Apostles, and perhaps others of the Apostles as well, extended to Paul and Barnabas "the right hands of fellowship."

In the original Greek of the Epistle to the Galatians, the word King James's translators rendered as "fellowship" is *koinonia*. It has the meaning of being a fellow participant in an association; a partner, comrade, or companion; one belonging to a select group.[13] It would seem that giving the right hand of fellowship would indicate admitting Paul and Barnabas as companions in a particular group. Since both were known to the presiding Brethren and had met them before, it seems unlikely that Peter welcomed Paul and Barnabas into the Christian fellowship for which Paul had been a leading missionary for more than a decade, and Barnabas a well-known figure even longer.

What group that included Peter, John, and James could Paul and Barnabas have been welcomed into? The answer is patently clear. After these chief Brethren of Christ's Church had worked in tandem to learn and put into effect the Lord's plan for Gentile freedom from Jewish observances, Paul and Barnabas were extended new callings. Henceforth, they would act as special witnesses of the Savior, possessing apostolic keys of authority. It seems likely despite Paul's modest recounting that this was the occasion when Paul and Barnabas were called to the Quorum of the Twelve Apostles.

Since the Greek word *apostolos* means in its most basic sense simply "one who is sent forth," many scholars of early Christianity interpret Paul's use of the term invariably to signify men, and for that matter, women, who are sent forth as missionaries or in some other capacity to accomplish the Lord's work.[14] Protestant scholars in particular prefer this interpretation because it can readily be linked to their doctrine of evocation. According to that teaching, individuals receive in their hearts a calling to serve God and subsequently act upon it on their own, without any additional authorization. One commentator suggests that in such a manner Paul assumed quite on his own the "apostolic" role of missionary, sending himself forth because "in his own consciousness it was the personal call of the risen Christ that made him an Apostle."[15] Certainly there are times when the word *apostle* is used in early Christian writings in a non-technical sense and may, indeed, simply indicate a missionary. The word is, however, also used in the technical way Christ employed it to indicate the Twelve, men called by authority to a particular priesthood office and ordained to the same by the imposition of hands. A native Greek speaker, Paul certainly knew the most basic meaning of the word, but as one who associated with certain of the original Twelve Apostles, clearly he would have understood how the term was employed in the Church to refer to the chief priesthood office that possessed the keys of authority. No reason mandates that Paul did not employ the term in the sense of priesthood office when he used it in reference to himself.

When Paul wrote that on an extended visit to Jerusalem he saw Peter, but none of the other Apostles save James, the brother of the Lord (Gal. 1:19), he used the term in its technical sense. Peter was one of the Twelve, as no doubt was James, who probably had replaced the martyred James, son of Zebedee, just as Matthias had earlier replaced Judas among the Twelve (Acts 1:22–26). Paul referred to himself as an Apostle in Galatians (1:1) and 1 Corinthians (9:1–2). Most significantly, in his Epistle to Timothy, Paul recounted how he was "ordained" an Apostle (1 Tim. 2:7). To be ordained implies the laying on of hands by someone in authority to ordain, very likely the Church official who extended the calling to the office for which the ordination was performed. In this instance, Peter, the presiding Apostle and very person in the position of authority to call other Apostles, issued the call for Paul to be ordained an Apostle when, as Paul related, Peter extended to him *koinonia* (Gal. 2:9).

Luke, who without exception used the term Apostle throughout his Gospel and Acts to refer strictly to those who belonged to the Twelve Apostles, identified as Apostles both Paul and Barnabas (Acts 14:14), the very two to whom Peter extended *koinonia* (Gal. 2:9). We may surmise that by A.D. 49 two other vacancies had occurred among the Twelve, and that they were filled by Paul and Barnabas.

Paul's Later Missionary Journeys

As one of the Twelve Apostles, Paul performed great missionary labors throughout Asia Minor and Greece. He returned to Judea with monies to assist the Jerusalem Saints, only to meet arrest by the Jews. After exercising his right of appeal to Roman judicial authority not only in the province but also at Rome, Paul journeyed finally to Italy to resolve the charges against him. After securing his freedom, the Apostle seems to have traveled through areas of western provinces, particularly in Spain, in order to proclaim the glad tidings of faith in Jesus Christ.

From A.D. 49 through 52, Paul undertook his second great missionary journey. Silas was his principal companion in teaching the gospel. Paul's route was overland. Thus he passed through Syria and Cilicia in transit, strengthening the existing Christian communities of those areas (Acts 16:6). Paul brought his message to areas of Lyaconia, Phrygia, Galatia, and Mysia before receiving a vision directing him to carry the gospel to the Roman province of Macedonia, thereby introducing to Europe the word of Christ (Acts 16:9–12). A quick crossing of the northern Aegean Sea brought Paul's company to Neapolis, the port of Macedon's provincial capital of Philippi.[16]

Paul's labor at Philippi provides one of the great success stories of the Apostle's ministry. Philippi was a Roman citizen colony in addition to being a provincial capital. Many of its residents were, therefore, Roman and thus Latin speakers. Today one can go visit the ruins of Philippi and see that the epigraphic monuments of the city are largely in Latin. No doubt some Greek speakers also resided there, but it is likely that much of Paul's teaching at Philippi was in Latin, rather than Greek. Many were baptized and wholeheartedly embraced the glad tidings of Christ. Later, writing to the Philippians, Paul mentions the bishops and deacons at Philippi (Philip. 1:1), indicating multiple congregations and, by implication, substantial numbers of Church members.

The branch of the Church established at Philippi was especially faithful and righteous. Professor Anderson notes that "the old Roman virtues were loyalty and reliability. These qualities certainly summarize the remarkable faithfulness of the Philippian Christians."[17] Paul declared that the Philippian Saints had received the favor of the Lord, because "from the very first day until now" they had abounded in the love of Christ one to another, and so were "filled with the fruits of righteousness" (Philip.

1:5,11). In part, the special spirit at Philippi may have initially derived from Paul's very first contacts in the city, a group of especially devout women whom he encountered at prayer. They seem to have been led by one of the great and dynamic women of early Christianity, Lydia, who from that time forward devoted herself to the work of the Lord, giving much of her considerable personal wealth to further the cause of Christ and support the missionary effort (Acts 16:12–15).[18] Clearly Lydia, the first European convert to the Church of Jesus Christ, was a great pillar of the Church at Philippi. Other Philippian members of the Church followed Lydia's example in their financial backing of the Lord's work, sending support to the beloved Apostle who had brought them to their knowledge of Christ (Philip 4:10–12, 16–18).

> They maintained a warm affection for their apostle, and showed it by sending him personal gifts from time to time. Paul was not too happy about accepting such gifts from his converts, but the generosity of his Philippian friends was so unanimous and spontaneous that he could do no other than accept their gifts in the spirit in which they were given and view them as an outward expression of their faith and love, and thus not only a donation to himself but also an acceptable offering to God.[19]

So great was Paul's love for the faithful branches of the Church at Philippi that he referred to the Philippians by unprecedented language. He called them "my brethren dearly beloved and longed for, my joy and crown" (Philip. 4:1), "fellowlabourers whose names are in the book of life" (Philip. 4:3). That he addresses as residing with the Saints at Philippi his "true yokefellow" (Philip. 4:3), "who Clement of Alexandria thought was Paul's wife, temporarily staying in a trusted branch of the Church," declares beyond doubt his trust in the faithfulness of Philippi.[20] It is not beyond speculation, however, that Paul's true yokefellow was none other than Lydia, who had become Paul's wife. The absence of Lydia's name from the faithful women and other members of the Church saluted by Paul in his Epistle to the Philippians, suggests that she may be the true yoke-fellow who is greeted.[21]

After departing Philippi, Paul journeyed through Macedonia, establishing the Church among the Greeks: at Thessalonica, where, in spite of much opposition from a sizeable local Jewish community, a great multitude of Greeks converted (Acts 17:1–9); at Berea, where much initial success was blunted by Jews from Thessalonica who followed Paul to undo his efforts (Acts 17:10–14). Next, Paul traveled to Athens for memorable disputation but had little known success in establishing the Church among a people where philosophic skepticism held sway (Acts 17:15–18:1).

Corinth was a place where Paul's missionary efforts were of extended duration, lasting from eighteen months to two years. The Roman capital of the province of Achaea, Corinth was a great center of trade, situated on the narrow isthmus between the Corinthian Gulf leading to the Adriatic Sea, and the Saronic Gulf leading to the Aegean. The great Greek city of Corinth had been destroyed in 146 B.C. Corinth was refounded by Julius Caesar as a Roman citizen colony in 44 B.C., and construction of a ship canal across the isthmus was begun, a project by no means beyond the abilities of Roman engineering. Thus, like Philippi, Roman citizens lived in Corinth and Latin was used, though to judge from the presence of Greek inscriptions as well, many more Greeks may be thought to have resided at Corinth, and the city possessed a significantly more Greek orientation than Philippi.[22] Corinth, as one of the greatest port cities of the Mediterranean world, was a place where cultures mixed, foreigners visited, and sailors frequented. Accordingly, its level of devotion to a variety of cults and a vast spectrum of sensual pleasures made it a place where living the gospel was perhaps somewhat more difficult. Such trials of faith are reflected in Paul's two Epistles to the members of the Church at Corinth, for whom "living in the world" was especially problematic and who, therefore, required more constant direction and encouragement from the Apostle. Indeed, one commentator has described Corinth as "a center of wickedness," likening it to "today's big cities in offering the best and the worst. . . . Yet the existence of bad society does not make all society bad. The Lord stood before Paul in vision and commanded him to stay and gather his people out of this worldly center."[23]

As was invariably the result of Paul's successful proselyting, local Jews attempted to create disorder and problems for which they could blame Paul before the local presiding magistrate. This time their strategy failed. F. F. Bruce explains the situation well.

In July of A.D. 51 (less probably, twelve months later), Lucius Junius
Gallio came to Corinth to take up his appointment as proconsul of
Achaia. Gallio (originally named Marcus Annaeus Novatus) belonged to
a well-known Roman family of Spanish origin: he was a son of Marcus
Annaeus Seneca, a distinguished professor of rhetoric, and a younger
brother of Lucius Annaeus Seneca, Stoic philosopher and at this time
tutor to the future Emperor Nero. His change of family name is due to
his having been adopted as heir by his father's friend Lucius Junius
Gallio. Not long after Gallio's arrival in Corinth, some members of the
local Jewish community charged Paul before him with propagating an
illegal religion. It is not said if the charge hinted at political implications
in Paul's preaching; perhaps he was simply accused of introducing a cult
of which Roman law took no cognizance. In any case, Gallio quickly
decided that there was nothing in this charge which called for action on
his part. The accused man was as self-evidently Jewish as his persecutors
were: this was a quarrel over the interpretation of disputed points in
Jewish law and theology. Crime and threats to the imperial peace fell
within his jurisdiction, but he had no mind to arbitrate in a Jewish religious controversy. Accordingly, without waiting to hear the defence
which Paul had prepared, he bade them begone from his tribunal. . . .
The Corinthian bystanders, pleased at seeing a snub administered to the
leaders of the Jewish community, seized the opportunity to assault the
ruler of the synagogue.[24]

Two important ramifications developed out of this incident. First,
through Paul's acquaintance and later apparently cordial relationship
with Gallio, arose the possibility of correspondence with Gallio's brother,
arguably the most important Roman intellectual of the day, L. Annaeus
Seneca. Fourteen short epistles exist which claim to be the letters written
between Paul and Seneca. The correspondence treats Christian doctrine,
offers mutual encouragement for ethical modes of living, and raises the
possibility of Seneca arranging for an audience with members of the
imperial family for Paul to explain his abandonment of Judaism to
become a follower of Christ. Although scholars date the composition of
the letters to the third century, it is not impossible that there was an
actual first-century correspondence between Paul and Seneca of which
the surviving letters may or may not be representative.[25]

Secondly, in ruling that the dispute between Paul and the Jewish leaders at Corinth was a religious dispute internal to Judaism, Gallio established a legal precedent on the grounds of which Christianity could have thereafter been legally taught. Bruce supports such an interpretation as follows.

> Gallio's refusal to take up the charge against Paul may have constituted an important negative precedent. Certainly, if he had taken up the charge and found Paul guilty of the alleged offence, such an adverse ruling by an influential governor would have been followed as a precedent by magistrates elsewhere in the Roman Empire, and Paul's apostolic work would have been seriously handicapped. Gallio's was no merely local and municipal authority, like that of the Philippian praetors or the Thessalonian politarchs. As it was, his inaction in the matter was tantamount to a ruling that what Paul was preaching was a form of Judaism, an association sanctioned by Roman law. The time was fast approaching, thanks mainly to Paul's own activity as apostle to the Gentiles, when it would no longer be possible for any Roman magistrate to regard Christianity as a form of Judaism; but for the present Paul was able to prosecute his ministry in Corinth and elsewhere without molestation from Caesar's representatives.[26]

After remaining up to two years at Corinth, Paul took ship for the East, ultimately arriving at Antioch, where he remained for a time (Acts 18:22–23). After this respite Paul returned to his labors in Asia Minor. In accordance with his custom when traveling westward, to avoid westerly winds adverse to shipping from Syria to Asia Minor, Paul journeyed overland through Galatia and Phrygia. The Apostle's destination was the great metropolis of Ephesus, where Paul would remain to build the Church there and in surrounding areas for the three years of 54, 55, and 56. At that time, Ephesus was the fourth largest city of the empire (behind Alexandria, Antioch, and Rome), a principle center of trade and commerce,[27] and a city made famous by its even then very ancient cultic center for the worship of the old Anatolian mother goddess, called by the Greeks Artemis and somewhat erroneously syncretized with the Roman Diana.

Paul's tremendous success in making many converts at Ephesus became a cause of concern for devotees of Artemis, particularly the guild of silvermakers who exploited the lucrative enterprise of idol-making and marketing to pilgrims and tourists who came to Ephesus to behold the great temple of Artemis, one of the seven wonders of the ancient world.[28] Paul's miracles of healing took immeasurable toll on the worship of Artemis and turned many to faith in Christ, so that they destroyed their idols and burned their books of magical arts, real-izing them to be empty and of no legitimate value (Acts 19:11–19), "so mightily grew the word of God and prevailed" (Acts 19:20). Finally, by threatening economic ruin, the silvermakers incited the populace of Ephesus to rioting against Paul and other Christians, claiming "that not alone at Ephesus, but almost throughout all Asia, this Paul hath persuaded and turned away much people, saying that they be no gods, which are made with hands" (Acts 19:26).

Paul's friends saved him from the murderous mob and helped him depart from Ephesus and travel to Philippi by sea (Acts 20:6). The length of time Paul remained at Philippi is not known but may have been of considerable duration. In a sense, Philippi perhaps more than any other place had become home for Paul. With only a slight Jewish population, most of whom had probably converted to Christianity anyway, and with the protection of Roman officials in a city of Roman citizens, Philippi was a safe haven for Paul. He was much loved by the branches of the Church at Philippi and if his wife was to be found there, whether Lydia or someone else left for safety's sake at Philippi, surely Paul would have returned for rest and renewal to this place of protection and love.

Finally Paul departed for Jerusalem, sailing along the way to the ports of Asia Minor, visiting and strengthening the Saints at Troas, Assos, Mitylene, Chios, and Samos. Not surprisingly, Ephesus was bypassed, though Paul met church leaders from Ephesus at Miletus where he disembarked and remained for some time (Acts 20:15–38). Paul may well have formulated by this time a plan to go to Rome and Spain for a Latin-speaking mission of spreading the gospel message. Were this the case, the meetings he had arranged with Church leaders from throughout Asia Minor no doubt had the appearance of a "wrapping up" of the Apostle's affairs in that region where he had labored for so many years.

To contemplate the success Paul experienced in proclaiming the glad tidings that Jesus was the Christ, the Son of God, the Savior, almost transcends credibility. What unparalleled courage this Lion of God displayed again and again! Can one really grasp what it must have been like to enter a strange city, call sufficient attention to oneself to bring together large segments of the population, and raise a voice of witness and testimony, all the while knowing that local Jewish leaders would soon begin to attack or falsely accuse when their congregants began to accept Jesus as the Messiah? Paul was also unsure that even the prized Roman citizenship would protect him from summary judgment by local magistrates who themselves might not have been Roman nor even have possessed Roman citizen status. All this and much more by way of adversity confronted Paul on each occasion that he entered a new place to which he was but a stranger. But the great missionary Apostle never displayed a moment's hesitation. His witness of the Master he had come to love so much brought thousands and tens of thousands directly, and so many more indirectly, into the fold of the Shepherd. Paul's effort was indefatigable, his courage dauntless, for he knew and expressed to his much loved Philippian Saints "to live is Christ" (Philip. 1:21).

Endnotes

1. Bruce, *Paul,* 72.

2. Ibid., 75.

3. King James translators employed the names of similar, but by no means identical Roman gods, Jupiter (Jove) and Mercury. The original Greek text used Zeus and Hermes for whom the mythological situation was more apt.

4. Welch and Hall, *Charting the New Testament,* chart 15-4.

5. Murphy-O'Connor, *Paul,* 194–98.

6. In view of the Roman senatorial and imperial policy of sending members of particular families to administer particular areas of the empire, it is difficult to resist the speculation that the presence of a Sergius Paulus but a short distance from Tarsus connects the Sergii Pauli at the very least, to Paul's part of the world and raises the possibility that it was an ancestor of this governor who was instrumental in procuring citizenship for the family of Paul, which then adopted the nomenclature of the aristocratic Sergii Pauli. Were this supposition demonstrable, Paul's family name would have been Sergius Paulus.

7. Murphy-O'Connor, *Paul,* 81.

8. Ibid., 82.

9. Welch and Hall, *Charting the New Testament,* chart 15-3.

10. Murphy-O'Connor, *Paul,* 84–86, discusses in detail Paul's aversion to manual labor, typical of the man of wealth and education.

11. Bruce, *Paul,* 133.

12. Welch and Hall, *Charting the New Testament,* chart 15-3.

13. Kittel, *Theological Dictionary of the New Testament,* 3:797–809.

14. Ibid., 1:407–13.

15. Bruce, *Paul,* 145.

16. For a brief outline of the locations visited by Paul and the chronology of his ministry see Welch and Hall, *Charting the New Testament,* charts 15-2 and 15-3.

17. Anderson, *Understanding Paul,* 291.

18. Witherington points out that "Lydia, a devout Jew from Thyatira . . . was a worshipper of the one true God, i.e., she was a practicing Jew. This may have been a lifelong commitment since there was a colony of Jews in Thyatira (Josephus, *Ant.,* 12.119). That she was meeting beside a stream on the Sabbath for prayer suggests that there were not enough Jewish men in Philippi to make up a quorum and establish a proper synagogue." Ben Witherington, "Lydia," *Anchor Bible Dictionary,* 4:422–23.

19. Bruce, *Paul,* 222.

20. Anderson, *Understanding Paul,* 292.

21. Paul would by Jewish custom have been married as a young man to have been able to function in a rabbinical capacity. Whether his wife followed him into Christianity, whether she remained a devout Jew, divorcing Paul as one who had left the Jewish faith, whether she had passed away in the fifteen years between Paul's conversion and his work at Philippi, or whether she was the "true yokefellow" temporarily residing at Philippi, have all been variously speculated. Absolutely no evidence exists to lend credence to any of such speculations.

22. For background on Roman Corinth see J. Murphy O'Connor, "Corinth," *Anchor Bible Dictionary,* 1:1134–39; and Jeffers, *Greco-Roman World,* 262–65.

23. Anderson, *Understanding Paul,* 93.

24. F. F. Bruce, *Paul,* 253–54.

25. D. A. Thomason, "Epistles of Paul and Seneca," *Anchor Bible Dictionary,* 5:201.

26. F. F. Bruce, *Paul,* 254–55.

27. Welch and Hall, *Charting the New Testament,* chart 6-2.

28. Bean, *Aegean Turkey,* 160–79; also see Murphy-O'Connor, *Paul,* 166–73.

CHAPTER THREE

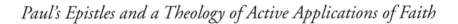

Paul's Epistles and a Theology of Active Applications of Faith

The letters Paul addressed to branches of the Church located in individual cities were not only designed to provide counsel for specific difficulties that confronted these places, but taken as a whole offer a theological framework of early Christianity that endures to the modern era. Moreover, it is by no means impossible that, although Paul never endeavored to systematize a theology of any kind, the Apostle may have been aware that his writings would not only provide guidance in respect to the problems of his own era, but would also orient and encourage Christians of later periods.

> In the thirteenth article of faith, Joseph Smith declared, "Indeed we may say we follow the admonition of Paul." The writings of Paul were deeply meaningful to and fully embraced by the Prophet Joseph Smith. . . . The essence of each of the Articles of Faith can be found, often verbatim, in the writings of Paul. . . . Paul admonished the people in Ephesus to be united in "one Lord, one faith, one baptism, one God and Father of all" (Eph 4:5–6). The congruence between the teachings of Joseph Smith and Paul shows them to be of one mind and one will as apostles of Jesus Christ.[1]

Paul's Epistles comprise a substantial part of the New Testament. In the present context neither scope nor space allows for analysis of each Epistle. Many comprehensive volumes have been written to treat such matters for each and every one of Paul's letters.[2] When viewed as a composite corpus of thought, Paul's Epistles seem to emphasize repeatedly several crucial themes for the practicing Christian. First, belief in the Lord Jesus Christ serves as the sure foundation for all. Second, the believer in Christ must actively exercise faith to obtain the gifts and inspiration of the Spirit and, in time, to develop charity or the true love of Christ. Third, those possessed of Christ's love will become increasingly Christlike and ultimately partake of the fulness of the Father.

Paul's Spiral: A Functional Epistemology of Personal Progression

In the third chapter of his Epistle to the Ephesians, the Apostle Paul reveals "the mystery, which from the beginning of the world hath been hid in God, who created all things by Jesus Christ" (Eph. 3:9). As he offers up his eloquent petition to Heavenly Father that followers of Christ may truly come to experience "the love of Christ, which passeth knowledge" (Eph. 3:19), Paul provides certain key information about how we can learn to act in a way that will enable us to receive the "fulness of God." For this reason, Paul's method is epistemological in regards to proper functioning to ensure personal progression.

First we learn that the method is, not surprisingly, Christ centered.

> And to make all men see what is the fellowship of the mystery, which from the beginning of the world hath been hid in God, who created all things by Jesus Christ: To the intent that now unto the principalities and powers in heavenly places might be known by the church the manifold wisdom of God, According to the eternal purpose which he purposed in Christ Jesus our Lord: In whom we have boldness and access with confidence by the faith of him (Eph. 3:9–12).

Through Christ each and every person can attain his highest potential.

The mechanism by which the powers of heaven, centered in Christ, can be accessed with confidence is faith. The active application of faith, both in specific instances and also in the living of life in general, lifts one from knowing about Christ, or knowing Christ in an intellectual way, or even believing in Christ, to an elevated plane of knowing Christ spiritually. Faith is the means, when proactively applied, to ascend in levels of spiritual awareness so that the Savior, and through Him, His Father, can be understood more fully. Paul makes allusion to this process as he offers up in behalf of the Saints, his prayer of love.

For this cause I bow my knees unto the Father of our Lord Jesus Christ, Of whom the whole family in heaven and earth is named, That he would grant you, according to the riches of his glory, to be strengthened with might by his Spirit in the inner man; That Christ may dwell in your hearts by faith (Eph. 3:14–17).

As Paul suggests, when Christ dwells in a person's heart, there develops in that person an awareness of the love of Christ, both the love Christ proffers us and the love we feel toward the Savior and our Heavenly Father. To be rooted and grounded in the love of Christ passes knowledge, provides true comprehension of all things, and ultimately leads to the fulness of God. Through possessing the love of Christ, an individual's highest potential is attained and his personal progression is accomplished, for all will be his, even the fulness of God. "That ye, being rooted and grounded in love, May be able to comprehend with all saints what is the breadth, and length, and depth, and height; And to know the love of Christ, which passeth knowledge, that ye might be filled with all the fulness of God" (Eph. 3:17–19).

In summary, this process of progression that Paul relates begins with belief in the Lord Jesus Christ as Son of God and Savior. Through the active application of faith, the Spirit in the inner man will make it possible for Christ to dwell in the heart. In this manner, Christ is understandable through the Spirit. Thus the individual comes to know Christ on a higher spiritual plane. The result of knowing Christ spiritually is to be possessed of the true love of Christ. As the love of Christ fills each person, the person follows Christ—the great exemplar—in almost automatic fashion. Transformed by the love of Christ, the person becomes increasingly Christlike.

The process is almost circular, one progression leading to another. In this way, disciples of Christ continually progress from one level of faith, knowledge, and love to another. The process is always upward, ever higher, grace for grace, as spiritual growth occurs. Accordingly, it is better referred to as a spiral, a spiral of continued spiritual growth and personal progression, centered in Christ and accelerated by the motivating catalysts of faith and love. We may, perhaps, refer to this outline for progressing as *Paul's Spiral*. From it will develop "the new man, which is renewed in knowledge after the image of him that created him" (Col. 3:10), to whom "is the righteousness of God revealed from faith to faith" (Rom. 1:17).

Christ-centered Faith

Paul's pointed and didactic metaphor that the follower of Christ is "become dead to the law by the body of Christ" (Rom. 7:4) sets forth without ambiguity the proposition that the law of Moses can no longer provide salvation, but that Christ's Atonement has provided the means of man's fulfillment in exaltation. After Christ "by the deeds of the law there shall no flesh be justified in his sight . . . not the righteousness of God without the law is manifested, . . . even the righteousness of God which is by faith of Jesus Christ unto all and upon all them that believe" (Rom. 3:20–22). It is by faith in Jesus Christ, and the proactive application of that faith to become spiritually alive in Christ, that, as outlined in Paul's Spiral, righteous men can partake of the fulness of the Father.

Beset by harassing Judaizers who sought to turn Paul's converts throughout Galatia, especially Jew but also Gentile, to the observance of Mosaic law, the Saints of Galatia were hard pressed to maintain their faith in Jesus Christ as the principal instrument of their salvation. Paul attempts to support their faith by explaining:

> A man is not justified by the works of the law, but by the faith of Jesus Christ, even we have believed in Jesus Christ, that we might be justified by the faith of Christ, and not by the works of the law: for by the works of the law shall no flesh be justified. . . . For I through the law am dead to the law, that I might live unto God. I am crucified with Christ: nevertheless I live; yet not I, but Christ liveth in me: and the life which I now live in the flesh I live by the faith of the Son of God, who loved me, and gave himself for me. I do not frustrate the grace of God: for if righteousness come by the law, then Christ is dead in vain" (Gal. 2:16, 19–21).

Regrettably, the Judaizers failed to understand the central role of Jesus Christ in the plan of salvation. Their centuries-long ingrained devotion to Mosaic law and practice apparently prevented many Jewish Christians from differentiating between traditional, and often erroneous, Jewish concepts of the Messiah, and the eternal and cosmic scope of the mission of Jesus Christ. Paul sought to explain that for a Christian who does not grasp the salvatory aspect of the true Messiah, "Christ is dead in vain." Moreover, it is noteworthy that Paul linked to the Father's plan of salvation the principles of faith and love, prefiguring in his remark to the Galatians the aforementioned teaching he would later communicate to the Ephesians.[3]

Paul was clear that "the gift of God is eternal life through Jesus Christ our Lord" (Rom. 6:23). Belief in Christ as Redeemer is prerequisite to the necessary exercise of faith that will lead to salvation, but it must be a truly Christ-centered faith. Paul endeavored to assist the Saints at Philippi to understand that basic doctrinal concept of the gospel when he wrote:

> I count all things but loss for the excellency of the knowledge of Christ Jesus my Lord: for whom I have suffered the loss of all things, and do count them but dung, that I may win Christ, And be found in him, not having mine own righteousness, which is of the law, but that which is through the faith of Christ, the righteousness which is of God by faith: That I may know him, and the power of his resurrection, and the fellowship of sufferings, being made conformable unto his death (Philip. 3:7–10).

In addressing the members of the Church at Corinth, Paul asserted that there could be no faith except that Christ had risen from the dead. For Paul, all hope of continued life and salvation is centered on the Savior's successful completion of the process of Atonement by His conquest of death through the Resurrection. From knowledge of the truthfulness of this event begins the development of faith in Christ and the initial stages of Paul's Spiral.

> If Christ be not risen, then is our preaching vain, and your faith is also vain. Yea, and we are found false witnesses of God; because we have testified of God that he raised up Christ. . . . And if Christ be not raised, your faith is in vain; ye are yet in your sins. . . . in this life only we have hope in Christ. . . . But *now is Christ risen from the dead,* and become the firstfruits of them that slept (1 Cor. 15:14–20, italics added).

For Paul, the proactive exercise of faith was an essential aspect of individually accessing the Atonement of the Savior. Through faith, and the resultant changes of action and obedience that derive from the exercise of faith, an individual could be lifted up to follow Christ's teachings and example. In this sense of accessing the gifts of the Atonement and the blessings of eternity, Paul instructed the members of the Church at Rome that "being justified by faith, we have peace with God through our Lord Jesus Christ: By whom also we have access by faith into this grace wherein we stand, and rejoice in hope of the glory of God" (Rom. 5:1–2). Once again, Paul expressed his vision of the goal of progression, which is to partake of the fulness or glory of God. It was Jesus Christ whose Atonement makes this possible, and Jesus Christ in whose fulfillment of the Father's plan of salvation faith must continually be exercised.

The Love of Christ and the Pathway to Perfection

The Apostle John, as the Beloved Disciple, is typically connected with teachings concerning the love of Christ. Paul's emphasis, however, of the importance of being filled with and acting toward others in the love of Christ was no less. Paul was convinced that the love of Christ is an eternal constant. For this reason he considered it an indispensable attribute of those who will ultimately partake of the fulness of God.

> For I am persuaded that neither death, nor life, nor angels, nor principalities, nor powers, nor things present, nor things to come, Nor height, nor depth, nor any other creature, shall be able to separate us from the love of God, which is in Christ Jesus our Lord (Rom. 8:38–39).

The most complete explanation of the importance of possessing the true love of Christ is, of course, found in the thirteenth chapter of 1 Corinthians. The word "charity" is the English transliteration of the Greek *charitas*, which signifies the true love of Christ. Even in King James's English the word charity means love, rather than giving to the poor, its typical usage in the parlance of modern English. Paul's famous dissertation on charity explains the nature and qualities of that virtue. He eloquently reiterates the point that one can possess many good qualities—even gifts from God—but without charity, the true love of Christ, one is nothing.

> Though I speak with the tongues of men and of angels, and have not charity, I am become as sounding brass, or a tinkling cymbal. And though I have the gift of prophecy, and understand all mysteries, and all knowledge; and though I have all faith, so that I could remove mountains, and have not charity, I am nothing. And though I bestow all my goods to feed the poor, and though I give my body to be burned, and have not charity, it profiteth me nothing (1 Cor. 13:1–3).

Paul enumerated characteristics displayed in the love of Christ as long-suffering, kind, unenvying, not proud, not unseemly, not easily provoked, avoiding evil, and rejoicing in truth (1 Cor. 13:4–6). Moreover, the love of Christ makes what seems impossible, possible, because it "beareth all things, believeth all things, hopeth all things, endureth all things" (1 Cor. 13:7). The often-quoted dictum "charity never faileth" highlights the eternal nature of Christ's love. It is eternal because its source is eternal.

When Paul wrote that prophecies, languages, and knowledge will all reach a fulfillment and so not continue, he was in essence comparing these things to the love of Christ, which will go on forever. "For we know in part, and we prophesy in part. But when that which is perfect is come, then that which is in part shall be done away" (1 Cor. 13:9–10).

These sentences of Paul hardly seem related to his discussion of charity, yet they are integral to it. They are perhaps made less understandable by the rendering of King James translators. The phrase translated as "in part" was in Paul's original Greek *ek merous*, literally *out of (ek) the whole (meros)*, in other words, *not whole, not complete*.[4] The incompleteness of prophecies, languages, and knowledge is in one sense a temporal incompleteness, in that they will not continue forever through eternity, but will be fulfilled in time. Moreover, these aspects of truth are also incomplete because they are insufficient in and of themselves to cause one to become Christlike. They are therefore not whole or perfect by themselves.

On the other hand, Paul asserts that the love of Christ is perfect. As King James translators render it in English, the word perfect derives from the Latin verb *perficio,* meaning *thoroughly done* or *complete.* This Latin word was employed by Jerome to translate into the Vulgate Bible Paul's original Greek phrase *to teleion.* The latter term has many meanings in many different contexts. *Teleios* can in a basic meaning signify *whole, without blemish,* or *perfect.* In Greek philosophy the adjective *teleios,* used substantively, denotes "the perfect man." The word derives from *telos,* which signifies the end.[5] Therefore, to be perfect or whole suggests that one has attained the goal, arrived at the end, is complete. Accordingly, Paul must mean that the love of Christ is eternal even in a temporal setting, but more importantly that, as an actuating principle, it will bring individuals to the end, where they will attain their goal of being complete and becoming whole. For Paul this completeness is "to know the love of Christ, which passeth knowledge, that ye may be filled with all the fulness of God" (Eph 3:19). The love of Christ will enable us to become Christlike, and so ultimately partake of the fulness of God.

The love of Christ seems connected to the ability to progress in imitation of Christ's example. Love functions as a catalyst for acquisition of the divine because it is itself an integral component of the divine. John understood this as well as Paul, and recorded as the final part of Christ's great Intercessory Prayer for His disciples—itself a tremendous expression of the Savior's love—the Son's petition to His Father "that the love wherewith thou hast loved me may be in them, and I in them" (John 17:26). The passage suggests that the love of Christ is inseparable from the person of Christ, and the person of Christ inseparable from that love.

Paul conveys much the same meaning as he reveals to the Colossians this great mystery, or hidden knowledge, that will assist men and women to fulfil their destiny as children of a divine Father in Heaven.

> Even the mystery which hath been hid from ages and from generations, but now is made manifest to his saints: To whom God would make known what is the riches of the glory of this mystery among the Gentiles; which is Christ in you, the hope of glory: Whom we preach, warning every man, and teaching every man in all wisdom; that we may present every man perfect in Christ Jesus (Col. 1:26–28).

Perfection, or completion of spiritual development, is accomplished through Jesus Christ who helps us become like Him. Faith and love are essential to the process.

The application of the principles of faith and love did not elude Paul as he instructed the Saints by means of his Epistles. The love of Christ should be applied toward one another just as Jesus would do. "Now the God of patience and consolation grant you to be like-minded one toward another according to Christ Jesus: That ye may with one mind and one mouth glorify God, even the Father of our Lord Jesus Christ. Wherefore receive ye one another, as Christ also received us to the glory of God" (Rom. 15:5–7).

Faith functions as a principle of belief and a principle of motivation or actuation in a myriad of ways. Most importantly, it seems to facilitate the functioning of the Spirit. For Paul, personal guidance by the Spirit was essential. It made conversation possible. "And my speech and my preaching was not with enticing words of man's wisdom, but in demonstration of the Spirit and of power: That your faith should not stand in the wisdom of men, but in the power of God" (1 Cor. 2:4–5).

The workings of faith, the Spirit, and the love of Christ intertwine to produce righteous living that will eventually lead to a perfected state and the fulness of God. "For we through the Spirit wait for the hope of righteousness by faith. For in Jesus Christ neither circumcision availeth any thing, nor uncircumcision; but faith which worketh by love" (Gal. 5:5–6). In this manner, man can fulfil his divinely ordained destiny of eternal life. Paul declared with great fervor of testimony, "I am not ashamed of the gospel of Christ: for it is the power of God unto salvation to every one that believeth. . . . For therein is the righteousness of God revealed from faith to faith" (Rom. 1:16–17).

Endnotes

1. Welch and Hall, *Charting the New Testament,* chart 15–16.

2. Anderson's *Understanding Paul* remains in print and constitutes an excellent single volume treatment of Paul's writings, especially for a Latter-day Saint reading public. Moreover, the volume's notes provide an adequate guide to the more important scholarly works about individual Epistles.

3. For an in-depth analysis of Paul's teachings on these themes to the Galatians see F. F. Bruce, *Epistle to the Galatians,* 135–227. For Jewish popular misconceptions of the Messiah, see James H. Charlesworth, ed., *The Messiah: Developments in Earliest Judaism and Christianity* (1992).

4. Kittel, *Theological Dictionary of the New Testament,* 4:594–98.

5. Ibid., 8:54–60, 67–78.

CHAPTER FOUR

The Consuming Fire of God

Paul traveled from Jerusalem, to Rome, and through western provinces of the Empire during the last years of his life. This was partially to secure exoneration from false charges, but always primarily to proclaim Jesus Christ as Son of God, Savior, and Lord. The faithful Apostle's strength and motivation were centered in Christ Jesus, whom Paul now knew just as well as did the special witnesses of Christ who had been the Master's personal friends and relatives. Paul's knowledge of the majestic being who was Jesus Christ derived from the visions he had received and from living by the Spirit, which enabled Paul, as it can all men and women, "as many as are led by the Spirit of God" (Rom. 8:14), to be true sons and daughters of God. Paul was never separated, neither by tribulation, distress, nor persecution, and finally by "neither death, nor life, nor angels, nor principalities, nor powers, nor things present, nor things to come . . . from the love of God, which is in Christ Jesus our Lord" (Rom. 8:38–39). Because Paul had served God "acceptably with reverence and godly fear," he had been accorded that great gift bestowed on only a few, to know "our God is a consuming fire" (Heb. 12:28–29).

Paul's Captivity

The final passages of Acts treat the so-called captivity of Paul. Luke's account of the events of the last decade of Paul's life, from his being seized by the Jewish mob in A.D. 59 through his death, possibly in 68, is far less detailed than when Luke relates other periods of Paul's activities. As to the initiating events at Jerusalem, when Paul was accused of bringing Gentiles into the temple, among scholars "there is a growing consensus that Luke had only a very rudimentary idea of what actually happened to Paul."[1] Luke did have knowledge of a sequence of events that explains how Paul came from Jerusalem to Rome, and he relates this information.

> This basic framework probably comprised no more than the following elements: Roman intervention saved Paul from a Jewish mob. The tribune in Jerusalem, Claudius Lysias, transferred the responsibility to his superior in Caesarea, Felix, who had not disposed of the case when he was replaced by Festus. Eventually Paul claimed his right as a Roman citizen to be tried by the emperor and was sent to Rome.[2]

The disposition of Paul's case was long in coming. As a Roman citizen, Paul possessed the *ius appellationis ad Caesarem,* or right of appeal to Caesar.

> According to the great 3d-century jurist, Ulpian, the right of appeal was guaranteed to all Roman citizens, whether residents of Italy or the provinces under the provisions of a *lex Iulia de vi publica,* enacted at the beginning of the Empire by Augustus, who thereby instructed Roman magistrates and officials that citizens should not only have the right of appeal from local judicial authority to Rome, but should also not be inflicted with death, scourging, prolonged imprisonment, or torture without full due process of law, including the right of *appellatio* (*Dig.*, 42–6.7).[3]

Although Felix had accepted jurisdiction over the case, so protecting Paul from injustice at the hands of the high priest and Sanhedrin, the Roman procurator postponed trial until witnesses from Jerusalem could appear. Since they did not appear and since Felix awaited a testimonial affidavit from Claudius Lysias, he suspended the case, keeping Paul under house arrest in his own governor's palace. Paul actually would have enjoyed rather luxurious accommodations under such circumstances and would have been free to teach throughout Caesarea. It is possible that Felix had hoped to receive a bribe to release Paul, but since none was forthcoming the case lingered on (Acts 23–24). All that Luke tells us of Paul's tedious period of custody in Caesarea is that from time to time Felix called him to his presence for conversation. For, strange as it appears, Felix, according to Luke, had "a more perfect knowledge of that way" (Acts 24:22). Nothing that is otherwise known about Felix prepares the reader for this statement, but it must be linked with his marriage to the youngest daughter of the elder Herod Agrippa. Indeed, the Western text says quite explicitly that it was Felix's wife "who asked to see Paul and hear him speak."[4]

Festus, the procuratorial successor of Felix, received leading Jews who had finally come down from Jerusalem to accuse Paul of offending Jewish law as regards the temple. In the face of their accusation Paul exercised his right of appeal to Caesar, an action which would prolong adjudication even more (Acts 25:6–12).[5] Festus was required to send paperwork summarizing the case with Paul to Rome. Since Festus was clearly no expert on Jewish matters, Paul appeared before the younger Herod Agrippa, who was temporarily present at Caesarea and had agreed to assist Festus in composing the required *litterae dimissoriae,* or explanatory legal briefs. To Herod Agrippa, Paul recounted the story of his life as a Pharisee, the vision on the road to Damascus, his conversion to Christ, and the long years of his ministry. He explained how Christ was the promised Messiah and how He fulfilled the law and the prophets. To all this "Agrippa said unto Paul, Almost thou persuadest me to be a Christian" (Acts 26:28).

Afterward, when Herod Agrippa and Festus were in private, "they talked between themselves, saying, This man doeth nothing worthy of death or of bonds. Then said Agrippa unto Festus, This man might have been set at liberty, if he had not appealed unto Caesar" (Acts 26:31–32). It seems very unlikely that a Roman governor would have actually convicted Paul of any offense. Paul did not exercise an appeal when Felix was governor "because Felix had virtually decided on his innocence and was simply postponing the formal acquittal and release. One day Paul would be discharged and carry out his long-cherished plan of traveling to Rome and the west."[6] With Festus, Paul may not have been as confident of his release. His appeal to Caesar was no doubt exercised not for reasons of Paul's own safety but as part of Paul's strategy for proclaiming the glad tidings of Christ. Indeed, it is entirely plausible that Paul appealed to Caesar, not merely to be able to carry the gospel message to Rome, but to present it directly before the person of the emperor.[7] At this period of Nero's reign the emperor had yet to fall prey to bad counselors and the indulgence of personal excesses. His administration was still fair and sound, and Seneca, brother of Paul's protector Gallio and also possible correspondent of Paul, was still Nero's principal advisor, the architect of much good throughout the Roman world. As for the disposition of the charges against Paul, he might have been confident of exoneration, especially as "seven or eight years previously he had experienced the benevolent neutrality of Roman law in the decision of Gallio that there was nothing illegal in his preaching."[8]

Acts reports that Paul arrived in Italy at Puteoli on the north shore of the Bay of Naples.[9] Though approximately a hundred miles south of Rome, the city was the standard port for shipping from the eastern Mediterranean and North Africa. From there he journeyed up the Appian Way and was met by brethren who, upon hearing of Paul's advent, had come out from Rome to meet the Apostle. After arriving in the city, the centurion who had accompanied Paul from Caesarea turned him over to the "captain of the guard" (Acts 28:13–16). The Greek text names this officer as *stratopedarchos,* or garrison commander. Fitzmyer suggests this man was the commander of the *Castra Praetoriana,*[10] the permanent camp of the Praetorian Guard on the eastern edge of the city. If so, he would have been a *praefectus castrorum,* prefect of the camp, rather than the commander of the guard, the Praetorian Prefect. Indeed, under Nero the Praetorian Prefect, Burrus, was a principal advisor of state who assisted Seneca in guiding the young emperor. It is doubtful that he would have received prisoners.

There was no permanent facility of imprisonment in Rome. The Mamertine Prison, made famous in Petrine tradition, functioned at various periods either as a holding facility before arraignment in the nearby *curiae,* or lawcourts of the Forum, or, as is likely in the first century, served as a place of brief imprisonment for those awaiting execution, which was swift in the Roman system. Accordingly, it is not surprising that Paul was placed under the Roman version of house arrest. This entailed living in a house that Paul procured for himself and lived in for two years under the supervision of a single guard (Acts 28:16, 30). Paul received all who came to visit him as the Acts account relates (Acts 28:30). This passage is sometimes wrongly construed to mean Paul had to remain in the house, could have visitors, but was confined in a manner closer to modern concepts of house arrest than to actual Roman practice, which would have allowed Paul the complete freedom of the city. Accordingly, in Rome Paul could have preached and testified of Christ with impunity as he awaited adjudication of his case. Luke accurately confirms the conditions that would have been allowed under Roman law, and describes Paul as "preaching the kingdom of God, and teaching those things which concern the Lord Jesus Christ, with all confidence, no man forbidding him" (Acts 28:31).

These are the last words of Acts. Luke provides no information about the course or outcome of Paul's trial. Sherwin-White opines that the fact "that Paul was not brought to trial for two years . . . may be connected with the failure of his accusers to continue their accusation at Rome. But it may also be due to the congestion of the court list."[11] If Paul's case were finally heard toward the end of his two years at Rome, and if as Sherwin-White observes, "under Nero the necessary personal jurisdiction of the emperor . . . was delegated to other persons and confirmed by him afterwards,"[12] it is unlikely that Nero, who thus seldom heard appeals in person, would have listened to Paul's plea, unless Seneca, Gallio, or some other influential Roman known by Paul intervened to persuade the emperor to hear a common citizen from the eastern provinces, a Jew of Tarsus. It is important to put Paul's case in proper historical context. "From the perspective of a Roman official, Paul was not a particularly important prisoner and . . . he may have benefitted from a purely casual release."[13] Scholars vary in their theories of the judgement rendered for Paul. Some believe that no trial ever took place and the matter was simply dismissed, others that no trial occurred and the matter was left pending, others that Paul was acquitted, and still others that he was convicted and that his death should be linked to the outcome of the trial rather than to any connection with the A.D. 64 Great Fire and the subsequent Neronian police action against Christians at Rome.[14] What should be clear is that insufficient evidence exists to allow other than speculation as to the outcome of Paul's case.

Paul's Final Missionary Journeys

Paul's pastoral Epistles to Timothy, Titus, and Philemon are sometimes identified as the "captivity epistles" because they are believed to have been written during the Apostle's Roman imprisonment. Often these writings are scrutinized for indication of what may have happened to Paul at Rome, or what he intended to do after

his trial. Understanding this group of letters is a matter of some difficulty, however. 2 Timothy, in particular, produces diverse interpretations of meaning and significance, as well as differing views
regarding its date and place of composition. It is construed to prove
Paul's release; or to demonstrate a two-tiered legal action against
Paul, making release possible after two years for additional journeys
and a second imprisonment that resulted in completion of Paul's
trial, with the outcome of conviction and death; or, quite differently,
as evidence, after missions in Spain and Illyricum, of further
missionary activity in the form of an Aegean-spanning sea voyage in
which Timothy and others are instructed to come to Paul not at
Rome, as traditionally supposed, but to meet the Apostle at
Ephesus.[15] It is probably prudent to avoid considering these writings
as evidence relating to Paul's posttrial activities and searching for
other indications of journeys to Spain or anywhere else.

Years before, when he wrote to members of the Church at Rome,
Paul expressed his desire to come westward, passing through Rome en
route to his principal destination of Spain (Rom. 15:24, 28). For Paul
to complete that goal, if he were at all able, would be natural after
departing Rome. Because such an action is so logical and since the
Apostle himself suggested it, scholars exhibit caution in accepting later
sources that seem to corroborate an actual missionary journey to Spain.

The earliest reference to the event derives from a text of the era of
the apostolic fathers, known as First Clement. Its author is the
Clement whom tradition considers the third bishop of Rome, and
who may be associated with Titus Flavius Clemens, first cousin of the
emperor Domitian, executed on charges of atheism possibly because
he was Christian. In any case, this Clement would certainly have been
in an excellent position as a bishop at Rome to know whether Paul
had departed for Spain several decades before. Clement claimed that
Paul "taught righteousness to the whole world," and "reached the
farthest limits of the West."[16] For someone living in the Roman
Empire, "the farthest limits of the West" clearly indicated Spain.
Clement also notes Paul's sufferings and includes exile among them.[17]
Such a reference to an event not known from the writings of Luke or
Paul strengthens the case for the independent nature of Clement's
knowledge about Paul's life, thus increasing the likelihood that

Clement may be correct about Paul's Spanish mission.[18] Luke's record gives no indication of Paul having been condemned to exile, nor even a circumstance where he would have been subject to exile. Only his trial at Rome could have resulted in such a punishment. It must be remembered that exile under Roman law usually did not mean transportation to a particular place, but simply exclusion from a place for a time. In this instance, for Paul, Rome would have been the place from which exclusion had been effected.

The Muratorian Canon, a table of contents of the New Testament traditionally dated to the late second century with brief comments about each of the books, specifically notes that in Acts Luke omits reference to events he did not witness, including the death of Peter and Paul's journey to Spain. "Luke tells the 'most excellent Theophilus' that the various incidents took place in his presence, and indeed he makes this quite clear by omitting the passion of Peter, as well as Paul's journey when he set out from Rome to Spain."[19] Bruce suggests that this is a source independent from Clement, arguing that the source for these two pieces of information omitted by Luke, the passion of Peter and Paul's journey to Spain, was the apocryphal *Acts of Peter,* "which begins by describing Paul's departure from Italy by sea for Spain, and goes on to recount Peter's controversy in Rome with Simon Magus, ending with a description of Peter's crucifixion."[20]

These sources are insufficient to confirm a missionary journey by Paul to Spain, but certainly admit the possibility. The voyage from Rome to Spain was only seven days long. Travel to Spain would not have been rigorous, nor would residency in Spain. "The Iberian peninsula was the most Romanized of all territories under Roman control."[21] Of the Spaniards, Strabo writes that they "have completely changed over to the Roman way of life, not even remembering their own language anymore . . . so that they are not far from being all Romans."[22] Being in Spain would be like being in Italy. Paul could have accomplished much good work, but of his efforts, of course, nothing is known whatsoever by way of fact or legend. Other possibilities for Paul's activities during the period between his departure and return to Rome include a mission to Illyricum, where earlier efforts had been interrupted, a journey through the Aegean region, and work in Italy.[23]

Paul's Death

Little evidence of any kind exists regarding the time, place, or circumstances of Paul's death. Again, the earliest reference to this aspect of Paul's life is Clement, who writes that when Paul "had given his testimony before the rulers, he thus departed from the world and was taken up into the holy place, having become an outstanding example of patient endurance."[24] The reference to delivering a testimony before the rulers suggests a legal proceeding at which Paul had the right to speak. Moreover, in accordance with tradition, "the manner of Paul's death, beheading, is understood to imply that he was condemned by a regularly constituted court."[25] Roman citizens condemned to death were typically executed by beheading. Torture or more heinous forms of execution, such as crucifixion, were prohibited by law for those possessing citizen status. Whether any kind of court appearance Paul may have made was related to the charges that he had originally appealed to Rome, or whether it was in connection with another matter, cannot be known through evidence that presently exists.

The next surviving reference to Paul's death is that of Eusebius, written more than two hundred years after Clement. "It is recorded that in Nero's reign Paul was beheaded in Rome itself, and that Peter likewise was crucified . . . That they were both martyred at the same time Bishop Dionysius of Corinth informs us in a letter written to the Romans."[26] The linking of Peter and Paul as martyrs may be real or invented. If accurate, it places Paul's death in the context of the Neronian persecution. Indeed, as noted above in connection with Peter's death, later martyrologies link Peter and Paul in death with the seventy-seven traditionally claimed as executed by Nero. The deaths of all involved need not have occurred at the same time to be connected to the action of Nero; nor is it necessary that all occurred immediately after the Great Fire of 64. The procedures involved and trials held in the case of Roman citizens like Paul may have taken considerable time. Moreover, it is possible that Paul was not even in Rome in 64 and returned later to a situation in which Paul, as a known Christian leader, may have been subject to prosecution.

The late second-century Roman presbyter, Gaius, is quoted by Eusebius as indicating that Paul was beheaded on the Ostian Way, the road to Rome's harbor, Ostia, at the mouth of the Tiber, at a site known as Aquae Salviae, and buried a mile farther away from the city where Constantine later erected the Basilica of St. Paul Outside the Walls.[27] The floor underneath the high altar of the basilica is formed by two slabs of stone, inscribed in the style of the fourth century, one bearing the inscription *Paulo* (to Paul) and the other the inscription, *apostolo mart* (apostle and witness). They suggest that Paul is buried at this spot. Whether this is the final resting place of the great missionary witness of Christ can probably never be known. Nevertheless, it has been noted that "a point in favor of the authenticity of the site" is that it is "located in a pagan necropolis, not the environment that later piety would have chosen,"[28] but the very place the Romans might have been expected to bury Paul indiscriminately among the dead of all faiths and nations.

Paul and the Cosmic Christ

Paul had said that "to me to live is Christ, and to die is gain. But if I live in the flesh, this is the fruit of my labour. . . . I am in a strait betwixt two, having a desire to depart, and be with Christ; which is far better" (Philip. 1:21–23). The missionary Apostle had run his race and run it well. Death brought him fulfillment through returning to the presence of the Master whom he had come to know well as he labored so long and hard in His behalf.

Paul's life and being were centered in Christ, and throughout his writings he taught those whom he had converted to follow the example of Christ. Such is the work of a true witness of Christ. Paul expounded this principle to the Corinthians by asking, "have I not seen Jesus Christ our Lord? are not ye my work in the Lord?" (1 Cor. 9:1). Paul's vision of Christ must have been a powerful source for testimony. As Paul learned so must all followers of the Savior learn, that the glad tidings are founded upon the Resurrection of Jesus Christ. Paul taught this doctrine by enumerating the many persons who had beheld the majesty of the resurrected Lord and stood as witnesses that the Redeemer lived again. With the sincerest humility Paul concluded the list of witnesses, testifying that "last of all he was seen of me also, as of one born out of due time. For I am the least of the apostles" (1 Cor. 15:8–9).

Paul's knowledge of the nature and person of Christ was received directly through revelation from the Savior in much the same way as the boy prophet of this dispensation. Paul testified to the Galatians that in relation to the gospel which he had instructed them in, "I neither received it of man, neither was I taught it, but by the revelation of Jesus Christ" (Gal. 1:12). In addition to Paul's accounts in his own writings of some of these visions and revelatory experiences, in Acts 9 Luke preserves the story of Paul's great vision of the resurrected Lord and also records in Acts 22 Paul's own recounting to the Jews of his life-altering experience with Jesus of Nazareth, revealed in His majesty as the Son of God.

Perhaps the greatest visionary experience Paul was blessed to receive is one that has been shared in various dispensations by a number of the select servants of God. Paul mentions it briefly but is constrained not to divulge details. He does not even identify himself as the recipient of the vision, though it is hard to conceive that it could have been anyone else. Paul refers to himself as "a man in Christ" who "(whether in the body or out of the body, I cannot tell: God knoweth;) such an one caught up to the third heaven. . . . How that he was caught up into paradise, and heard unspeakable words, which it is not lawful for a man to utter. Of such a one will I glory: yet of myself I will not glory, but in mine infirmities" (2 Cor 12:2–5). The last passage suggests not that Paul did not receive this vision, only that he cannot reveal the "man in Christ" as himself, lest he glory in a blessing which should be treated with humility. Indeed, Paul will instead glory in his infirmities about which he must be humble and pray for the Lord to help him overcome. Paul understands that despite the blessings of the Spirit that the Lord has bestowed on him, he remains an imperfect man seeking perfection through Jesus Christ. Nevertheless, the Prophet Joseph Smith had knowledge that Paul was, in fact, the "man in Christ" referred to. He explained,

> Paul ascended into the third heavens, and he could understand the three principle rounds of Jacob's ladder—the telestial, the terrestial, and the celestial glories or kingdoms, where Paul saw and heard things which were not lawful for him to utter. I could explain a hundred fold more than I ever have of the glories of the kingdoms manifested to me in the vision, were I permitted, and were the people prepared to receive them.[29]

Joseph knew what Paul had seen because he had seen it too.

Paul's vision is hardly alluded to, much less explained. It is, however, in many respects similar to the vision given several decades later to John the Revelator. Moreover, Paul, as well as John, presents throughout his teachings a Christ who is Lord. These two faithful witnesses testify of Christ in His divine nature as Son of God. Their writings teach Christ as Redeemer, the only name by which salvation may be obtained, since it is Jesus Christ who brought about the Atonement and so fulfilled the role with which He had been commissioned by the Father in the Great Premortal Council. Paul and John reveal a Christ who was and is the Creator of worlds without number. They portray the Savior not merely as teacher, prophet, or even the long foretold Messiah of Israel, but proclaim Jesus as Lord and King, Master of all things that are. For them Jesus is not riveted to the cross, nor limited by the bounds of this world which He overcame, but encompasses the universe (in Greek, the *cosmos)*. Paul envisions the Lord of Creation with arms outstretched, offering the means of eternal progression to the children of the Father.

Such doctrine is categorized as "high Christology" in scholarly analyses, because Christ fills a role higher than that of man. In the present day, when revisionist secular and sectarian scholarship increasingly seeks to see in the Savior only a man, just an enlightened teacher and thinker, the views of Paul relating to Christ as divine Lord approach the heretical in the minds of some modern-day teachers of Christianity. For them Christ has little connection with salvation except that He teaches a moral lifestyle that is in and of itself salvatory. No wonder such teachings among the early Christians gives pause to those whose Christianity is much departed from that of John and Paul.[30]

Paul expounds upon the divine person and calling of Jesus Christ throughout his teachings. For example, in Ephesians the Apostle explains "the mystery, which from the beginning of the world hath been hid in God, who created all things by Jesus Christ" (Eph. 3:9), the Christ-centered spiraling process of applying faith and exercising the love of Christ as a method to partake of the fulness of God the Father, all "according to the eternal purpose which he purposed in Christ Jesus our Lord" (Eph. 3:11). For, according to Paul, the Father made the Son the instrument of salvation and exaltation. Because the Son willingly humbled Himself and submitted to death, so overcoming it, "God also hath highly exalted him, and given him a name which is above every name: That at the name of Jesus every knee should bow, of things in heaven, and things in earth, and things under the earth" (Philip. 2:9–10). This is a Christ whose kingdom, given by the Father, truly transcends this world to embrace all things.

Paul develops this doctrine nowhere so completely as in his Epistle to the Colossians. He instructs the Colossians to give thanks to the Father for His plan of salvation, "which hath made us meet to be partakers of the inheritance of the saints in light" (Col. 1:12). The plan provides a Savior, through whose Atonement forgiveness can come to those who repent. "Who hath delivered us from the power of darkness, and hath translated us into the kingdom of his dear Son; In whom we have redemption through his blood, even the forgiveness of sins" (Col 1:13–14). This Savior has provided the means whereby all others may progress to be like Him and His Father. "Who is the image of the invisible God, the firstborn of every creature" (Col. 1:15). The Firstborn is the Creator and, as such, all things are subject to Him. Moreover, all things continue to exist in their spheres because of Him. "For by him were all things created, that are in heaven, and that are in earth, visible and invisible, whether they be thrones, or dominions, or principalities, or powers: all things were created by him, and for him: And he is before all things, and by him all things consist" (Col. 1:16–17). He is the first, the head of the Church, the first resurrected, the preeminent one with whom the Father has shared His fulness. "And he is the head of the body, the church: who is the beginning, the firstborn from the dead; that in all things he might have the preeminence. For it pleased the Father that in him should all fulness dwell" (Col. 1: 18–19). Through Christ alone may come the salvation and exaltation of all, everywhere. His object is to bring to pass the presentation to the Father of all in a holy state. "And, having made peace through the blood of his cross, by him to reconcile all things unto himself; by him, I say, whether they be things in earth or things in heaven. And you, that were sometime alienated and enemies in your mind by wicked works, yet now hath he reconciled In the body of his flesh through death, to present you holy and unblameable and unreproveable in his sight" (Col. 1: 20–22).

Paul teaches that in Christ "is the plenitude of the divine essence" and that those who are followers "of Christ realize their plenitude in him; they need not seek, for they cannot find, perfection anywhere else."³¹ Jesus Christ is the only mediator for man. The Gospel of John preserves this truth as Jesus declares "no man cometh unto the Father, but by me" (John 14:6), and Paul proclaims straightforwardly, "For there is one God, and one mediator between God and men, the man Christ Jesus" (1 Tim. 2:5). In describing those who will inhabit the celestial kingdom, the Prophet Joseph Smith taught the same doctrine as Paul: "These are they whose names are written in heaven, where God and Christ are the judge of all. These are they who are just men made perfect through Jesus the mediator of the new covenant, who wrought out this perfect atonement through the shedding of his own blood" (D&C 76:68–69).

In a visionary experience where the heavens were opened to reveal the same third heaven Paul beheld, the Prophet Joseph Smith described the role and mission of Christ in terms astoundingly similar to Paul's. He too speaks of the cosmic Christ who partakes of the fulness of God and so possessed the power to bring redemption to man. In such terms Joseph defines the gospel,

> And this is the gospel, the glad tidings, which the voice out of the heavens bore record unto us—That he came into the world, even Jesus, to be crucified for the world, and to bear the sins of the world, and to sanctify the world, and to cleanse it from all unrighteousness; That through him all might be saved whom the Father had put into his power and made by him (D&C 76: 40–42).

Like John and Paul, the Prophet Joseph Smith beheld Jesus in his glory and majesty, as Lord of the universe, having received of the fulness of God. "We beheld the glory of the Son, on the right hand of the Father, and received of his fulness; And saw the holy angels, and them who are sanctified before his throne, worshiping God, and the Lamb, who worship him forever and ever" (D&C 76:20–21). This was the great Creator whom Joseph beheld, and he testifies to this aspect of Jesus' eternal role: "by him, and through him, and of him, the worlds are and were created" (D&C 76:24). Because He made all things, Christ has power over all things and so can provide the means, just as Paul taught, for men and women to partake of the fulness of the Father. In this manner and through the atoning sacrifice of the Savior, "the inhabitants thereof are begotten sons and daughters unto God" (D&C 76:24).

The Consuming Fire of God

The Apostle Paul testified repeatedly that Christ continued to live, for he himself had seen the resurrected Lord. The Prophet Joseph Smith provides a similar witness, eloquent in its simplicity and powerful in its sincerity. "And now, after the many testimonies which have been given of him, this is the testimony, last of all, which we give of him: That he lives! For we saw him, even on the right hand of God; and we heard the voice bearing record that he is the Only Begotten of the Father" (D&C 76:22–23).

The New Testament witnesses of Christ, the four pillars of early Christianity, spent their lives fulfilling apostolic callings to testify and bear witness that Jesus is the Christ, the Son of God, the Savior. For their devotion they suffered again and again, finally sealing their testimony with their life's blood, all save John, whose faithful ministry has endured for twenty centuries and continues still. Joseph Smith followed the same path and sealed his testimony with his life's blood as the great witness of this latter-day dispensation, to which Paul attributes the distinction of being the time when the work of the Lord will come to full fruition. "In the dispensation of the fulness of times he might gather together in one all things in Christ, both which are in heaven, and which are on earth; even in him" (Eph. 1:10).

The four pilliars of early Christianity, the Prophet Joseph Smith, and prophets from all dispensations of time have been impelled to share their witness of the Master whom they serve. Such men who have come to know the Savior, whether in life or through revelation and vision as the resurrected Lord, are possessed of a burning testimony of Christ and His work. This testimony is sufficient to carry them through the adversities they may face as they labor in His behalf, and grows ever stronger, burning with increasing intensity and urgency to bring the souls of men to a knowledge of the Lord of the heavens and of His sacred and holy Father.

Such burning testimony drives strong men like Alma to cry out, "O that I were an angel, and could have the wish of mine heart, that I might go forth and speak with the trump of God, with a voice to shake the earth, and cry repentance unto every people" (Alma 29:1). It causes gentle men like Nephi to utter prayers of indescribable love and sweetness: "My God hath been my support. . . . he hath filled me with his love, even unto the consuming of my flesh. . . . He hath heard my cry by day, and he hath given me knowledge by visions in the nighttime. . . . O Lord, I have trusted in thee, and I will trust in thee forever" (2 Ne. 4:20–21, 23, 34).

Paul described this phenomenon well. After uttering the prayer that "we may serve God acceptably with reverence and godly fear," the faithful Apostle constructs an aptly descriptive metaphor—"For our God is a consuming fire" (Heb. 12:28–29). Paul in very fact knew the consuming fire of God. He had lived with it since the day he beheld his Lord on the road to Damascus, and for the very first time, understood. Not only did Paul's knowledge and understanding increase through the years, but more importantly his love of the Savior and his devotion to the Master's work expanded to fill the hearts of persons he met in the course of his ministry as he traversed the nations. Paul burned with the consuming fire of God. So did Peter, John, and James. With no thought for themselves, but only with devotion to the Master they loved so completely, all four great witnesses of the New Testament era labored tirelessly to proclaim the good news that Jesus is the Christ.

Endnotes

1. Murphy-O'Connor, *Paul,* 348.

2. Ibid.

3. John F. Hall, "Appeal to Caesar," *Anchor Bible Dictionary,* 1:317.

4. Bruce, *Paul,* 360–61.

5. An outline of legal causes of action and their consequence, as suggested in Acts, can be found in Welch and Hall, *Charting the New Testament,* chart 15-6.

6. Bruce, *Paul,* 365.

7. Professor John W. Welch has suggested to me the possibility that Paul exercised his right of appeal to Caesar in order to procure for himself the opportunity of proclaiming Christ before the emperor.

8. Bruce, *Paul,* 366.

9. See S. T. Carroll, "Puteoli," *Anchor Bible Dictionary,* 5:560–61.

10. Fitzmyer, *Acts of the Apostles, 788.*

11. A.N. Sherwin-White, *Roman Society and Roman Law in the New Testament,* 118.

12. Ibid., 111.

13. Murphy-O'Connor, *Paul,* 355.

14. Summaries of such views can be found in Bruce, *Paul,* 366–67, 376–78; Sherwin-White, *Roman Society,* 110–119; Murphy-O'Connor, *Paul,* 354–55.

15. Bruce, *Paul,* 441–47; Murphy-O'Connor, *Paul,* 363–66; J.N.D. Kelly, *A Commentary on the Pastoral Epistles* (1963), 9.

16. I Clement 5.7.

17. I Clement 5.6.

18. Murphy-O'Connor, *Paul,* 361.

19. Bruce, *Paul,* 449.

20. Ibid.

21. Murphy-O'Connor, *Paul,* 362.

22. Strabo, *Geography,* 3.2.15. Also see Murphy-O'Connor, *Paul,* 362.

23. Ibid., 363–68.

24. I Clement 5.7

25. Murphy-O'Connor, *Paul,* 371.

26. Eusebius, *Ecclesiastical History,* 2.25.

27. Ibid.

28. Bruce, *Paul,* 450–51.

29. Smith, *Teachings of the Prophet Joseph Smith,* 304–305.

30. Summaries of various scholarly positions on the subject can be found in Bruce, *Paul,* 417–421; and in Murphy- O'Connor, *Paul,* 237–248.

31. Bruce, *Paul,* 417.

BIBLIOGRAPHY

Achtmeier, Paul J. *Anchor Bible Dictionary,* s.v. "Gospel of Mark," 4:542–43.

Adamson, James B. *James the Man and His Message,* (Grand Rapids: Eerdman's, 1989).

Anderson, Richard L. *Understanding Paul* (Salt Lake City: Deseret Book, 1983).

Applebaum, Shimon. *Anchor Bible Dictionary,* s.v. "Jews in North Africa," 3:1072–73.

Attridge, Harold. *Anchor Bible Dictionary,* s.v. "The Acts of Thomas," 6:531–34.

Ballif, Jae R. *Encyclopedia of Mormonism,* s.v. "Restoration of the Melchizedek Priesthood," ed. Daniel H. Ludlow, 4 vols. (New York: Macmillan, 1992), 2:885–87.

Balsdon, J. P. V. D. *Romans and Aliens* (Chapel Hill: University of North Carolina Press, 1979).

Bauckham, Richard. *Jude and the Relatives of Jesus in the Early Church* (Edinburgh: T&T Clark, 1990).

Bean, George E. *Aegean Turkey* (New York: Praeger, 1966).

Beard, Mary, John North, and Simon Price. *Religions of Rome,* 2 vols. (Cambridge: Cambridge University Press, 1998).

Beckwith, Roger. *The Old Testament and Canon of the New Testament Church* (Grand Rapids, MI: Eerdman's, 1986).

Beer, Moshe. *Anchor Bible Dictionary,* s.v. "Judaism: Babylonian," 3: 1076–83.

Betz, Hanz-Dieter. *Galatians: A Commentary on Paul's Letter to the Churches in Galatia* (Philadelphia: Fortress, 1979).

Bickerman, Elias J. *The Jews in the Greek Age* (Cambridge: Harvard University Press, 1988).

Boismard, M. "Stephen," *Anchor Bible Dictionary,* 6:207–11.

Borgen, Peder. *Anchor Bible Dictionary,* s.v. "Judaism: Egypt," 3: 1061–72.

Brandon, S. G. F. *The Fall of Jerusalem and the Christian Church* (London: S. P. C. K., 1951).

Brown, Raymond E., Karl P. Donfried, and John Reumann. *Peter in the New Testament* (Minneapolis: Augusburg Press, 1973).

Brown, Raymond E. and John P. Meier. *Antioch and Rome* (New York: Paulist Press, 1983).

Brown, Raymond E. *The Chronicles the Apostles Left Behind* (New York: Paulist Press, 1989).

_____. *The Churches the Apostles Left Behind* (New York: Paulist Press, 1984).

_____. *The Death of the Messiah* (New York: Doubleday, 1994).

_____. *The Epistles of John,* vol. 30 of Anchor Bible, (NewYork: Doubleday, 1982).

_____. *The Gospel of John,* vol. 29 of Anchor Bible, (NewYork: Doubleday, 1966).

Brownrigg, Ronald. *The Twelve Apostles* (New York: Macmillan, 1974).

Bruce, F. F. *Commentary on Galatians* (Grand Rapids, MI: Eerdman's, 1982).

_____. *The Epistle to the Galatians* (Grand Rapids, MI: Eerdman's, 1982).

_____. *The Epistles of John* (Grand Rapids, MI: Eerdman's, 1970).

_____. *The Gospel of John* (Grand Rapids, MI: Eerdman's, 1983).

_____. *Paul, Apostle of the Heart Set Free* (Grand Rapids, MI: Eerdman's, 1977).

_____. *Peter, Stephen, James & John* (Grand Rapids, MI: Eerdman's, 1979).

Buchanan, C. W. "Jesus and the Upper Class," *Novum Testamentum 7* (1964), 195–209.

Cameron, Ron. *Anchor Bible Dictionary,* s.v. "Gospel of Thomas," 6:535–40.

_____. *Anchor Bible Dictionary,* s.v. "The Apocryphon of James," 3:619–20.

Chilton, Bruce. *Anchor Bible Dictionary,* s.v. "Gamaliel," 2:903–06.

Clark, J. Reuben, Jr. *On the Way to Immortality and Eternal Life* (Salt Lake City: Deseret Book, 1949).

Claybaugh, John D. "What Latter-day Scriptures Teach about John the Beloved," *The Testimony of John the Beloved* (Salt Lake City: Deseret Book, 1998), 16–35.

Collins, Raymond F. *Anchor Bible Dictionary,* s.v. "John," 3:886–87.

_____. *Anchor Bible Dictionary,* s.v. "Thomas," 6:528–29.

Corbo, Virgilio C. *Anchor Bible Dictionary,* s.v. "Capernaum," 1:866–69.

Corley, Kathleen. *Anchor Bible Dictionary,* s.v. "Preaching of Peter," 5:282.

Cousar, Charles B. *Anchor Bible Dictionary,* s.v. "Council of Jerusalem, 3:766–68.

Culpepper, R. Alan. *John, the Son of Zebedee,* (Minneapolis: Fortress Press, 2000).

Dallman, William. *John, Disciple, Evangelist, Apostle* (St. Louis: Concordia, 1932).

Daniels, Jon B. "Barnabas," *Anchor Bible Dictionary,* 1:610–11.

_____. *Anchor Bible Dictionary,* s.v. "Gospel of Bartholomew," 1:615–16.

Davies, W. B. *Paul and Rabbinic Judaism* (London: S. P. C. K., 1955).

de Satge, John. *Peter and the Single Church* (London: S. P. C. K., 1981).

Donfried, Karl P. *Anchor Bible Dictionary,* s.v. "Peter," 5:251–63.

Donfried, Karl P. and Peter Richardson. *Judaism and Christianity in First Century Rome* (Grand Rapids, MI: Eerdman's, 1998).

Downey, Glanville. *History of Antioch in Syria* (Princeton: Princeton University Press, 1961).

Draper, Richard. *Opening the Seven Seals* (Salt Lake City: Deseret Book, 1991).

Dumezil, G. *Archaic Roman Religion,* 2 vols. (Chicago: University of Chicago Press, 1970).

Dunn, James D. G. *Unity and Diversity in the New Testament: an Inquiry into the Character of Earliest Christianity* (Harrisburg: Trinity Press International, 1990).

Eller, Vernard. *The Beloved Disciple* (Grand Rapids, MI: Eerdman's, 1987).

Elliott, John H. *Anchor Bible Dictionary,* s.v. "First Peter," 5:241–83.

_____. *Anchor Bible Dictionary,* s.v. "Second Peter," 5:282–87.

England, J. Lynn and W. Keith Warner. *Encyclopedia of Mormonism,* s.v. "First Presidency," ed. Daniel H. Ludlow, 4 vols. (New York: Macmillan, 1992), 2:512–14.

Feldman, L. H. *Jew and Gentile in the Ancient World* (Princeton: Princeton University Press, 1993).

Ferguson, John. *The Religions of the Roman Empire* (Ithaca: Cornell University Press, 1989).

Ferguson, Everett. *Backgrounds of Early Christianity*, 2nd ed. (Grand Rapids: Eerdman's, 1993).

Fiensy, David. "The Composition of the Jerusalem Church," in *The Book of Acts in its Palestinian Setting*, ed. Richard Bauckham. (Grand Rapids, MI: Eerdman's, 1993).

Fitzmyer, Joseph A. *The Acts of the Apostles* (New York: Doubleday, 1998).

Fraade, Steven D. "Judaism: Palestinian," *Anchor Bible Dictionary*, 3:1054–61.

Freyne, Sean. *Galilee, Jesus and the Gospels: Literary and Historical Approaches* (Grand Rapids, MI: Eerdman's, 1988).

Freedman, David Noel, ed. *Anchor Bible Dictionary*, 6 vols. (New York: Doubleday, 1992).

_____. ed. *Eerdman's Dictionary of the Bible* (Grand Rapids, MI: Eerdman's, 2000).

_____. ed. *Eerdman's Dictionary of the Bible*, s.v. "Prochorus," (Grand Rapids, MI: Eerdman's, 2000), 1085.

Frend, W. H. C. *Martyrdom and Persecution in the Early Church* (New York: New York University Press, 1968).

_____. *The Rise of Christianity* (Philadelphia: Fortress Press, 1984).

Garnsey, Peter. *Social Status and Legal Privilege in the Roman Empire* (Oxford: Clarendon Press, 1970).

Goldenburg, Robert. *Anchor Bible Dictionary*, s.v. "Hillel the Elder," 3:201–02.

Grant, Michael. *The History of Ancient Israel* (New York: Scribner's, 1984).

Grant, Robert M. "The Oldest Gospel Prologues," *Anglican Theological Review* 23 (1941), 241–42.

Gruen, Erich S. *The Hellenistic World and the Coming of Rome* (Berkeley: University of California Press, 1984).

Hagner, Donald A. *Anchor Bible Dictionary*, s.v. "James," 3:616–18.

Hall, John F. *Anchor Bible Dictionary*, s.v. "Appeal to Caesar," 1: 317.

_____. ed. *Etruscan Italy* (Provo: BYU Press, 1996).

———. *Encyclopedia of Mormonism,* s.v. "Peter," ed. Daniel H. Ludlow. 4 vols. (New York: Macmillan, 1992), 3:1077–79.

———. "The Roman Province of Judea: A Historical Overview," *Masada and the World of the New Testament,* ed. Hall and Welch, (Provo: BYU Press, 1997).

Hall, John F. and John W. Welch, eds. *Masada and the World of the New Testament,* (Provo: BYU Press, 1997).

Hedrick, Charles W. *Anchor Bible Dictionary,* s.v. "Second Apocalypse of James," 3: 632–33.

Hendriksen, William. *A Commentary on Galatians* (London: Banner of Truth Trust, 1969).

Hennecke, E. and W. Schneemelcher. *New Testament Apocrypha* (Philadelphia: Westminster, 1964).

Holzapfel, Richard. "King Herod," in *Masada and the World of the New Testament,* ed. Hall and Welch, (Provo: BYU Press, 1996), 35–73.

Hornblower, Simon, ed. *The Oxford Classical Dictionary,* 2nd ed. (Oxford: Oxford University Press, 1970).

Horsely, A. Burt. *Peter and the Popes* (Salt Lake City: Deseret Book, 1989).

Horsely, Richard A. *Archaeology, History, and Society in Galilee* (Valley Forge: Trinity Press International, 1996).

Jackson, Foakes and Kirsopp Lake. *The Beginnings of Christianity: The Acts of the Apostles* (London: Macmillan, 1933).

Jackson, Kent P. "Revolutionaries in the First Century," in *Masada and the World of the New Testament,* ed. John F. Hall and John W. Welch (Provo: BYU Press, 1997), 129–40.

Jackson, Samuel Macauley, ed. *The New Schaff-Herzog Encyclopedia of Religious Knowledge,* 15 vols. (Grand Rapids: Baker Book House, 1977).

Jaegar, Werner. *Paideia: the Ideals of Greek Culture,* 3 volumes. (Oxford: Oxford University Press, 1957–1965).

Jeffers, James S. *The Greco-Roman World of the New Testament Era* (Downer's Grove: InterVarsity, 1999).

Kennedy, George A. *New Testament Interpretation through Rhetorical Criticism* (Chapel Hill: University of North Carolina Press, 1984).

Kimball, Spencer W. "Peter, My Brother," *BYU Speeches of the Year* (Provo: BYU University Press, 1971).

Kittle, Gerhard, ed. *Theological Dictionary of the New Testament,* 10 volumes (Grand Rapids: Eerdman's, repr. 1995).

Koch, K. "Ezra and the Origins of Judaism," *Journal of Semitic Studies,* 19 (1974), 173–79.

Koester, Helmut. *Introduction to the New Testament,* vol. 1, *History Culture and Religion of the Hellenistic Age,* 2nd ed., (New York: Walter de Gruyter, 1995).

Kraabel, A. R. "The Diaspora Synagogues: Archaeological and Epigraphical Evidence," *Aufstieg und Niedergung der Römische Welt,* vol 2.19.1 (Berlin: De Gruyter, 1979), 477–510.

Kunke, Wolfgang. *An Introduction to Roman Legal and Constitutional History,* 2nd ed., trans. J. M. Kelly (Oxford: Clarendon Press, 1973).

Lentz, J. C. *Luke's Portrait of Paul* (Cambridge: Cambridge University Press, 1993).

Levinskaya, Irina. *The Book of Acts in Its Diaspora Setting* (Grand Rapids: Eerdman's, 1996).

Lightfoot, J. B. *The Apostolic Fathers* (Grand Rapids: Baker House, repr. 1996).

Ludlow, Daniel H., ed. *The Encyclopedia of Mormonism,* 5 vols. (New York: Macmillan, 1992).

MacDonald, Dennis R. *Anchor Bible Dictionary,* s.v. "Andrew," 1:242–43.

Malina, Bruce J. and Jerome H. Neyrey. *Portraits of Paul* (Louisville: Westminster John Knox, 1996).

Marsh, David B. "Give Unto Me Power Over Death," *The Testimony of John the Beloved* (Salt Lake City: Deseret Book, 1998).

Mattingly, Harold. *Christianity in the Roman Empire* (New York: W. W. Norton, 1967).

Mayor, Joseph B. *The Epistle of St. James* (London: MacMillan, 1910).

McConkie, Bruce R. *Doctrinal New Testament Commentary,* 3 vols. (1965; reprint, Salt Lake City: Bookcraft, 1971), 2:143.

MacDonald, Lee M. *The Formation of the Christian Biblical Canon* (Peabody, MA: Hendrickson, 1995).

Meier, John P. *Anchor Bible Dictionary,* s.v. "Gospel of Matthew," 4:622–41.

Meyer, Eduard. *Ursprung und Anfange des Christentums* (Darmstadt: Wisesnschlafliche Buchgesellschat, 1968).

Meyer, Marvin. *Anchor Bible Dictionary,* s.v. "Letter of Peter to Philip," 5:265–66.

Mirecki, Paul. *Anchor Bible Dictionary,* s.v. "Gospel of Peter," 5:278–81.

Murphy-O'Connor, Jerome. *Anchor Bible Dictionary,* s.v. "Corinth," 1:1134–39.

_____. *Paul, A Critical Life* (Oxford: Oxford University Press, 1996).

Newport, Kent. *Anchor Bible Dictionary,* s.v. "Martyrdom of Matthew," 4:643–44.

Neusner, Jacob. *A History of the Jews in Babylonia,* 5 vols. (Leiden: Brill, 1965–1970).

Nibley, Hugh. *Apostles and Bishops in Early Christianity,* ed. John W. Welch and John F. Hall (forthcoming).

_____. *Lehi in the Desert* (Salt Lake City: Bookcraft, 1952).

_____. *When the Lights Went Out* (Salt Lake City: Deseret Book, 1970).

_____. *The World and the Prophets* (Salt Lake City: Deseret Book, 1987).

North, Robert. *Anchor Bible Dictionary,* s.v. "Ezra," 2:725–28.

Novak, Ralph M. *Christianity and the Roman Empire* (Harrisburg: Trinity Press International, 2001).

Overman, J. A. and W. S. Green. *Anchor Bible Dictionary,* s.v. "Judaism: Greco-Roman Period," 3: 1037–54.

Painter, John. *Just James, the Brother of Jesus in History and Tradition* (Minneapolis: Fortress, 1999).

Parrot, Douglas. *Anchor Bible Dictionary,* s.v. "The Acts of Peter and the Twelve Apostles," 5: 264–65.

Penna, Romano. *Anchor Bible Dictionary,* s.v. "Judaism: Rome," 3: 1073–76.

Perkins, Rheme. *Peter, Apostle for the Whole Church* (1993; reprint Columbia: University of South Carolina Press, 1999).

Peters, F. E. *The Harvest of Hellenism* (New York: Simon and Schuster, 1970).

Powell, C. "'Faith' in James and its Bearing on the Problem of the Date of the Epistle," *Expository Times 62* (1950–51), 311–14.

Rajak, Tessa. "The Location of Cultures in Second Temple Palestine: The Evidence of Josephus," in *The Book of Acts in Its Palestinian Setting,* ed. Richard Bauckham. (Grand Rapids: Eerdman's, 1993).

Rawson, Beryl, ed. *The Family in Ancient Rome: New Perspective* (Ithaca: Cornell University Press, 1986).

Roberts, Alexander and James Donaldson, eds. *The Ante-Nicene Fathers,* 10 vols. (Grand Rapids: Eerdman's 1996), 1:31.

Roberts, B. H. *The Outlines of Ecclesiastical History* (Salt Lake City: Deseret Book, repr. 1979).

Rook, J. T. "Boanerges, 'Sons of Thunder' (Mark 3:17)," *Journal of Biblical Literature* 100 (1981), 94–95.

Schmithals, Walter. *Paul and James* (London: SCM Press, 1963).

Schoelel, William R. *Anchor Bible Dictionary,* s.v. "First Apocalypse of James," 3: 628–29.

Scullard, H. H. *A History of the Roman World, 753–146 B.C.,* 4th ed. (London: Routledge, 1980).

Sherwin-White, A. N. *The Roman Citizenship* (Oxford: Clarendon, 1973).

_____. *Roman Society and Roman Law in the New Testament* (Oxford: Clarendon, 1963).

Smith, Dennis E. *Anchor Bible Dictionary,* s.v. "Table Fellowship," 6: 302–04.

Smith, Joseph. *Documentary History of the Church,* 2:200; 4:207–09; 5:392; 6:478–79.

Smith, Joseph Fielding, ed. *Teachings of the Prophet Joseph Smith* (Salt Lake City: Deseret Book, 1938).

Smyth, H. W. *Greek Grammar* (Cambridge: Harvard University Press, 1920).

Snyder, Grayden F. "Survey and New Thesis on the Bones of Peter," *Biblical Archaeologist 32* (1969), 2–24.

Stoops, Robert F. *Anchor Bible Dictionary,* s.v. "Acts of Peter," 5:267–68.

_____. *Anchor Bible Dictionary,* s.v. "Simon Magus," 6:29–31.

Strange, James F. *Anchor Bible Dictionary,* s.v. "Bethsaida," 1:692–93.

Streeter, B. H. *The Primitive Church* (New York: Macmillan, 1929).

Talmage, James E. *The Great Apostasy* (Salt Lake City: Deseret Book, repr. 1968).

_____. *Jesus the Christ* (Salt Lake City: Deseret Book, 1972).

Thomason, D. A. *Anchor Bible Dictionary,* s.v. "Epistles of Paul and Seneca," 5: 201.

Torcan, Robert. *The Cults of the Roman Empire* (Oxford: Oxford University Press, 1989).

Townsend, G. B. *The Oxford Classical Dictionary,* s.v. "Suetonius," 2nd ed. (Oxford: Oxford University Press, 1970).

Trebilco, Paul. *The Jewish Communities in Asia Minor* (Cambridge: Cambridge University Press, 1991).

Tucker, Jeffrey T. *Eerdman's Dictionary of the Bible* s.v. "Andrew," (Grand Rapids: Eerdman's, 2002), 62.

Turcan, Robert. *The Cults of the Roman Empire* (Cambridge: Blackwell, 1989).

Turner, John D. *Anchor Bible Dictionary,* s.v. "Book of Thomas the Contender," 6: 529–30.

Vorster, William S. *Anchor Bible Dictionary,* s.v. "Protoevangelium of James," 3: 629–32.

Walters, James C. "Romans, Jews, and Christians," in Karl Donfried and Peter Richardson, *Judaism and Christianity in First Century Rome* (Grand Rapids: Eerdman's, 1998), 175–95.

Watson, Alan. *The Spirit of Roman Law* (Athens: University of Georgia Press, 1995).

_____. *The State, Law, and Religion: Pagan Rome* (Athens: University of Georgia Press, 1992).

Watson, D. F. *Anchor Bible Dictionary,* s.v. "Nicolaitans," 4:1106–07.

Watson, JoAnn Ford. *Anchor Bible Dictionary,* s.v. "Philip," 5:311–12.

_____. *Anchor Bible Dictionary,* s.v. "Thaddeus," 6:435.

_____. *Anchor Bible Dictionary,* s.v. "Zebedee," 6:1055.

Weidmann, F. W. *Polycarp and John* (Notre Dame: University of Notre Dame, 1999).

Welch, John W. and John F. Hall. *Charting the New Testament* (Provo: FARMS, 2002).

Westcott, B. F. *The Gospel According to St. John* (London, 1880).

Wilken, Robert L. *The Christians as the Romans Saw Them* (New Haven: Yale University Press, 1984).

Wilkins, Michael J. *Anchor Bible Dictionary,* s.v. "Bartholomew," 1:615.

Williams, David J. *Paul's Metaphors* (Peabody: Hendrickson, 1999).

Wilson, J. Christian. *Eerdman's Dictionary of the Bible* s.v. "Acts of the Apostles," (Grand Rapids, MI: Eerdman's, 2002).

Winter, Michael M. *Saint Peter and the Popes,* (Westpoint: Helicon, 1960).

Wisse, Frederik. *Anchor Bible Dictionary*, s.v. "Apocalypse of Peter,"
    5:268–69.

Witherington, Ben. *Anchor Bible Dictionary*, s.v. "Lydia," 4:422–23.

Worth, Roland H. *The Seven Cities of the Apocalypse* (New York: Paulist
    Press, 1999).

Young, Brigham. *Journal of Discourses*, 26 vols. (Liverpool: F. D. Richards,
    repr. 1967).

Zahavy, Tzvee. *Anchor Bible Dictionary*, s.v. "Judaism: Mishnaic Period,"
    3:1083–89.

Zoeckler, Otto. "Mary," *The New Schaff-Herzog Encyclopedia of Religious
    Knowledge*, 223.

Ancient Sources

Apostolic Constitutions

Ascents of James

Cassius Dio

Epiphanius, *Panarion*

Eusebius, *Historia Ecclesia*

Gospel of Thomas

Irenaeus, *Against Heresies*

Jerome, *Chronicle*

_____. *Concerning Illustrious Men*

Josephus, *Bellum Judaicum*

_____. *Jewish Antiquities*

Justin Martyr, *Dialogue with Trypho*

Kerygmata Petrou

Liber Pontificalis

Malalas, *Historia Chronica*

Martyrdom of Polycarp

Pliny, *Epistles*

Strabo, *Geography*

Suetonius, *Domitian*

_____. *Claudius*

Syncellus, *Chronographia*

Tacitus, *The Histories*

_____. *Annals*

Tertullian, *Apology*

_____. *On the Flesh of Christ*

_____. *On the Prescription against Heretics*

Theodoret of Cyprus, *Homily I, Immutabilis=Patrologia Graeca* 83.81

Xenophon, *Anabasis*

INDEX